HISTORY OF THE
US ARMY

HISTORY OF THE
US ARMY

JAMES M. MORRIS

JG
PRESS

Published by World Publications Group, Inc.
455 Somerset Avenue
North Dighton, MA 02764
www.wrldpub.com

ISBN 1-57215-313-X

Printed in China

5 4 3 2   03 04 05 06

Page 1: Training with a UH-60 Black Hawk
helicopter at the Army Assault School at Fort
Campbell, KY.
Pages 2-3: George Washington reviews his
ragged troops at the camp at Valley Forge.
This page: An Army Airforce B-25 Mitchell
bomber completes its attack run on a
Japanese escort vessel.

CONTENTS

INTRODUCTION

The United States Army may be said to have been formally born on 14 June 1775 when the Second Continental Congress created George Washington's Continental Army. Its antecedents, however, extend considerably farther back in time. The North American colonists had, after all, been intermittently engaged in various forms of organized warfare for much of the preceeding century. And in a broader sense, the colonists' understanding both of what an army is and of how war should be conducted was the product of ideas that had been developed in Europe yet another hundred years earlier, when warfare was forever transformed by the introduction of the portable firearm.

Modern warfare was born during the sixteenth and seventeenth centuries when the arquebus or 'shot,' a form of man-held artillery, came into use. The early arquebus could project a one-ounce ball for a distance of up to 200 yards, although it took as long as fifteen minutes to load and fire. Its successor, the musket, represented a major step forward in weapons technology, though it, too, was unwieldy and inaccurate – besides requiring 56 separate movements to reload.

It was during the destructive Thirty Years' War between 1618 and 1648 that the first true

America's first settlers still used the primitive matchlock arquebus.

modern army was created by Gustavus Adolphus. This Swedish leader introduced the *levée en masse* (large citizen army); the paper cartridge for use by his musketeers; and the three-rank, simultaneous-fire infantry formation for continuous volley fire. He also created well-disciplined 'divisions' of 4000-5000 men for greater maneuverability on the battlefield, cavalry units to be used as shock troops to charge enemy flanks, and three standardized classes of artillery (heavy siege guns; lighter, more mobile field guns; and regimental pieces, which could be drawn into position by a single horse). Gustavus Adolphus insisted on trained officers, regular pay for his soldiers and tighter military discipline (including banning whores from military encampments).

By the eighteenth century the technological outlines of modern warfare had clearly taken shape. Artillery (smoothbore, as opposed to later rifled artillery) now consisted almost exclusively of Gustavus' three basic types, and all were capable of firing relatively standard gauge solid iron shot for localized destruction and either grapeshot (small balls attached to one another and designed to spread on explosion) or cannister (loose pellets in a can also designed to spread) against personnel.

The flintlock musket was the standard infantry weapon. For example, the British army's 'Brown Bess' was a smoothbore musket with a 3-foot, 8-inch barrel that fired three-quarter-inch diameter balls. It had an effective range of 50 to 100 yards, and a trained musketeer could fire three rounds

per minute. Attached to the barrel of the musket was a 14-inch 'ring' or 'socket' bayonet that allowed the infantryman to turn the musket into a spear without plugging the muzzle. The bayonet could be used against cavalry or against enemy personnel.

As weapons became standardized, so too did tactics. The line, which had developed out of the Greek phalanx, was the standard infantry formation in battle. Troops would march onto the battlefield in columns and then, on command, form into firing ranks. To perform this evolution in the face of bloody battle and possible death demanded rigorous training, and thus close-order drill evolved to assure proper movement and maintenance of formation while under enemy fire.

Once the two enemies' lines were drawn up, four stages of combat would normally follow. First, the artillery behind the lines of infantry would open on the enemy. Next, the infantry would advance in ranks to within 50 to 100 yards of the enemy. Third, the infantry would fire in volleys on command, usually not bothering overmuch about marksmanship at such close range. Last, the musketeers would charge the enemy with their bayonetted weapons if his line seemed ready to break. The army that did not 'cut and run' under fire and bayonet charge won the battle.

Such formalization, plus the intellectual climate of the times, forced eighteenth-century warfare into certain moral postures regarding battle. In the first place, enlightenment humanism inclined Europe toward limited warfare. It was assumed, for instance, that civilians would be immune from the violence and destruction of war. Second, the times demanded that wars only be fought for highly specific political or economic ends, never for the destruction of the enemy, his land or his people. Third, it was generally assumed that the bulk of the armies would come from the less-productive or lower social classes, rather than from the more 'solid' citizenry, thus lessening the aggregate loss to the country by battlefield woundings

Firearms transformed tactics, making musketeer ranks the key battle units

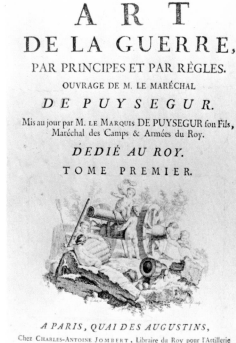

ART
DE LA GUERRE,
PAR PRINCIPES ET PAR RÈGLES.
OUVRAGE DE M. LE MARÉCHAL
DE PUYSEGUR.
Mis au jour par M. LE MARQUIS DE PUYSEGUR son Fils,
Maréchal des Camps & Armées du Roy.

DÉDIÉ AU ROY.

TOME PREMIER.

A PARIS, QUAI DES AUGUSTINS,
Chez CHARLES-ANTOINE JOMBERT, Libraire du Roy pour l'Artillerie
& le Génie, à l'Image Notre-Dame.

M. DCC. XLIX.
AVEC APPROBATION ET PRIVILEGE DU ROY.

and deaths. Total war was a concept yet to be developed.

Technology and attitudes affected tactics, as well. Since heavy casualties of highly-trained soldiers could be expected in confrontational modes of warfare based on death-dealing artillery and musket fire, it followed that wars should be won by maneuver whenever possible. A good general was one who by movement could put his enemy in an untenable position and thus force him to surrender, his means of escape being cut off and his supply lines being cut. Thus interdiction of lines of supply and reinforcement, not the 'butcher's bill,' became the criterion of superior generalship.

The new style of warfare also produced feats of defensive engineering, especially under the influence of the fortifications designed by Sébastien Vauban, chief engineer to King Louis XIV of France. Vauban and his disciples concentrated on building low-walled forts surrounded by moats and glacis, or downward-sloping banks of earth or masonry. The only way to attack such a fort was to approach it through laboriously-dug parallel and zigzag trenches and then to place it under effective fire to breach its walls. This type of prolonged siege warfare also tended to hold down casualties and force a surrender by investment.

The eighteenth century, then, saw wars of formation, muskets, bayonets, artillery, maneuver and siege. Within these military practices and moral assumptions, the US Army was born. It would change and change again in succeeding centuries, as new technologies changed the face of war.

Above left: Mobile artillery, c. 1630.
Above: Title page of a 1749 French treatise on tactics.
Below: Linear tactics in America: a battle of the French and Indian Wars.

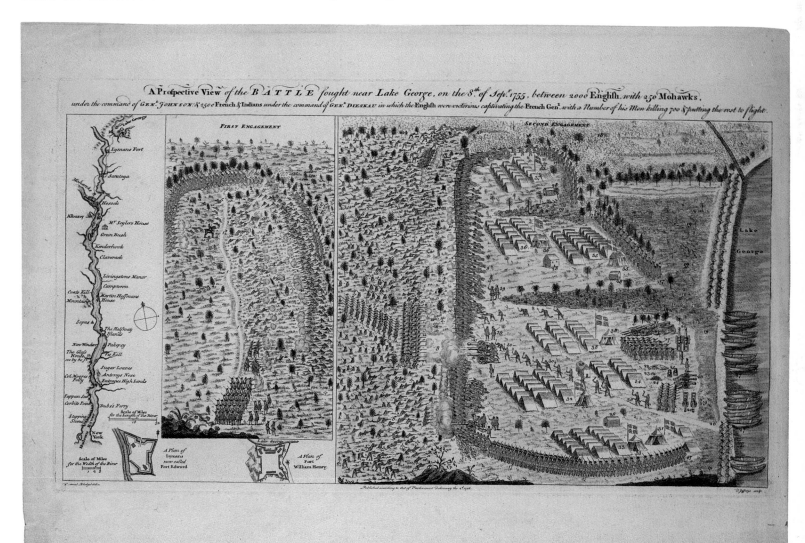

New World warfare: an Indian attack on an 18th century frontier camp.

BIRTH OF THE AMERICAN ARMY: 1607-1781

From their earliest beginnings the British colonies on the North American continent had been left largely to their own devices regarding defense against their enemies, especially against the Indian tribes along the Atlantic coast who resisted the continuing encroachments of the European settlers. The early English settlements were generally small and isolated, and most military defense, perforce, had to be local defense. Aid from distant settlements or from the entire colony was available only in case of major Indian uprisings. As a result, the colonists were obliged to develop local military units, the militia, to provide for their security.

Although the tradition of the militia in English history stretched back in time to the Saxon *fyrd*, the militia in the mother country had largely fallen into disuse with the rise of professional armies in the sixteenth and seventeenth centuries. But since maintenance of a professional army would be both unnecessary and prohibitively expensive for limited campaigns against the Indians on the American frontier, colonial assemblies opted instead for local-based militias, and gradually all thirteen colonies, with the singular exception of pacifist Quaker-dominated Pennsylvania, which opted for all-volunteer units, developed a compulsory militia system under the nominal control of their central governments.

Generally speaking, in the colonial militia all able-bodied men (with the exception of sheriffs, ministers, teachers, slaves and some others) between the ages of 16 and 60 were required to report for regular training at the town or county seat. They were expected to furnish their own muskets, ammunition and other supplies. Militia musters largely consisted of marching and target practice with muskets, and they were often as much social and festive as military. The commanding

Indian-fighting honed the martial skills of the early settlers.

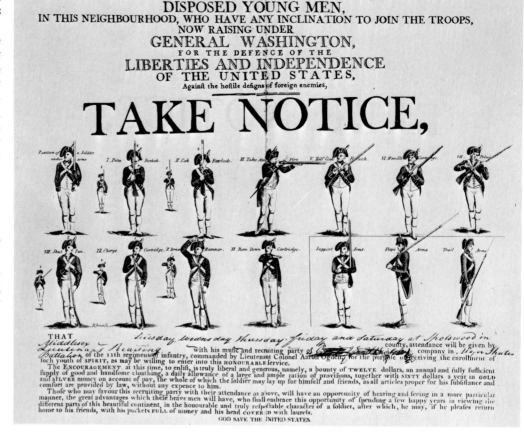

officers for a colony or a military district, the colonels, were appointed by the governor with the consent of the assembly, but company-grade officers, in the best English tradition, were elected by the men.

When trouble came – usually in the form of an Indian attack on some town or settlement – the militia would be called to drive off and punish the troublemakers. Very seldom, however, would entire local militia units, or 'trainbands,' be called into active service, since the trainbands functioned more as training units for soldiering than as fighting units. Rather, volunteers chosen from the

Above: The 10 steps to arm a musket.
Right: An early colonial rival: Spain.
Below: Militia, the original army.

various local units would assemble to engage in the campaign. If not enough volunteers who were sufficiently young and sturdy to engage in a campaign came forth to serve, the local commander had the authority to draft enough militiamen from his unit to fill out the necessary number of men called for by the governor. Since campaigns usually lasted for only a few days, the militiamen chosen had little need for much logistical backup other than what they could carry.

These militias were far from professional. Even the officers typically had no professional military training. But if unschooled in the niceties of conventional warfare, both the officers and their men knew their Indian adversaries and were content to forego doctrine in order to subdue opponents skilled in wilderness warfare. If the Indians fought with stealth and surprise, so too would the colonial militiamen. If the Indians used scouts to reconnoiter the path ahead to prevent a surprise of the main body, so too would the colonials employ friendly Indians or 'rangers' to do the same. If the Indians frequently slew all white men, including women and children, and burned their settlements to the ground, so would the militiamen slaughter and lay waste to Indian villages.

Despite the low level of training of the militias, whose drills became ever more casual as the Indian menace lessened, by sheer numbers and technological superiority the militiamen almost invariably defeated their Indian opponent in the colonial wilder-

ness. And thanks to this success, the militia as a defensive institution won the loyalty of the American colonists and soon became part of the social and traditional fabric of American colonial life.

Yet the colonial militia was not without its weaknesses. Since the units were uniformly seen as created for local defense, the militiamen were not inclined to respond to crises outside their own regions. This was especially noticeable in the eighteenth century as the Indian menace faded. In Virginia, for example, there was so little threat to the peace that the militia hardly existed for almost half a century, the Virginia Rangers being considered sufficient to watch the frontier. In 1713, when a threat arose from the Tuscarora Indians, Governor Alexander Spotswood was unable to raise the militia or even enlist volunteers and was forced to make peace with the tribe instead.

But even as the Indian threat receded, potential new enemies were emerging: the French and Spanish. Now the enemy would be more formidable but not near at hand, meaning that larger military forces would have to be recruited for longer times to serve at greater distances from home. Accordingly, the tendency arose to enlist recruits from outside the militia structure. Indians, free blacks and mulattoes, white servants and apprentices, plus landless whites – all were recruited as volunteers. As a result, the actual fighting that occurred was increasingly carried out by these new formations, while the old militia units became more and more social in function. If serious danger was close at hand, the militia would still respond; when it was not, the 'strollers,' 'vagabonds,' and 'drifters' were the first to be recruited for military service. How well these changes would work in practice was put to the test when the American colonies became embroiled in the English-French wars.

Colonial Wars Against the French and Indians

While the British colonists were building up their colonies along the Atlantic seaboard from Maine to Georgia in the seventeenth and early eighteenth centuries, they were not alone. To the north, along the St Lawrence River valley, the French had established colonies that eventually reached the Great Lakes country and extended down the Mississippi River to the Gulf of Mexico. To the south, the Spanish were also busy creating colonies in Florida, along the Gulf Coast, and in what is now the American southwest. Thus the English colonies were effectively ringed by potentially hostile settlements, against which they had to be on constant guard.

At the same time, the English colonists displayed a marked inclination to expand into the interior of the continent. They especially desired to cross the Appalachian mountain chain and move onto the lush, forested lands beyond. Yet this movement directly challenged the French to the north and west. The French, though fewer in number than the English, had established more favorable

relations with the Indian tribes with whom they traded for furs and were thus able to recruit the Indians as allies in their border conflicts with the ever-expanding English settlers and traders.

In Europe, the English and French monarchies were now engaged in a titanic struggle for domination, and soon Europe's 'Wars for Empire' spilled over into North America, initiating a period of colonial conflict that lasted for seven decades, from 1689 to 1763. The English and their colonists warred against the French both at home and in North America, with the Spanish (trying to maintain their European and colonial greatness) often siding with the French. In four successive wars the English colonial militias were called upon to aid the mother country and her regular military forces. Given their animosity toward the French, both for their encroachments on English colonial rights and for their willingness to use savage

A frontiersman with the first native firearm, the Pennsylvania long rifle.

Indians as allies, the American colonists were ready to stand beside the British land and naval forces, but often only if local grievances were involved or if the danger was perceived as affecting them seriously.

The first of the Wars for Empire was fought between 1689 and 1697. In Europe it was known as the War of the League of Augsburg; in America it was called simply King William's War. Here the northern colonies, which were most aggrieved by French attacks on their fishing rights and were most endangered by attacks by France's Indian allies on the frontier, led the way. While the British were willing to use their powerful navy to war on the French colonists in Canada in this first war, they were reluctant to supply the manpower necessary to carry out a land expedition against the French garrisons there. The New England colonies therefore accepted the task of raising a land army to attack their French neighbors. This was not strictly a militia operation, since militia units could not operate outside the colonies, but recruits were drawn largely from existing trainbands. Popular leaders were chosen to lead the operations, and the colonial assemblies put up the money for the attacks on the French. Two complementary operations were planned. One colonial expedition would attack Port Royal in Acadia (Novia Scotia) at the mouth of the St Lawrence; the second would march into Canada following the lake and river chain from the Hudson River valley to Montréal on the St Lawrence.

For the first of these operations the colony of Massachusetts raised a force of 700 men for a land and naval attack on Port Royal. Supported by the Royal Navy, the colonial troopers took the town early in 1690 but were unable to leave enough men there to retain it and it fell back into French hands. Undeterred, the Massachusetts volunteers tried again later in the same year. Now they assembled a 2000-man force, this time to take the fortress at Québec. Here they met nothing but frustrating failure. Failure also dogged the concurrent operation designed to take Montréal farther up the St Lawrence. Volunteers from New York and Connecticut were called to assemble at Albany, then move up the river chain to Montréal. Some units never arrived, and those that did march north made such slow progress through the wilderness that the whole expedition was called off. If the American phase of King William's War was inconclusive, so too was the European phase, and the French and British eventually made peace. But not for long.

Queen Anne's War, or the War of the Spanish Succession as it was called in Europe, took place between 1701 and 1713. Again it was a frustrating experience for the colonials. Again they attempted to subdue their French neighbors to the north by a two-pronged attack on the lower and upper St Lawrence citadels. The eastern prong was to sail from Boston to hit Québec by land and sea, with support from the British navy and five regiments of British regulars. The western prong was again to assemble at Albany and move overland against Montréal. Some 1500 volunteers gathered at Albany in 1709 to carry out the overland attack; an almost equal number gathered in Boston to move on Québec. Then came word that the British were not coming, as the troops were needed at home, and both expeditions had consequently to be abandoned. But the next year the colonists, with British naval support, were able to raise 1500 men and take Port Royal for a second time, and this time they held it as a permanent possession of the Crown.

The following year, 1711, the British promised naval and military aid, and the two-pronged attack scheme was revived. New England raised a force of 1500 men to join a British force of 7000 regulars. Considerable naval support was provided, but the sizeable expedition foundered on the rocks of the St Lawrence when the irresolute admiral commanding, Sir William Phips, lost his bearings in the fog in the mouth of the St Lawrence and, seeing a number of his ships go aground, gave up and brought the expedition back to Boston before sailing for home. This debacle meant that Sir Francis Nicholson, commanding the 2000 men assembled at Albany for the overland drive on Montréal, had to abandon his plans too. If the New England colonists were dismayed by these events, they were consoled by the fact that at the end of the war, in 1713, France was forced to turn over Newfoundland, Acadia, and the lands surrounding Hudson Bay to England.

Yet the French menace still remained to the north and west. Now the French began to rely more heavily on their Indian allies to harass the neighboring English colonists, especially in the Great Lakes and Ohio River regions, by supplying them with firearms. The French also maintained a string of forts designed to assure their hold on the North American interior and to protect their fur trade with their Indian friends.

After three decades of peace, the Wars for Empire broke out again in 1744, in what was called King George's War in the colonies and the War of the Austrian Succession in Europe. It ended in 1748, but in this short time the colonials demonstrated their military prowess by mounting a major expedition against Louisbourg ('the Gibraltar of the New World') on Cape Breton Island at the entrance to the St Lawrence. All of the 4000 men and most of the naval vessels in this successful operation were contributed by the New England colonies.

Predictably, colonies removed from the area of struggle were not interested in helping their compatriots: Fishing rights and French depredations were New England problems. Nevertheless, the expedition was a success, and Louisbourg fell to the colonial forces. Subsequently, when at the peace conference ending the war the British gave Louisbourg back to the French in exchange for the port of Madras in India, the colonists were outraged. Yet whatever the outcome, the colonial volunteers had proven in their typical eighteenth-century-style siege of Louisbourg that they could be a formidable fighting force, despite what the British generals thought of their rag-tag appearance and lack of professional military training.

After 1748 the French continued to strengthen their American possessions by expanding their network of forts along the Great Lakes and Ohio River valley. These included Fort Frontenac, at the eastern end of Lake Ontario, and Fort Niagara, along the crucial Niagara River. Especially important was their erection of Fort Duquesne at the confluence of the Allegheny and Monongahela Rivers (the site of present-day Pittsburgh) in 1753, thereby reinforcing their claim to the whole trans-Appalachian interior. If the mother country was still unsure whether it should push for complete French expulsion from the American interior, the colonists directly affected by the French presence had no such doubts, and conflict soon broke out anew. From 1754 to 1756 an undeclared war raged along the English-French frontier in colonial America.

Virginia, allowed by the crown to repel French encroachments upon territories claimed by her (which included western Pennsylvania), sent a militia force under Colonel George Washington to attack the French at Fort Duquesne and drive them from the area. This Virginia force was met by superior French numbers, compelled to surrender, and sent back home.

Undeterred by this loss, the British Crown dispatched a force of two regiments of regulars commanded by Major General Edward Braddock. Braddock, a veteran of four decades of honorable service on European battlefields, assembled a force of over 2000 men (which included a number of Virginia militiamen) and set out from Virginia in June 1755 through the wilderness to expel the French from Fort Duquesne.

Frustrated by being able to make only two miles per day, Braddock went ahead with an advance force of 1500 men to launch his attack. On 9 July 1755, when only seven miles from Duquesne, he and his army were suddenly attacked by an inferior force composed of less than 900 French regulars, Canadian militia and Indians firing from ambush. Braddock's forces tried vainly to form a line of fire to answer the enemy's withering fusillade. Unable to come to grips with the concealed enemy and soon facing further intense fire on their flanks, the British-militia forces suffered severe casualties, and after three hours retreated from the field in disarray, storming through their baggage train, even though no enemy was pursuing. Over 900 British and colonial troops had been killed or wounded, and 63 of 83 British officers were also casualties, including General Braddock, who was mortally wounded.

It was now obvious that highly-disciplined

Forced to surrender Fort Necessity to the French in 1754, young George Washington glumly returned to Virginia.

European troops marching in columns and firing in line on command could not be effective in the wilderness without serious modifications in tactics. Future fights would see the British regulars employing scouts, skirmishers, rangers and light troops (wearing brown and green clothing in place of the traditional British scarlet) to prevent a repetition of Braddock's costly lesson in frontier battle tactics.

The year 1755 also saw two expeditions by colonial troops against French forts in the wilderness: Crown Point on Lake Champlain and Fort Niagara between Lake Erie and Lake Ontario. Both were failures. Some 3000 colonials were assembled from New York and New England for the attack on Crown Point, but the volunteers got only as far as Lake George before they were repulsed by French forces. The expedition to Fort Niagara in the west was cancelled because of logistical problems.

In 1756 the French and British at last officially declared war. In America the con-

Britain captured Louisbourg, guardian of the St Lawrence, in 1745, only to return it to France in 1748 via the Treaty of Aix-la-Chapelle, and then to recapture it in 1758.

flict is remembered as the French and Indian War of 1756-1763. In Europe it is called the Seven Years' War. It was the final and decisive War for Empire. This time the British decided to concentrate their efforts on the American front. Eventually strong naval forces and 25,000 British troops were sent to the colonies for this all-out fight. These British forces were supplemented by a number of American colonial regiments placed in regular service and by colonial volunteer and militia units. The greatest number of colonial troops came from the more endangered New York and New England colonies, but most colonies fell far short of their requisitioned men, supplies and financial support.

Suffering only one important loss in the first three years of the conflict – this at Fort Ticonderoga on Lake Champlain when a combined British-colonial force of 16,000 attempted to take the fort and was repelled with heavy losses in 1758 – the British and colonial forces scored impressive victories over their French adversaries. In 1758 Louisbourg was taken in classic siege fashion by British army and naval forces, and in that same year a force of 3000 men, made up largely of colonials, captured Fort Frontenac on Lake Ontario, thus weakening the French

position at Fort Duquesne. As a result, when a British and colonial force made its way to the western fort near the site of Braddock's humiliating defeat three years earlier, they found it abandoned. Occupying the fort, the British renamed the installation Fort Pitt in honor of William Pitt, their great parliamentary war leader.

By now Britain was fully committed to deciding the issue with France on the American battlefields. Again a two-pronged attack was planned against the French bastions in Canada. One army of 9000 men under Major General James Wolfe, still in his early thirties, aided by a strong naval force, advanced up the St Lawrence River to the city of Québec. Discovering a path up the sheer cliffs in front of the city, Wolfe and his men daringly scaled the escarpment on the night of 12 September 1759 and suddenly appeared before the city in traditional battle line the next morning. The French commander, Major General Louis Joseph, le marquis de Montcalm, drew up his regular and militia troops in line to face the British foe on the Plains of Abraham. Shortly after, the greatest and most decisive battle of the Wars for Empire was fought in classic European style. The less disciplined French troops could not

A View of the Landing the New England Forces in ye Expedition against CAPE BRETON, 1745.
When after a Siege of 40 days the Town and Fortress of LOUISBOURG and the important Territories thereto belonging were recover'd to the British Empire.

Britain learned harsh truths about wilderness fighting in 1755 when General Braddock and 1500 regulars were ambushed by French and Indians near Fort Duquesne (*above*). Among the nearly 900 British killed was Braddock (*left*). Three quarters of the British officers were casualties.

stand up before the withering volley fire of the British regiments. Victory went to the British regulars, although both Wolfe and Montcalm fell mortally wounded that day.

In the meantime, as the western prong of the offensive, another army of 11,000 British regulars and colonial volunteers had assembled in New York under General Jeffrey Amherst. Their mission was to capture Fort Ticonderoga and Crown Point and then advance to the St Lawrence, there to take Montréal and move downriver to assist Wolfe at Québec. Amherst first sent a detached force to capture Fort Niagara. Its success there left Fort Detroit and the other western forts isolated. He then moved on Fort Ticonderoga and Crown Point. Although the French garrisons at these outposts decided to abandon them to the stronger enemy, they retreated only as far as the Richelieu River and there set up such an effective defense that Amherst was unable to make his rendezvous with Wolfe at Québec. Only in 1760 did Amherst take Montréal, thus bringing Canada under British control and ending the colonial phase of the Seven Years' War.

When the war was finally brought to a close in 1763 by the Treaty of Paris, the extent

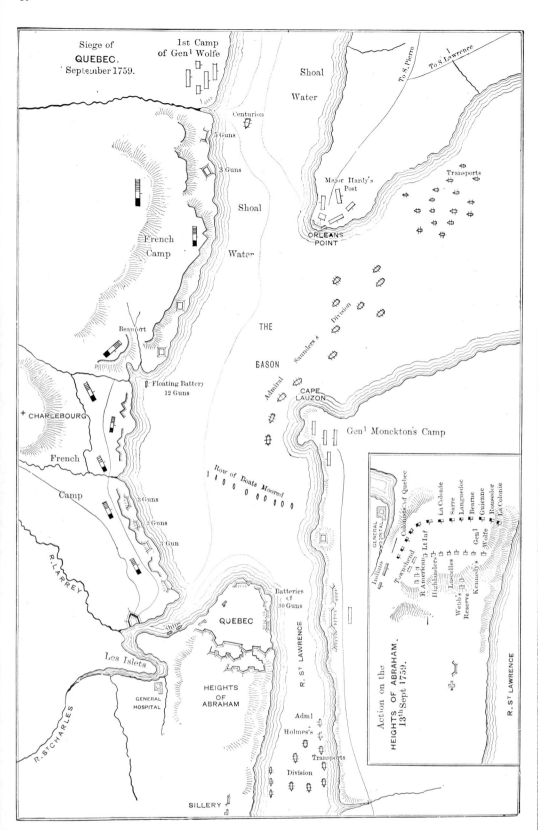

The siege of Québec, 1759. The French position in Canada was fatally affected by the loss of this fortress city.

evident in the course of the war that supplying an army in the wilderness presented special problems. Any army moving away from its base would inevitably encounter serious difficulties unless it took its food, ammunition, and all other necessities of war with it. In short, the colonial wars had demonstrated that whereas well-equipped, well-disciplined armies still dominated the open field, control of uncultivated hinterland might well fall to him who best mastered the new tactics of guerrilla.

The American Revolution

With the Treaty of Paris of 1763 and the end of the Wars for Empire, both the American colonists and the mother country looked for-

of French defeat was reflected in the terms of peace. France was forced to relinquish her entire American empire, with the exception of small islands, Miquelon and St Pierre, south of Newfoundland. Her ally, Spain, lost Florida to Britain, but received New Orleans and the vast lands west of the Mississippi as compensation. Britain was now the dominant power on the North American continent.

These conflicts had seen the colonial volunteer-militia units carry the brunt of the land fighting in the first three wars and also make sizeable contributions in the last and decisive conflict. In the process, much had been learned. It was not that traditional eighteenth-century European-style warfare of line fire and siege had been discredited: indeed, such tactics had proved decisive in key campaigns such as those at Louisbourg and Québec. But open-field battlefield tactics had to be modified whenever fighting took place in the wilderness and against non-conventional enemies. Scouts, skirmishers, camouflage clothing, and irregular formations were shown to be absolutely necessary off the open-field battleground where the enemy utilized surprise, maneuver, and ambush as primary tactics. It had also become ward to a time of peace, but differences soon arose between them over how the now-expanded American colonial territories should be governed. Britain was deeply in debt, thanks to the costs of the wars, yet at least 10,000 soldiers would now be needed to guarantee the safety of the new frontier regions and their Indian inhabitants, especially since the American colonists assumed that with the fall of New France those lands would be open to them for settlement. Since the colonists had obviously gained much by the

Right: Cap Rouge, nine miles north of Québec, was the initial base camp of British General James Wolfe.
Below: Benjamin West's famous painting of the death of Wolfe at Québec.

Two events that sparked the American Revolution: the Boston Tea Party (*top*) and the Boston Massacre (*top right*).

defeat of the French and the acquisition of their territories, it seemed only right to the Crown that some of the necessary tax burden should be borne by the colonists, especially as their taxes were significantly lower than those paid by citizens in the mother country.

Thus, as a matter of justice and fiscal responsibility, the decision was made by Crown and Parliament to raise both the internal and external taxes levied on the American colonists. The primary means employed would be both to increase taxes on trade in and out of the colonies through the Navigation Acts and to enforce these and existing tax measures far more rigorously than before. At the same time, the Crown made efforts to bring the colonies under much tighter governmental control to assure that their policies and practices would be favorable to the mother country and to the empire at large.

That was Parliament's point of view. The American colonists saw things in quite another way. They felt they had already made adequate contributions to the empire through existing taxes and through their miltiary service during the recent wars. And they did not want the British regulars on the frontier anyway. These soldiers might hold the Indians in check, but they might also keep the colonists out of coveted lands. Worse, in 1763 the government had established the Proclamation Line along the crest of the Appalachian ridge and declared the lands to the west to be a giant Indian reservation, thereby wiping out colonial land claims.

The raising of taxes and greater governmental control from London – which would lessen the amount of home rule enjoyed by the colonists – seemed to be turning the clock back and denying the colonists their legal liberties. The degree of self-government enjoyed by the colonists for a century and a half may technically have been a legal privilege, not a right, but the colonists did not see it that way. Privileges long enjoyed tend

to be looked upon as rights sanctioned by time and the colonists were not about to acquiesce in the retraction of their 'rights.'

As Parliament attempted to raise taxes through such measures as the Sugar and Stamp Acts, only to be met by protests and economic boycotts which forced the mother country to back down, it became obvious that many of the colonists were willing to resist with more than polite disapproval and remonstrance. But when the Tea Act was passed in 1773, and some Bostonians responded by unceremoniously dumping shiploads of tea into the harbor, the king and Parliament decided that it was time to call a halt. Parliament then passed a number of restrictive acts, including closing the port of Boston, designed to bring Massachusetts back into subjection. These acts soon became known collectively in the colonies as the 'Intolerable Acts.' When Massachusetts was also placed under military rule, in the

person of Major General Sir Thomas Gage, the stage was set for armed resistance.

The Massachusetts Provincial Congress, determined to resist coercion and military rule, ordered the colonial militia to prepare for action, if necessary, and began to collect ammunition and military supplies. These were stored at Concord, twenty miles outside of Boston. When General Gage found out through spies about the cache of forbidden supplies, he sent a force of 700 men to seize them on the night of 18 April 1775. But the minutemen, the elite among the militia, were warned of this expedition by Paul Revere and William Dawes and formed as a body on the village green at Lexington to block them. Early on the morning of 19 April the British regulars and the Massachusetts minutemen faced each other on Lexington Green. Someone – no one knows who – pulled a trigger. Immediately the regulars fired volleys and charged with their bayonets. The militiamen dispersed after suffering eight dead. The regulars marched on to Concord, destroyed what was left of the military stores, and began to march back to Boston. Along the way they came under attack by militiamen firing from houses and from behind walls and fences and were saved only by a relief force sent out from Boston by General Gage. British casualties for the day were almost 275 men; the American militiamen suffered 95, a tribute to their guerrilla tactics.

Word of what had happened spread like wildfire through the colonies. Charges of British military and governmental tyranny seemed to have been confirmed in blood. Militia from throughout Massachusetts and from the other New England colonies poured into the Boston area, and the British garrison

The beginning of the Revolutionary War: Minutemen and British regulars skirmish on Lexington Green.

operation. The Americans, roughly equal in numbers to Howe's forces, twice repelled British attacks on their fortified positions. Only on the third try was Howe successful, but he suffered a loss of over 1000 men in gaining his Pyrrhic victory. The Battle of Bunker Hill (as it mistakenly came to be called) really gained little for the British, for they were still surrounded by the 'rabble army' and unable to break out. The rebels, for their part, could not drive the British out of Boston, but they had helped create a myth (dubious, in the light of subsequent events) that an American militiaman was more than equal to any British regular.

The fighting in New England in the spring and summer of 1775 forced the Crown into a new military stance. If the colonies were determined on war, then war they would have. But it would be a conventional war fought along conventional lines, with mass British armies meeting their foes on the battlefield and the Royal Navy shutting down the colonies' commerce and supporting the British land armies up and down the coast. The British would either bring the rebellious colonial armies to decisive battle or destroy them by maneuver. Thus the rebellion would come to an end, and the pre-war political situation would be restored. In practice, the matter would not be so simple.

Bringing this British force to bear on America took some time. This left the colonies about a year to prepare themselves for the decisive conflict. Needing a regular military force to protect the colonies, the Second Continental Congress adopted the irregular New England army assembled around Boston as the Continental Army on 14

Lexington began as an American defeat: The British brushed aside the Minuteman, killing eight. But on their march back to Boston they lost 25 percent of their force to American snipers.

found itself surrounded by a ring of determined patriots. At the same time, militia forces under Benedict Arnold of Connecticut and Ethan Allen of Vermont seized the key British forts at Ticonderoga and Crown Point. The Second Continental Congress, meeting in Philadelphia, found that it now had to decide what to do with a *de facto* army surrounding the colonies' most important port and threatening to expel the British.

But events would not wait on prolonged deliberations. As weeks passed, with the forces facing one another (the militia being supplemented by volunteer units from the neighboring colonies, and the British receiving reinforcements of 6,500 men), both sides finally decided to make moves to break the stalemate. When the British began to fortify Dorchester Heights south of Boston, the colonists moved to fortify Bunker Hill, at the neck of the Charlestown peninsula to the north. But the working party foolishly decided to fortify Breed's Hill, just across from Boston, instead, and the British resolved to drive them off. On the afternoon of 17 June 1775 General Gage sent 2200 men under Major General William Howe to carry out the

In storming Bunker (actually Breed's) Hill the British won a worthless objective at a cost of 1000 casualties.

June 1775. Thus the US Army, the primary defender of the nation's rights and independence, was born in a season of need as the American colonies cast their lot for freedom and prepared to defend it with their lives. At the same time, the Congress also called for volunteers from the other colonies to join the Continentals, and the next day appointed the Virginian George Washington as Commander in Chief, a move to solidify support from the southern colonies.

Whatever their political intentions, the members of the Congress had chosen a first-rate leader, brimming with dedication to the American cause and able to inspire confidence in those around him. Washington had had only a little military experience during the French and Indian War, but now he set out, with the help of four newly-appointed major generals and eight brigadiers (two-thirds of the twelve being from New England and three chosen because of their experi-

ence in the British army) to create an army on the British model.

Plans called for an army of 20,000 men, but enlistments fell far short of that goal. Many colonists were reluctant to serve even a one-year enlistment period if it meant separation

from their families, farms or, businesses. By the end of the year New England militiamen were already beginning to leave the siege lines around Boston and return home, and Washington had to fill their places with other militia and volunteers. For crucial siege sup-

At Cambridge, Mass., on 15 June 1775, George Washington assumed command of the day-old Continental Army.

plies, Washington outfitted a small navy manned by army volunteers. It managed to capture a few British supply ships. He also sent Colonel Henry Knox to Ticonderoga to bring back the 50 cannon captured there.

In the meantime Washington launched a major expedition in the hope both of adding Canada to the coalition of rebellious American colonies and of gaining control of the northern axis of the potential northern invasion route from the St Lawrence down through Lake Champlain to the vital Hudson River valley. Major General Philip Schuyler from New York was given the responsibility for this expedition in June 1775, and soon 2000 men were gathered for the undertaking. The invasion, following the pattern of the earlier colonial wars against the French, was to be two-pronged. The western prong, under Brigadier General Richard Montgomery, would march from Ticonderoga north to take Montréal. The eastern prong, headed by Colonel Benedict Arnold, was to move up the Kennebec River and across the wilds of Maine to strike Québec. Montgomery managed to take Montréal by 13 November, but Arnold's forces were decimated by sickness and desertion while moving through the

Right: Overview map of the Revolution.
Below: On 17 March 1776 the British abandoned Boston to the Americans.

rugged Maine wilderness. Thus the army under Arnold numbered only 600 on that same day, 13 November, that his soldiers crossed the St Lawrence, climbed the escarpment below Québec, and encamped on the Plains of Abraham.

The British regulars and Canadian militia at Québec were unwilling to commit themselves to formal battle as Montcalm had done sixteen years before, so Arnold drew back to await reinforcement from Montgomery at Montréal. But Montgomery could bring only 300 men, and virtually no Canadians had come forward to join the American cause. With the enlistments of about half of the American force due to expire at the end of the year, Arnold and Montgomery decided to make a last desperate attempt to take the city on the night of 30 December 1775. Launched in a raging snowstorm, the attack was a dismal failure. Montgomery was killed; Arnold, wounded. When the British received reinforcements and launched a counter-attack in June 1776, the American army retreated without a credible fight. The Northern Army had failed. Canada and the St Lawrence were still firmly in British hands.

The only consolation the Americans could take from the campaigns of 1775-1776 was that on 17 March 1776 the British pulled out of Boston. General Howe, Gage's successor in command, decided to take his army to Hali-

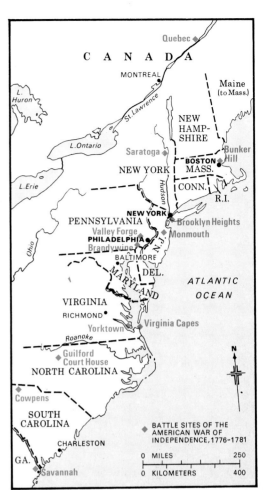

Trumbull's famous scene of Congress endorsing the Declaration of Independence. The war was already a year old.

fax, Nova Scotia, to refit and await reinforcements from home. His decision to abandon Boston was aided by the fact that Washington's army had taken Dorchester Heights and Nook's Hill and had placed artillery there to harass the British below. The evacuation of Boston was not of major military significance. The British enjoyed firm control of Canada, had a major base of operations at Halifax, and were able to control the coast with the Royal Navy. Yet psychologically, the abandonment of Boston was uplifting for the rebellious colonists and made them even more confident of eventual victory.

On 4 July 1776 the Declaration of Independence was proclaimed. In one stroke it transferred a war for limited home rule into a war for independence from the Crown. Yet the weak confederation of thirteen states still faced a difficult task before independence would become reality. The new Americans were only 2.5 million in number and held more local than national loyalties, each state being jealous of its powers and prerogatives. The people were divided in their views on the war itself, with probably only one-third in favor of the revolution, one-third opposed, and one-third unwilling to commit themselves to either government. Short on warmaking manufactures, the new United States

of America would be hard pressed to fight a sustained war even with unanimous popular support.

Given all of this, Washington wisely realized that the one symbol of unity and center of resistance was the Continental Army, and he was determined to keep it intact at all costs. But the states were more solicitous of their own particular volunteer and militia forces (their 'lines') than toward the national military efforts. Furthermore, enlistments were short-term, desertions were frequent, opportunities for training were minimal, and the Congress insisted on playing an interfering role in running the war both through appointments of generals and determination of strategy. Military supplies were never sufficient for the army, and the Continental currency with which the soldiers were paid and supplies were purchased continually declined in value throughout the war.

Washington's Continental army was eventually authorized to consist of 110 battalions of infantry, or about 80,000 men, but it never numbered more than 30,000 men, and seldom could more than 15,000 be mustered for battle. As a result, Washington was constantly forced to use the militia units of the states to supplement his regulars. Sometimes these militia units provided sterling service; more often they did not. But though Washington bemoaned both the states' failure to support his Continentals and his need to rely on undependable militia units, this exceptional

military leader somehow kept his forces together, maintained good relations with the Congress, and by patience and skill finally won the day against the British army and naval forces.

What was this Continental Army on which Washington – and the nation – depended so much? How was it organized, equipped and trained? In the beginning it was still very much a congeries of semi-local forces. Massachusetts contributed 26 battalions; Connecticut, 10; Rhode Island, three; and New Hampshire, three. The composition of each battalion, both in terms of the number of companies it included and its total strength, varied wildly. Suffice it to say that in 1775 the grand total came to about 17,000 men and officers. British regular forces in North America at the same time numbered only about 8500, but this establishment rose steadily throughout the war, reaching a total of 48,647 in 1781. Total American strength, as noted earlier, never exceeded 30,000, but this was sometimes enough to confer local superiority.

As a combat force, the Continental Army was at first almost entirely composed of infantry, the functions of cavalry and artillery being left to militia units. Indeed, it was not until 1777 that Congress finally got around to authorizing the creation of the first four regular cavalry regiments (each consisting of 360 light dragoons organized in six troops), but the need for a regular artillery branch

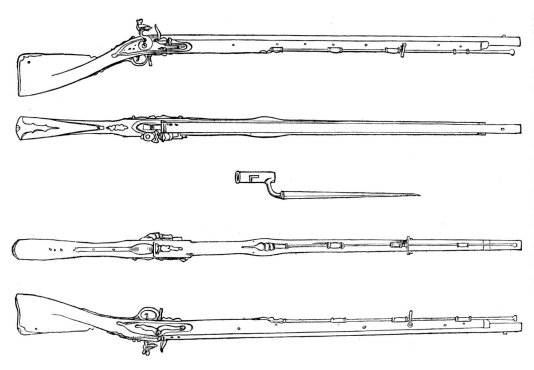

Probably the shoulder arm most widely used by both sides: Britain's Long Land ('Brown Bess') Musket.

24- and 36-pound siege guns; and eight-, 12- and 16-inch mortars.

As to dress, there was an insistent, but never very successful, drive towards uniformity. At first there was no standard at all. Then, in 1775, Congress recommended that all Army uniform coats be brown, with the color of the facings on the lapels and the number and arrangements of coat buttons to serve as distinguishing badges for the battalions. This recommendation was only notionally followed, some units insisting on retaining their own blue, green and even *red* coats; and in any case, the dyes used to produce the supposedly uniform brown coats were so variable that the results ranged from light sand to dark umber. Again, in 1779, Congress ordered that the standard infantry coat be blue, with distinctively-colored lapel facings for troops from each of four geographic regions (New England – white; New York and New Jersey – buff; Pennsylvania, Delaware, Maryland and Virginia – red; the southern states – blue, trimmed with white). Although this uniform often appears in later pictorial, film, and stage representations of Continental soldiery, it was never universally adopted because by 1779 the purchase of so many new uniforms was virtually beyond the government's financial means. For the remainder of the war most Continental units continued to have to cobble together what uniforms they could from existing supplies, including the nearly 30,000 uniforms provided by the French between 1776 and 1778.

Until 1778 training in the Continental Army was as haphazard as most other things about it. The low levels of training that had been

was recognized almost from the onset of the fighting. In mid-1776, that same Colonel Henry Knox whom Washington, a year earlier, had sent scurrying to Ticonderoga to take charge of the captured British cannon, was ordered to establish a Continental Artillery. What Knox produced were four battalions, 10 companies each, armed with from six to 10 guns or howitzers per company. The contribution that this artillery branch made to American victory was of a high order and set high standards for the future.

The equipment of the Continental Army was, throughout most of the war, chaotic. Since the army had not existed before 1775 there was of course no standard infantry weapon. Captured stores of the British army's 'Brown Bess' muskets (a .753-calibre flintlock with a 44-inch-long barrel) may have formed the nucleus of the infantry's original firepower, but the majority of the Continentals'

shoulder weapons was a mixed bag of odd-calibre muskets, fusils and carbines (varieties of short muskets), and the rare, deadly Pennsylvania long rifles so favored by marksmen. As the war progressed increasing numbers of French .69-calibre Charleville muskets found their way into American hands, and some American manufacturers began producing copies of both the Charleville and the Brown Bess for the Army. But at no point could Continental infantrymen be said to have had a standard shoulder arm.

The same was true of artillery. Although American manufacturers eventually began to produce standard four-, 12- and 18-pound cannon, the Continental Artillery was always primarily dependent on weapons of foreign origin, and these came in all sizes and shapes. Very loosely speaking, American artillery tended to follow the French patterns – four-, eight-, and 12-pound field guns; 16-,

Below left: A Rhode Island artilleryman. At first only the militia served cannon.
Below: A long 6-pounder field gun.

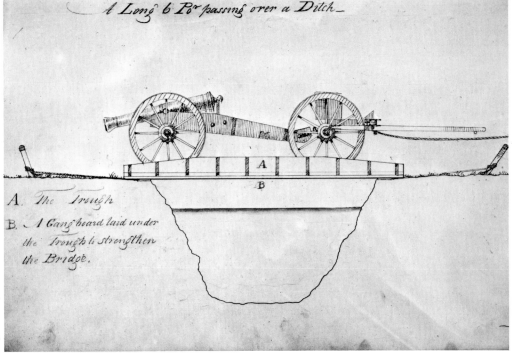

A Long 6 Por passing over a Ditch

A. The Trough
B. A Gangboard laid under the Trough to strengthen the Bridge.

American army uniforms, 1776-9: *right*, a brown-clad infantryman; shooting, a member of 'Morgan's Rifles.'

furnished by the pre-war militias guaranteed that Washington's new army would be largely innocent of discipline and all but the most basic military skills. The soldiers' dedication and enthusiasm may have offset some of these liabilities, but throughout the early years of the war the Continental Army was obliged to do a great deal of learning while on the job.

This state of affairs improved considerably when, at the beginning of 1778, Washington appointed Friedrich Wilhelm, Baron von Steuben, to the post of Inspector General of the Army. A former staff officer in the army of Frederick the Great of Prussia, von Steuben quickly set up at Valley Forge a training program that was at once highly professional, comprehensive, and specifically adapted to American conditions. Men trained personally by von Steuben returned to their own units and inaugurated local training programs based on what they had learned from the master, and in this way the effect of von Steuben's teachings spread through the Army with remarkable rapidity. The follow-

ing year the Baron published his *Regulations for the Order and Discipline of the Troops of the United States*: it would remain the Army's official manual for the next 33 years.

So great was von Steuben's influence that it even prompted a restructuring of the Army's basic formations. After 1778 the standard battalion was to consist of eight companies of about 60 men each. The standard tactical unit would be two companies, the theoretical maximum that a single man could command by voice in the heat of battle.

Yet von Steuben was not a magician. Though he had helped to make the Continental Army far more formidable than it had previously been, it still had to confront a highly dangerous and professional adversary. And whether the Americans could ever hope to achieve victory on the battlefield continued to depend on a great many considerations that were less tactical than strategic.

That the Americans did finally prevail can in part be explained by the fact that the British were fighting a war 3000 miles from their home base, and in part by the fact that they were fighting for a cause over which public opinion at home was badly divided. The Royal Navy might assure control of the

American waters and blockade the Americans' major ports, but the British army still had to destroy an army, aided by militia, that could refuse to fight and move back into the interior toward its own bases of supply almost at will. And the longer the American military forces held out, the more difficult would be the political problem of maintaining support for the war on the home front. Furthermore, as both sides realized, sitting in the wings waiting for a chance to strike if the opportunity presented itself, was France, still smarting from her losses in the Wars for Empire and hoping for an opportunity to regain her lost territories and weaken her mortal enemy across the Channel. The outcome of American war for independence, like most wars, would depend almost as much on time and will as it did on military struggle. Whether the Americans would have enough of either was the question.

In 1776 the British were finally able to bring their military and naval power to bear, but at year's end the American rebels had not been subdued and, indeed, were showing remarkable vitality. After the evacuation of Boston, General Howe remained in Halifax awaiting reinforcements for his intended attack on New York City. From there he would move north along the Hudson into Canada, thus effectively cutting off New England, the center of resistance, from the other states. From March until June Howe tarried, but in the meantime the British government ordered an expedition into the south to encourage Loyalists there to bring this section of the United States back under British rule.

The southern expedition, to be transported by a fleet under Admiral Sir Peter Parker, was delayed in starting and did not arrive in American waters until May, by which time numerous Tory forces in the south had been defeated by patriot forces. Despite this, Parker decided to attack Charleston, the largest and most influential city in the south, but his attack on the American Continental and militia army failed miserably. The Americans had established their defenses on Sullivan Island in the form of a palmetto log fort, dubbed Fort Moultrie, at the mouth of the harbor. The British landed on nearby Long Island in June but found they could not ford the waters to attack Sullivan Island and had to sit idly by while American artillery pounded the British invasion fleet. Parker was forced to give up the effort and sail north to join Howe in Halifax. For three years thereafter the south was virtually untouched by the war.

Howe, after further frustrating delays, finally set off with his invasion force for New York in late August. It was so late in the year that all he could hope to do at this point was to seize the city and its vicinity and use them as a staging area for a campaign up the Hudson-St Lawrence route the following year. Howe had an army of 32,000 men for the invasion. He was also ably supported by a powerful naval force under his brother, Admiral Richard Howe, giving him control of the critical Hudson, Harlem and East Rivers around New York. Washington, with his Continentals and militia, had only about 19,000 men to resist this British land-sea operation.

Washington made a fundamental mistake in trying to defend Manhattan Island by fortifying Brooklyn Heights on Long Island, across the East River. Brooklyn Heights, he reasoned, could dominate the lower tip of Manhattan and keep it secure. But by standing at Brooklyn Heights the American army was subject to being cut off from behind, and although the land behind Brooklyn Heights was defended by American troops, Major General John Sullivan had left the crucial Jamaica-Bedford road unguarded. Landing on 22 August 1776, Howe attacked the American position by the unguarded road and forced the defenders back upon the fortifications on Brooklyn Heights. Fortunately for the American cause, Howe delayed his main attack long enough to allow Washington to escape with his forces across the East River on the night of 29 August.

Two weeks later Howe hit the remainder of Washington's forces on Manhattan and forced them to flee north. But again his delay in pressing the attack allowed the Americans to dig in at Harlem Heights and hold off the British for another month. When, in mid-October, Howe landed behind Washington at Pell's Point, the Virginia general evacuated Manhattan and moved north to White Plains, leaving some 6000 men to guard the Hudson River at two forts situated on each side of the river: Fort Washington on the east and Fort Lee on the west bank. Howe came after Washington, forcing him to send half his

Right: Continental infantry, 1779-83.
Below: Battle of Valcour Island, 1776. The Continental Army fought a naval battle in a fruitless effort to break Britain's hold on Lake Champlain.

November, 1776: Lord Cornwallis' troops scaled New Jersey's Hudson Palisades, forcing the Americans out of Fort Lee.

army across the Hudson into New Jersey while the other half remained to delay Howe at the passes through the New York highlands upriver at Peekskill. Howe then seized Fort Washington and 3000 prisoners and forced Major General Nathaniel Greene to abandon Fort Lee. Washington's army was by now in full retreat, out of New York, across New Jersey, and down into Pennsylvania. Stragglers and deserters so sapped his forces that he had only 2000 effectives when he finally halted. The 8000 men he had left in the highlands above New York City just drifted away from the war.

The only bright spot on the American scene as 1776 campaigning came to a close was the spirited defense Benedict Arnold had made against a flotilla of boats Major General Guy Carleton had constructed to bring his sizeable force down Lake Champlain to seize Fort Ticonderoga. Carleton wanted to take 'Fort Ti' in the fall to use it as a base for a move down the Hudson the follow-

ing spring. Arnold and his men built their own flotilla to challenge Carleton and, although losing in the subsequent naval action at Valcour Island in Lake Champlain, so delayed Carleton that he gave up the idea of laying siege to Fort Ti for that year and returned to winter quarters in Canada, a welcome respite for the Americans.

Despite this victory by Arnold, the American cause looked dim as the winter of 1776-1777 settled in. The British army was in control of the central reaches of the eastern seaboard, having established themselves in winter quarters in Newport, Rhode Island; in New York City; and in Perth Amboy, New Brunswick, Princeton, Trenton and Borden-

Washington crossing the Delaware on Christmas night 1776, the prelude to his brilliant surprise attack on Trenton the next morning.

town in New Jersey. Howe had every reason to be satisfied.

But Washington was not done. Hastily and desperately assembling a force of about 7000 men, both Continentals and Pennsylvania militia, he made plans to hit the British in their winter quarters. He had to do this before the end of December because many enlistments expired on the last day of the year. His plan was to make a surprise attack on the British on Christmas night at Trenton, southwest of Howe's New York base. A second force under Colonel John Cadwalader was to do the same at Bordentown, farther south. A third force was to cross opposite Trenton and prevent any escape from Washington's attack. The second and third phases of the plan misfired, but Washington's attack on Trenton was superbly effective.

Crossing the Delaware River at McConkey's Ferry, a few miles above Trenton, the American force proceeded down the east bank of the river, then split into two columns to enter the town at each end on the morning of 26 December at 0800 hours. The Hessian mercenaries were taken completely by surprise and surrendered after a fight lasting only an hour and a half. Washington took over 900 prisoners. The Hessians had lost 40 killed; the American casualty list was only four dead and four wounded.

Encouraged by this success, Washington again made an incursion with 5000 men across the Delaware on the night of 30 December. This time he found his way blocked by British garrisons under Major General Charles Cornwallis at Trenton. Delaying battle until the next day because his troops were exhausted, Cornwallis was sure that Washington had fallen into a trap and would have to fight. But Washington and his men slipped away during the night, leaving their campfires burning to deceive their enemies, and struck Princeton, to the northeast of Trenton, the next morning, inflicting heavy casualties on two British regiments.

Washington then pulled back into winter quarters at Morristown, New Jersey, and the British pulled in their outpost to positions closer to New York City for the rest of the winter. Washington had won two notable, if small, victories at Trenton and Princeton, but they had hardly changed the strategic scene in and round New York. They had, however, convinced many American British doubters of his prowess as a military commander.

The year 1777 did not produce significant victories in the field or the crushing of Washington's army that the British had expected. Instead, only Pyrrhic victories were gained, and the British grand scheme to cut off New England from the other colonies ended in defeat.

General Howe decided to capture the capital of Philadelphia, even though he was promised only 5500 reinforcements from home, instead of the 15,000 he requested. Facing him would be Washington's army of about 8000. The bitter Morristown winter had taken its toll of his troops, but replacements had been found with the coming of spring. Of equal importance, numerous foreigners had

thrown in their lot with the undermanned and poorly-officered Continental forces. Some were men of limited ability on the battlefield but with pompous claims to rank and privilege; others would make valuable contributions to the war effort: Thaddeus Kosciuszko, a fine military engineer from Poland; Friedrich Wilhelm, Baron von Steuben, from Germany, who would train Washington's army at Valley Forge; and Marie Joseph du Motier, le marquis de Lafayette, from France, who became a trusted leader at Washington's side.

During June and July 1777 Washington kept his main army between Philadelphia and New York to bar Howe's path to the capital, but the British commander loaded his army on ships and sailed down to Hampton Roads and then up Chesapeake Bay to Head of Elk, southwest of Philadelphia. Washington rapidly shifted his covering army south to meet Howe and took up a blocking position at Brandywine Creek. At Brandywine on 11

Mortally wounded in the fighting at Trenton, Hessian Col. Rall lived long enough to surrender to Washington.

September Washington's forces were flanked by Lord Cornwallis' troops, which had marched upstream and moved behind the American position, and Washington was forced to retreat to Chester, below Philadelphia. By 26 September the capital itself had fallen (the Congress having fled to York, Pennsylvania), and Howe marched into the city and disposed his troops around the surrounding area in a defensive perimeter. Washington attempted to break Howe's lines as he had done at Trenton the year before, but his attack at Germantown on 4 October misfired. Howe then tried to lure Washington

Two of Washington's foreign advisors: Friedrich Wilhelm, Baron von Steuben (*left*) and Marie Joseph du Motier, le marquis de Lafayette (*below*).

and his army out into decisive combat at Whitemarsh, but the American commander would have none of it. Eventually Howe withdrew into winter quarters in Philadelphia, while Washington set up winter quarters at Valley Forge, twenty miles northwest, in a state of material and human exhaustion.

Thus by the end of Howe's 1777 campaign the British commander had successfully taken Philadelphia, but in the process he had unwittingly lain the groundwork for one of the most crucial British defeats of the war. While Howe had been carrying out his amphibious operation from the Chesapeake to take Philadelphia, he had left only a small contingent of troops in New York City, not enough to move north and join in a large operation then being carried out by Major General Sir John ('Gentleman Johnny') Burgoyne. Although apparently aware of Howe's intention of

Left: At Valley Forge von Steuben taught Continentals military drill.
Below: The Battle of Bemis Heights, 7 October 1777, the American victory that decided the Saratoga campaign.

Saratoga proved how effective the American long rifle could be in battle.

moving southwest against Philadelphia in the summer of 1777, the Crown had approved of Burgoyne's separate movement down from Canada to strike at the Americans via the Lake Champlain-Lake George route. He planned to reach Albany by the fall. His main body of almost 8000 British regulars, Hessians, Tories, and Indians would come down Lake Champlain, take Fort Ticonderoga, and then move down Lake George to the Hudson and Albany. A secondary force of about 1700 regulars and friendly Indians under Colonel Barry St Leger would sail to Oswego on the shore of Lake Ontario, move down to the Mohawk River valley to take Fort Stanwix on the upper Mohawk, just to the east of Oneida Lake, and attack Albany from the west. Facing this dual invasion force were only about 3000 Continentals led by the unpopular General Schuyler of New York.

Ticonderoga fell easily to Burgoyne's forces on 27 June 1777. Pursuing the defeated American enemy to Skenesborough, Burgoyne decided, despite his heavy baggage and artillery trains, to continue overland through the wilderness. Schuyler did all he could to slow down the advancing Burgoyne, and Washington sent all possible help in the form of Continentals, but it was the New England militia, incensed at Burgoyne's use of Indians and by reports of a beautiful white woman, Jane McCrea, being scalped by one of Burgoyne's Indians, who made the difference. At Bennington, Vermont, on 16 August, the New Hampshire militia savaged a sizeable British foraging force and its relief column, Burgoyne losing about 10 percent of his command.

In the meantime the British force moving down from Oswego into the Mohawk Valley toward Fort Stanwix was running into serious difficulties. The small Fort Stanwix garrison was determined to withstand St Leger's siege, even though a courageous attempt to relieve them by New York militia under Brigadier General Nicholas Herkimer met with failure. Schuyler sent Benedict Arnold west with 900 Continentals to aid the defenders at Fort Stanwix. Arnold took advantage of a half-witted Dutchman and a friendly Oneida Indian to convince the superstitious Indians, who treated the words of madmen with special concern, that a great number of reinforcements were on their way. This caused the Indians to abandon the fight, and St Leger soon afterward gave up the siege of Fort Stanwix. Thus Burgoyne's flanking

Burgoyne's surrender at Saratoga was the war's turning point: Because of it France joined the American cause.

movement from the west had failed, and his left flank was now in serious jeopardy.

Yet Burgoyne was still determined to fight on to Albany. He crossed back to the west side of the Hudson on 13-14 September to continue south. Major General Horatio Gates, who had now replaced Schuyler by order of the Congress under pressure from New England, was waiting for him at Bemis Heights, just below Saratoga, New York. On 19 September Burgoyne attacked the positions skillfully prepared for Gates by Brigadier General Kosciuszko, in what is called the 'Battle of Freeman's Farm' and suffered serious losses.

Burgoyne had all the while been hoping for relief from New York City, but the ever-cautious Major General Henry Clinton refused to make a major move to help him. So Burgoyne was faced with an American force becoming ever stronger while his was becoming weaker, and no relief was on its way. On 7 October he tried to break out of the encircling American lines but was badly battered by the riflemen of Colonel Daniel Morgan's Continentals in what has come to be called the 'Battle of Bemis Heights.' Then, as Burgoyne withdrew back toward Saratoga, American militia worked around behind him and cut his supply lines. He was

soon trapped, and surrendered on 17 October 1777, along with 6000 of his men and great quantities of supplies.

The victory at Saratoga more than made up for the loss of Philadelphia, for it was the type of clear victory the French had been awaiting before openly throwing in their lot with the American rebels. By February 1778 an alliance had been made between the two countries, and Britain's local war against her colonies had taken a giant step toward becoming a resource-draining world war.

The fortunes of war had been swinging wildly both for and against the American patriots. Now in the winter of 1777-1778, the tides of fortune seemed to be swinging against them again as George Washington and his men suffered the most agonizing months of the war in winter encampament at Valley Forge. The supply system run by the government had broken down almost completely, and without adequate food, clothing and shelter, Washington's rag-tag army endured great hardship. Yet the American army persevered and even gained strength. General Nathaniel Greene took over the post of Quartermaster General and introduced order into the chaotic supply system; and Baron von Steuben accepted the position of Inspector General and instituted his system of training to teach the men of the army the military skills they so desperately needed.

By spring 1778 General Howe had resigned his command in America and had

returned to England. His successor, General Clinton, was under orders to abandon Philadelphia, to send some of his men to the West Indies and Florida to counter a new French threat there, and then to return to New York by sea. In the event, Clinton decided to return to New York by land instead, and Washington hoped a harassing action might weaken him as he came. This turned out badly when, on 27 June, an American advance force under Major General Charles Lee attacked Clinton near Monmouth Court House, New Jersey, and was badly bloodied in the day-long fight that ensued. That night Clinton's forces slipped away and within days were safely back in New York. Lee was court-martialed for incompetence.

Nor did things go better when Washington, seeking to cooperate with his new French allies, attempted to take Newport, Rhode Island, in late July and early August 1778, supported by the French fleet of Admiral Charles, le comte d'Estaing. This operation was interrupted by the arrival of a British fleet under Admiral Richard Howe. The two fleets maneuvered for battle position on 12 August but got scattered in a gale, after which Howe returned to New York, d'Estaing went to Boston and then to the West Indies, and the American land force was left to extricate itself as best it could.

After these inconclusive actions the focus of the war shifted to the south, leaving the northern armies to confront one another in a sort of stalemate. The shift reflected a change in British strategy, a return to the south where, it was still believed, Tory strength was greater. The British army, supported by the navy, was to take the key southern ports and then move inland, pacifying the outlying areas as it went, destroying any rebel armies, and bringing the population into loyalty to the Crown both by giving them protection against the rebels and by using them in keeping the peace in loyal militia units.

At first the new British strategy worked well. Charleston almost fell to British siege in May 1779, being barely saved by the return of Major General Benjamin Lincoln and his troops from Georgia. Then, in September, an attempt by d'Estaing's French fleet with 6000 troops, and 1300 Americans under Lincoln to take back the British base at Savannah resulted in an overwhelming British victory. The Americans had suffered appalling losses in an ill-conceived direct assault on the British defensive positions, and because d'Estaing thereafter sailed off to the West Indies, Clinton was free to move down the coast unmolested.

Accordingly, he drew 14,000 men from New York and Savannah in an attempt to take Charleston. His carefully-planned attack by land and sea began in February 1780. His forces first landed on John's Island, the south of the city, and then crossed over the Ashley River to put Lincoln, unwisely situated at the end of the neck of land between the Ashley River and the Cooper River to the north, under attack from behind. On 8 April 1780, the Royal Navy forced its way past lightly-defended Fort Moultrie guarding the harbor, and Lincoln was completely cut off. Under siege and with no way to get out, he was forced to surrender on 12 May. His entire force of over 5000 men was lost to the cause. This most crushing American defeat of the war was complemented by an attack on Colonel Abraham Buford's relief force of 350 Virginians by Lieutenant Colonel Banastre Tarleton's cavalry at the Waxhaws, near the North Carolina-South Carolina border. Most of the Americans were slaughtered, despite Buford's attempts to surrender.

Clinton returned to New York with about one-third of his forces, leaving Major General Cornwallis to police and pacify the south, especially South Carolina. But despite his control of the seaports and the aid of Tory units who cooperated with his forces, Lord Cornwallis found it very difficult, if not impossible, to bring the area into loyal subjugation. There were no Continentals in the area, but guerrilla bands led by Thomas Sumter, Andrew Pickens, and Francis Marion continued to operate and keep resistance alive. Realizing that the local citizenry could not be wooed back to loyalty to the Crown if the British army could not effectively protect their lives and property, Congress quickly formed a Southern Army of 4000 men under

Horatio Gates. Cornwallis intercepted this Continental-militia force at Camden, South Carolina, on 16 August 1780 and badly defeated it. Gates, the hero of the northern fighting at Saratoga three year before, this time distinguished himself by fleeing 160 miles in three days after the battle. Thus by the summer of 1780 the British were beginning to have reason to think that they might win at last, despite their tenuous control over the interior of the southern states, for things were going just as badly for the Americans in the north as in the south.

The Continental currency had become worth almost nothing, and the Congress could neither pay the soldiers nor procure

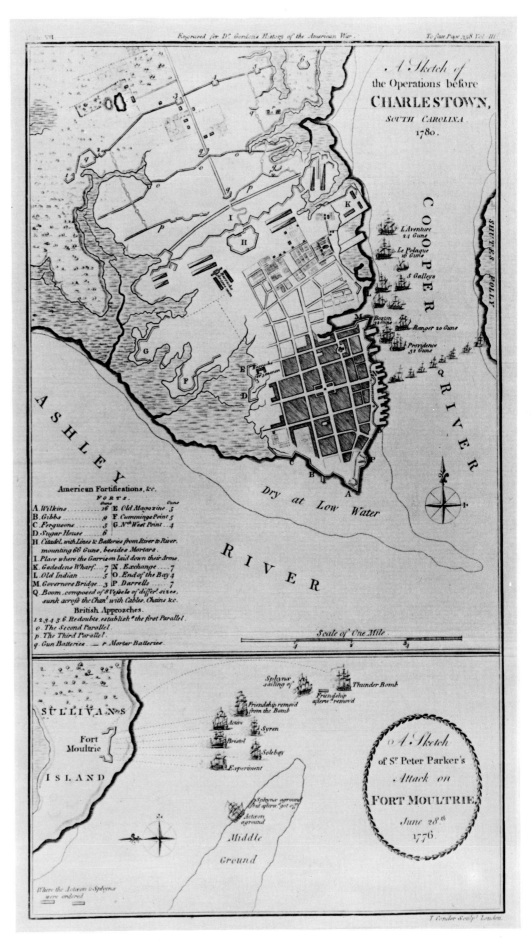

This 1780 British map of Charleston shows the campaigns of 1776 and 1780. By 1780 Britain saw in the invasion of the South a likely key to victory. In fact it proved a prescription for defeat.

necessary supplies. Recruiting for the Continental army became almost impossible, even for one-year service. Army morale sank, and there were mutinies in both 1780 and 1781 that had to be put down by force. In September 1780 the hero of Québec, Lake Champlain, and Fort Stanwix, Benedict Arnold, was discovered to be a traitor. Apparently angered by lack of what he considered proper recognition of his talents, and assured of money by the British, Arnold, as commander at West Point, made arrangements to turn over that vital post on the Hudson to the enemy. His treachery was discovered before it was carried through, but Arnold got away, later to serve the British as a general officer for the last years of the war.

At this lowest point in the fortunes of the American patriots, matters suddenly began to improve in the war in the south. In October 1780 a force of Tory militia commanded by Major Patrick Ferguson was sent by Cornwallis into the interior of South Carolina to pacify the region. On 7 October this force

In August 1780 the British defeated Horatio Gates, hero of Saratoga, at Camden, South Carolina, a victory that augured well for the Southern strategy.

was met by mounted militia from western North Carolinia and Virginia at King's Mountain, on the Carolinas border, and wiped out. Cornwallis had to halt his movement in the Carolina interior and retreat to Winnsboro, South Carolina, with militia dogging him every mile of the way.

Two months later General Nathaniel Greene, at last freed of his onerous duties as Quartermaster General and back on the field, arrived in Charlotte, North Carolina, to direct the continued resistance to any British moves into the interior. Cornwallis now sent a part of his army under Banastre Tarleton to find and destroy an army under Brigadier General Daniel Morgan, while Cornwallis himself led the remainder of the army cautiously into North Carolina.

Tarleton caught up with Morgan on 17 January 1781 at an open area called Cowpens, near the North Carolina border. Morgan's force was three-fourths militia, but he used them, his Continentals and his cavalry well. Placing his Continentals on a hill, with two lines of militia in front of them, he instructed the militia to fire volleys until pressed by the British advance and then to fall back through the Continentals and act as a reserve. When the British moved on the center of Morgan's

line, and the militia, as instructed, fell back through the Continentals and behind the hill, it appeared to Tarleton that he had won the day. But Morgan then sent the militia around the hill to assault Tarleton's left flank, while Morgan's cavalry, under Lieutenant Colonel William Washington, came charging into Tarleton's right flank. Tarleton's forces were virtually wiped out by this classic double envelopment, though Tarleton himself managed to escape.

Morgan now joined forces with Greene in North Carolina, and together they led the over-committed Cornwallis on a futile chase through North Carolina, into Virginia, and back again, finally stopping at Guilford Court House in North Carolina to do battle on a site of Greene's choice. By this time Cornwallis had only about 2000 men, and though the ensuing battle on 15 March 1781 went to the British, their casualty count was high and their supplies were exhausted. Yet instead of moving back to Charleston to resupply and refit, Cornwallis headed for Virginia to join reinforcements sent by General Clinton. While Cornwallis moved north, Greene moved into South Carolina; soon all British posts except Charleston and Savannah had been seized by American regulars or militia.

While General Cornwallis had been busy trying to pacify the Carolinas by occupation, Clinton had been trying to do much the same in Virgina. He had had limited success until, in 1781, he sent an expedition of 1600 men into Virginia under Benedict Arnold, who raided up the James River to beyond Richmond. Clinton reinforced this contingent with another of 2600 men under Major General William Phillips. Then, in May 1781, Cornwallis unexpectedly arrived from North Carolina and took over command. All told, Cornwallis now had about 7000 men. Against such strength, General Lafayette and his 1200 Continentals, even with the aid of the Virginia militia, could do little to stop British raids throughout central Virginia.

Clinton eventually ordered Cornwallis to return to the coast to establish a base for evacuating at least part of this force back to New York. Cornwallis chose the little tobacco port of Yorktown on the York River, in from Chesapeake Bay, because of its deep anchorage. There he would await a British fleet. Lafayette, having been reinforced by 1000 men of the Pennsylviania Line under Brigadier General Anthony Wayne, followed him down from Richmond, always keeping a respectful distance. Then Washington re-

ceived word that a French fleet under Admiral François, le comte de Grasse, would be coming not to New York but to the Cheasapeake from the West Indies. If de Grasse could hold off the British fleet due to sail from New York, while the American army held Cornwallis' army under siege at Yorktown, Washington might be able to compel Cornwallis to surrender before Clinton could send relief.

Washington ordered Lafayette to put Cornwallis under siege at Yorktown. He then made a feint toward New York to mislead Clinton, and, in combination with a French army of 4000 under Lieutenant General Jean Baptiste de Vimeur, le comte de Rochembeau, made a rapid march toward Yorktown. On 20 August de Grasse arrived with 24 ships in the Chesapeake and debarked 3000 French troops to aid Lafayette. When the 19 ships of the Royal Navy, under Admiral Thomas Graves, arrived at the Virginia Capes on 5 September, they found de Grasse already in the bay and waiting for them. The

Right: Washington and Rochambeau at Yorktown, as painted by Howard Pyle.
Below: Daniel Morgan, who first broke Britain's chain of Southern successes.

Morgan's victory at Cowpens in early 1781 initiated the reversal of British fortune that culminated at Yorktown.

ensuing 'Battle of the Chesapeake' may have been indecisive from a naval point of view, but Graves was not able to force his way into the Chesapeake. Meantime, a second French fleet under Admiral Louis, le comte de Barras, arrived at the Chesapeake from Newport with reinforcements and slipped safely into the bay. There was no way that Graves could now aid the besieged Cornwallis at Yorktown; he returned to New York.

Washington now had a total of 9000 American troops (both Continentals and Virginia militia) and 6000 French at Yorktown. A formal siege began, with the digging of complex entrenchments and ever-increasing pressure on Cornwallis from the slowly advancing artillery. Cornwallis could not escape by land, and he was cut off by sea. Clinton was dilatory about sending a fleet with 4000 troops from New York to relieve him. On the very day Clinton's relief force finally left for Virginia, Cornwallis, with no other option available, began surrender talks with Washington's representatives. Two days later, on 19 October 1781, the 7000 British troops at Yorktown formally surrendered to the American commanders and their French allies, while a British band played 'The World Turned Upside Down.'

This surrender ended the formal fighting in the War for Independence. The defeat at Yorktown finally convinced the Crown and Parliament that the war against the colonists was futile. Six years of conflict had not

brought the American Continental army and its militia allies to bay. The will of the colonists to resist had been bent but never broken. The French were now fully in the war, joined by the Spanish and the Dutch. British power was being challenged in two hemispheres and on half the oceans of the world. The costs were simply too high to continue the fight. The defeat at Yorktown led directly to the overthrow of the ruling British cabinet, and the new government was dedicated to bringing the war to an end on honorable terms. Avoiding possible future losses in the West Indies and in India was now considered more important than the recognition of American independence.

The peace talks that began shortly after Yorktown ended in 1783 with the Treaty of Paris, wherein Britain recognized the independence of the United States of America. A new nation had been born out of successful military conflict. It would now have to maintain its fragile independence and find its place in the family of nations. The work of the US Army was just beginning.

Right: Plan of the siege of Yorktown.
Below: When Cornwallis surrendered the 7000-man Yorktown garrison Britain in effect lost the war. The American victory was mostly Washington's doing, but French help had been crucial.

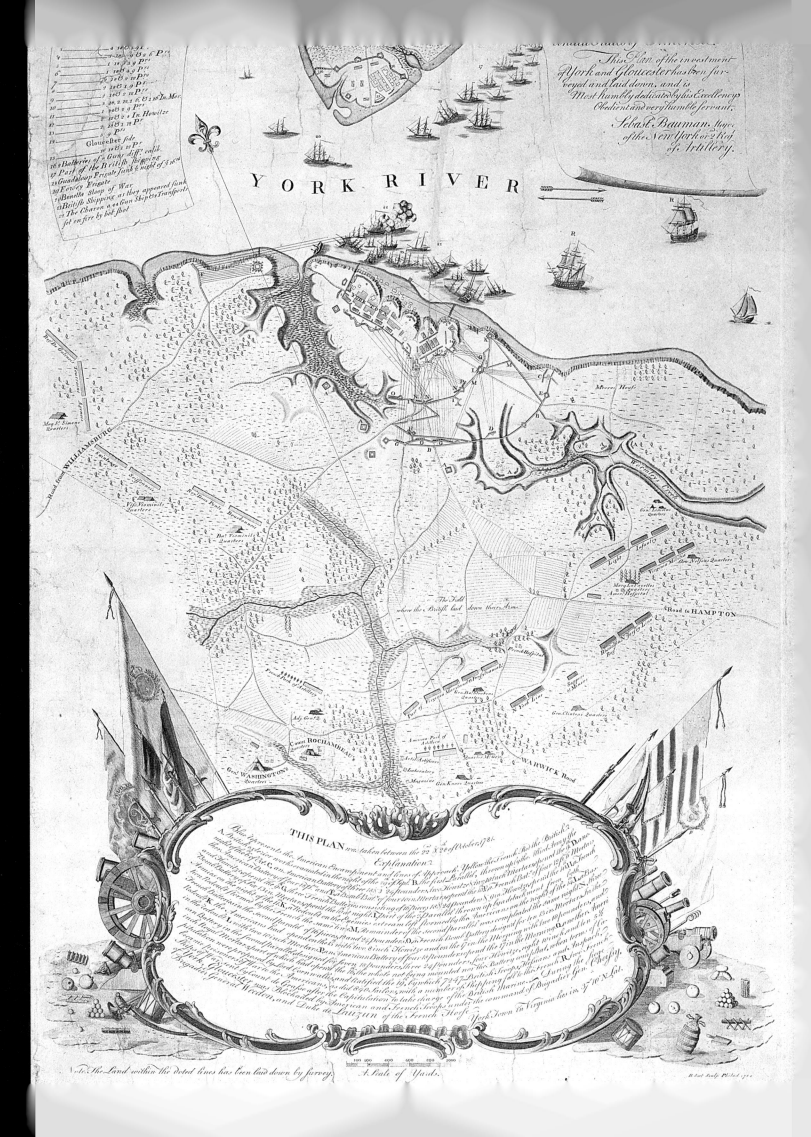

YEARS OF TESTING: 1783-1860

It was in the professionally-conducted Mexican War that the US Army came of age. Shown here, the storming of the city of Monterrey, 24 September 1846.

Once the war for independence had been concluded by the Treaty of Paris in 1783 the need for a standing army of any appreciable size ended, and Congress was quick to order a radical reduction in its numbers. This haste to cut the army was aided by the memory of the 'Newburgh Conspiracy' of 1782. This 'conspiracy' had begun with grumbling by some officers stationed at Newburgh, New York, about arrears in their pay. Certain of the officers had urged their peers both not to obey orders if the fighting was renewed and to refuse to disband, if so ordered by Congress, until they were paid. Washington had intervened and promised to intercede for the officers with Congress. When Congress decided to grant them their back pay and offered them full pay for five years, instead of half-pay for life, the issue evaporated. But memories of threatened military disobedience to civil authority still lingered.

A basic question facing the new nation at the end of hostilities was how large an army it needed and how that army should be constituted. Obviously a sizeable standing army, with no major enemies to fight, was both unnecessary and prohibitively expensive. What sort of force was needed to guard military supplies, control the Indians on the frontier, and generally be available to protect domestic peace? Should it be a small regular force, to be supplemented by militia in case of major trouble? This seemed to be the favored solution, but it raised the question of control of the militia, which were state forces. How much direction should the central government have over their training and use if they were to be effective militarily?

The Congress appointed a committee to come up with recommendations. Alexander Hamilton was chosen as chairman, and the committee's first major witness was George Washington. The revered general suggested that the nation would be best served by volunteer state militia units under federal control, plus a small regular army of 2630 officers and men to control the Indians and protect the nation's borders. Hamilton's committee adopted most of Washington's ideas, but Congress turned them down, primarily because of cost (at the time the regular army consisted of only 600 men guarding military supplies at West Point and other outposts). The committee then recommended the alternative of a larger force that could cost less. This would be achieved by cutting the pay of the officers. Congress again rejected its ideas.

Finally, in late June 1784, with time running out on its session, Congress agreed on an army plan. Disbanding the one existing infantry regiment and the one battalion of artillery (although leaving 80 artillerymen to

Above: Washington's mounted guard, 1784. In fact, though Congress had authorized 700, the army had but 525 men in 1784.

Below: The Battle of Fallen Timbers, 1794. 'Mad Anthony' Wayne's legion still wore uniforms much like those of 1779.

guard the military stores at West Point), the parsimonious Congress called for a new force of 700 men to constitute a regular army, the men to be drawn from volunteers from four states (Pennsylvania, New Jersey, New York, and Connecticut), under Lieutenant Colonel Josiah Harmar as commanding officer. This puny force soon proved to be inadequate to the tasks imposed upon it.

In 1786 the farmers in western Massachusetts, faced with severe economic problems, began to riot for relief from their debts. Congress responded by authorizing a 1300-man volunteer force to serve for three years, but by the time any of them reached the scene, a group of rebels led by Daniel Shays had already attacked the Springfield arsenal in January 1787. 'Shays Rebellion' was suppressed by the Massachusetts militia, but the incident clearly revealed that the tiny force of Army regulars was hardly enough to ensure domestic peace. The event, in addition to revealing the nation's military weakness, also clearly illustrated the impotence of the central government, denied taxing and enforcement powers under the Articles of Confederation. A convention, called to revise the Articles, ended by revising them out of existence and writing a new constitution.

Under the Constitution, a national army independent of the states was created, but its control was vested in both the legislative and executive branches of the federal government. Congress was given the power to declare war and to raise an army and a navy, but the Commander in Chief, in both peacetime and wartime, was the president. Congress, subsequent to the promulgation of the new Constitution and the election of executive officers and congressmen, created a single Department of War for Army and Navy. This department would persist until it became the Department of Defense after World War II.

In 1789 the new government took over the existing army of 800 men and confirmed now-Brigadier General Harmar in his rank and authority. Major General Henry Knox was appointed the first Secretary of War. While the organization of this new army was relatively simple, and procurement of supplies for the force was left in the hands of civilians for years to come, Congress did see fit to authorize creation of two federal armories for the manufacture of weapons. Armories at Springfield, Massachusetts, and at Harper's Ferry, Virginia, opened in 1794, although the nation still purchased most of its armaments abroad because of the lack of manufacturing facilities in the country.

A militia to assure domestic peace and to repel invaders having also been provided for in the Constitution, Congress passed a militia law in 1792. It provided for state militia forces to be made up of all able-bodied white men between the ages of 18 and 45, but left compliance up to the states. As a result, the state militia units were neither well-disciplined nor well-trained. Furthermore, Congress specified that members of the militia could not be compelled to serve for more than three months in any given year and forbade their use outside the United States. Although the militia was called to service by President Washington to put down a local insurrection called the 'Whiskey Rebellion' in western Pennsylvania in 1794, no real test of its effectiveness could come for a number of years.

Indian Troubles and Explorations in the West

The Indian menace in the Old Northwest had not vanished with the explusion of the French from America and the defeat of the British in 1783. If anything, it had become worse. One source of trouble was that the British, correct-

ly arguing that the monies owed to Tories for their lost properties during the Revolution had not been paid off, as specified in the Treaty of Paris, had refused to give up the forts in the western territories. And from these forts the Indians received arms and supplies with which they stoutly resisted the incursions of the hordes of settlers now pouring into the trans-Appalachian west. For their part, the new settlers soon began issuing veiled threats that if the federal government did not protect them from the Indians they might turn to England or Spain for support. These none-too-subtle hints at secession could not be ignored by the government if it wanted to keep the nation intact.

Congress responded to President Washington's request for greater military forces to garrison the frontier by raising the number of authorized regular Army troops to 2283, but something more had to be done to curb the Indian menace. Secretary of War Knox offered an answer in the form of a major show of strength in the 'Ohio Country'. He ordered General Harmar, cooperating with Arthur St Clair, governor of the Northwest Territory, to move against the Miami Indian tribes. Their dilatory two-pronged attack, in 1790, from Fort Washington (now Cincinnati) on the Ohio River against the Miamis failed completely. The next year St Clair and Harmar assembled 600 regulars and 1400 militiamen at Fort Washington and prepared to move out once again. This punitive expedition, contrary to Knox's order for a 'rapid and decisive' stroke, traveled as sluggishly as its predecessor. In two months it had moved only 100 miles to the north, having stopped to build forts along the way and being encumbered

From Fallen Timbers to his death in 1813 Shawnee chief Tecumseh was a relentless foe of the government.

A View of Col. Johnson's Engagement with the Savages (commanded by Tecumseh) near the Moravian Town, October 5, 1812.

1 Col. Johnson heroically defending himself against the attack of an Indian Chief.
2 The American Infantry firing upon a body of the enemy on the left
3 A dismounted Dragoon personally engaged with one of the enemy

5 Tecumseh rallying his men, and encouraging them to return to the attack.
6 A savage in the act of scalping a wounded drummer of the American Infantry.
7 The savages pursued by the cavalry, retreating to a swamp on the left.

Date on print incorrect, should

by its large baggage train, laden with the 'necessities' of civilized campaigning, including 300 women, many of them prostitutes. This force, by this time down to 1400 men, encamped on the night of 3 November near the headwaters of the Wabash River with virtually no security provided. Just before dawn the next morning, it was attacked by about 1000 Indians, who slew 600 whites and inflicted another 300 casualties. St Clair survived but soon retired from the Army, his reputation forever blemished.

Many Americans wanted to abandon the

William Henry Harrison's victory over the Indians at Tippecanoe in 1811 helped him to become president in 1840.

Indian wars after this painful defeat on the Wabash, but President Washington knew the issue had to be joined and resolved. So, as Commander in Chief, he ordered a third expedition against the Indians. Congress was now willing to authorize an army of 5000 men, and Washington appointed the Revolutionary War hero from Pennsylvnia, 'Mad Anthony' Wayne, as brigadier to succeed St Clair. Hardly 'mad,' although decidedly impetuous and blustery. Wayne insisted that the operation be carefully planned and that his troops be carefully trained and disciplined before his force began venturing into the wilderness.

Wayne moved his troops to Fort Washington in 1793, and the following year, with 3000

picked men, he moved north. He marched to within a few miles of Fort Miami, a recently-established post built by the British on the site of present-day Toledo, at the western tip of Lake Erie. There, on 20 August 1794, his force was attacked by Indians almost within gunshot of the fort. After repelling the first assault, Wayne and his men moved out in a bayonet charge and succeeded in driving the Indians out of their cover of fallen trees (hence the name 'Battle of Fallen Timbers') and onto the open prairie. Here his mounted militiamen decimated the Indian ranks, after which Wayne burned the Indians' villages and destroyed their crops. Cowed by this show of force, the western tribes in the Ohio Country agreed to make peace with the United States and to cede their lands to the nation. The treaty of Greenville, August 1795, ended the Indian menace for a time on the frontier, and pioneers flooded into the Northwest in unprecedented numbers.

Inevitably, settlers soon began spilling over onto lands never ceded by the Indians. To resist them, the Indians, under the leadership of Tecumseh, chief of the Shawnees, along with The Prophet, his brother, organized a defensive Indian confederation. William Henry Harrison, governor of the Indiana territory and former army officer, decided at the urging of the settlers to strike the Indians before they could mount effective resistance, and in the summer of 1811 he organized a force of 300 regulars and 650 militia to wipe them out. Moving from Vincennes in September, and stopping to build a fort on the edge of the Indian country, Harrison and his men moved on toward Tippecanoe Creek in western Indiana, the site of Tecumseh's main village. On the morning of 7 November 1811 the Indians attacked Harrison's encampment in a wild charge that soon degenerated into furious hand-to-hand combat. Organizing a counterattack, the American forces drove the Indians from the field with the aid of their mounted militia. Harrison lost almost 70 men killed in this minor engagement. It had secured only temporary peace on the frontier, but it gained for Harrison a military reputation that would stand him in good stead when he ran for president three decades later.

The Army was also active in these years in areas beyond the Northwest territory. Spain's sale of Louisiana to France in 1800 had caused great concern in America, and especially in the West. That the immense territories west of the Mississippi should be under the domination of feeble Spain was one thing; their ownership by expansive and strong France was another. It meant, among other things, that free transit for the Western farmers down the Mississippi to New Orleans might be endangered. Worse, Spain had suspended the right of deposit of goods at New Orleans (guaranteed to America by treaty) just before transferring the land to France, meaning that American trade down the Mississippi for sale at New Orleans might be completely cut off.

When President Thomas Jefferson, therefore, approached the French government in

1803 about buying New Orleans for $2 million and found that Napoleon was willing to sell the whole territory for only $15 million, he overcame his constitutional scruples, partially in deference to his Western voters, and agreed to the purchase. The Army took formal possession of the territory in December 1803 and established a garrison at New Orleans. Brigadier General James Wilkinson was appointed as the first governor of the Louisiana Territory.

Now that the Louisiana Territory belonged to America, Jefferson was determined to have it explored and mapped. Accordingly, he chose Captain Meriwether Lewis and Lieutenant William Clark, both army veterans, to lead the expedition. The Lewis and Clark expedition left St Louis early in 1804, travelled up the Missouri River, crossed the Rocky Mountains, and descended to the Pacific via the Columbia River in November 1805. The explorers returned through central Montana, arriving in St Louis in September 1806. Their findings were of immense value geographically, scientifically, and politically. In the meantime, Captain Zebulon Pike was sent on a similar mission to the headwaters of the Mississippi, and then on another into present-day Colorado. As with the work of Lewis and Clark, the explorations of Pike added much to the nation's store of knowledge and established legal claim to the

lands that had been traversed. But the role of the Army in the opening of the West was just beginning. It would not end until almost a century had passed, the Indians had been removed, and the trans-Mississippi territories all the way to the Pacific had been fully incorporated into the mainstream of the expanding nation.

Undeclared War with France

In 1789, the year the new Constitution was put into force in the United States, the Bourbon monarchy in France was openly challenged by the middle class, which demanded fundamental change in the government, many of the reformers taking the American Revolution as their inspiration. This was the beginning of a world-shaking French Revolution that would end only in 1799 with the coming to power of Napoleon Bonaparte. By 1793 the French had declared war against a European coalition of powers, including Britain, which were determined to restore the Bourbon monarchy to France. As France and Britain each needed to cut off supplies flowing to the other from colonies and from neutrals, both navies began to interdict trade and seize vessels on the high seas. As an emerging neutral trader, the United States soon found itself embroiled in Europe's war.

Since the British had taken the lead in

In fact, Tippecanoe was 'a near run thing.' A bayonet charge finally won the battle, but Harrison's losses were painfully high.

seizing American merchant vessels, the Washington administration attempted to keep the United States out of war by negotiating Jay's Treaty in 1794. Although in this treaty Britain did not actually renounce the right to make seizures on the high seas, she did agree to evacuate the outposts in the American West at long last. Seeing this treaty as pro-British in intention, France now began to seize American vessels. As the nation moved into John Adams' presidency in 1797, relations between the two countries were becoming precarious. Faced with French depredations and the possibility of war, Congress was willing to re-build the neglected Navy but would only authorize the president to call out 80,000 militia for three months to augment the Army of 3300 officers and men. (This Army had only four infantry regiments of eight companies each.)

Only in 1798, with an undeclared war at sea taking place, was Congress willing to expand the infantry and the harbor defense and ordnance units and create a Provisional Army. Although the Provisional Army, headed by George Washington as lieutenant general (the aging ex-president being persuaded to come out of retirement for the

Lewis and Clark on the Columbia River. The Louisiana Purchase opened a new theater of operations for the US Army.

emergency), eventually grew to 4000 men during the next two years, it had little to do except assume a passive defense against a French enemy that never came. The Provisional Army was disbanded in June 1800, three months before the undeclared Quasi-War with France was ended by treaty.

Conflict with Britain

Thomas Jefferson, who came to the presidency in 1801, was dedicated to creating a presidency of peace and economy. The Navy was scaled back almost to nothing, and the Army was soon down to only 3000 men. Yet it was during these years that the institution most responsible for the creation of a professional army in the United States was born. In 1802 Congress authorized the organization of a Corps of Engineers, to make up for a need for trained military engineers, and assigned its ten cadets and seven officers to West Point. The resulting engineering academy evolved into the United States Military Academy, a school not only for military engineers but also for professional army officers.

Despite Jefferson's efforts to keep the United States out of Europe's wars by the use of diplomacy, his purpose was frustrated by events. The war between Britain and France resumed in 1803, and soon the harassment of American merchant ships began again, this time with the added provocation (on the part of the Royal Navy) that some American sailors were being seized from their ships and involuntarily impressed into British naval service.

Jefferson's main weapon was to deny the offenders aid by forbidding them shipments from the United States, but this embargo stratagem was a two-edged sword and hurt the American shippers and manufacturers more than it injured either the French or the British, forcing Jefferson to abandon his attempts at economic coercion. The loci of most of the rising war fever for retaliation against Britain (who most openly interfered with American neutral rights) were the American South and West. The Northeast was willing to live with occasional confiscation of American ships and cargoes by the British, but the Western and Southern farmers blamed Britain for their economic recession, allegedly because her actions prevented American agricultural products from reaching their overseas markets. The Westerners were also inflamed by rumors that the British were stirring up the Indians on the frontier. There was talk of striking back at the British by taking Canada from them.

Jefferson's successor, James Madison, actually did manage to exert sufficient pressure on Britain, through the Non-Intercourse Act, to force her to agree to respect American neutral rights on the high seas, but this was not known to the American Congress when it passed a declaration of war on Great Britain on 18 June 1812. Thus the United States entered into a war whose causes were insubstantial and ephemeral and which the nation could not and did not win.

At the outset of the War of 1812 it appeared that the United States had taken on a nation of vastly superior strength. Britain had almost 300,000 men in her regular army, plus a home militia. Her navy consisted of 700 ships (of which at least 125 were formidable ships of the line) and 150,000 men. The American army, on the other hand, had only 11,000

troops, 5000 of whom were very recent recruits. The nation was able to call up a half-million men, including 56,000 regulars and 10,000 volunteers from the militia, but the 450,000 militia called to the colors served for only very short terms and could not be used outside the country. The American navy had less than 20 ships (including only six frigates) and 4000 men, this in a war where control of the sea could be critical.

On the other hand, Britain was forced to use most of her regulars against Napoleon in Europe and in her various colonies. In Canada, a major area of wartime contention, she had only 6000 regulars, 2000 militia, and perhaps 3500 Indians to protect a frontier that stretched from the Great Lakes along the entire length of the vital St Lawrence to Québec. And because of Canada's sparse population, Major General Isaac Brock, governor of Upper Canada, was able to enlist the aid of only 10,000 Canadian militia during the war. The British navy, too, was forced to use the bulk of its strength in the war against Napoleon. In 1812 the Royal Navy had only 80 vessels in American waters, and these had to cover the Atlantic coast all the way from Halifax to Florida, escorting merchant ships, blockading American ports, and fighting off American frigates and privateers along the long coastline. Yet despite Britain's preoccupation with her greater challenge in Europe, the American challenge – whatever its strength – had to be neutralized so as not to interfere with the greater war effort. Britain committed as many forces as she could to the American war, hoping either to dispose of

Throughout the Napoleonic wars the US had troubles with Britain and France. This 1809 proclamation was premature.

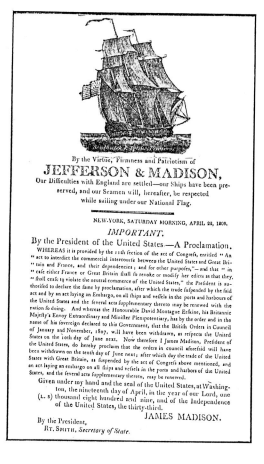

Sailors at mess. Britain's policy of impressing US tars enraged Americans.

the American military threat entirely, or, better, to hold the Americans at bay until the causes for their going to war were automatically removed with the defeat of Napoleon.

One way or another, the US Army would be called upon to do some heavy fighting. How well prepared it was to assume this responsibility is moot. In some respects the Army of 1812 was only a little better off than Washington's Continental Army had been in

Naval incidents multiplied in the 15 years before 1812.
Right: A US frigate *vs.* a British Sloop.
Below: An attack on a merchantman by a French corsair.

Infantry uniforms evolved steadily. By 1810 soldiers were wearing cotees and (for a few years) top hats.

1775. Years of penurious neglect had left it short of supplies, training, experienced officers, and morale. And of course it was pitifully small. Yet it enjoyed *some* advantages. Infantrymen now had a plentiful supply of standard American-made weapons, primarily the regulation .69-calibre flintlock musket and the .59-calibre flintlock cavalry pistol, furnished by the Springfield and Harpers Ferry armories, respectively. Artillery was still in a relatively chaotic state, but soon after the war began Congress created an Ordnance Department, and by 1814 the US Corps of Artillery had been born.

Also during the course of the war, some enterprising officers, such as Generals Winfield Scott and Jacob Brown – much in the manner of von Steuben before them – undertook to give their own troops intensive courses in military training. Though such professional training was never Army-wide, it produced individual units of sufficient effectiveness to cause (according to the story) one British officer at the Battle of the Chippewa River to exclaim, 'These are regulars, by God!'

In the matter of uniforms, too, the new US Army was in somewhat better case than the Continentals had been, though throughout the war uniform material was always in short supply. Now the regulation infantry uniform consisted of a short waist-length blue jacket (called a cotee) adorned with a high red

collar and red cuffs, as well as a tall black leather shako and gray or white trousers. The Artillery uniforms were essentially similar, as were those of the cavalry, except that instead of the shako the cavalry's headgear was the characteristic crested and plumed dragoon's casque. If nothing else, the US Army was now beginning to *look* like an army.

And, in fact, it would behave like an army. Its performance during the war of 1812 would be spotty, at best, but at least some of those spots would be bright enough to add lustre to a burgeoning tradition in which the nation could take pride.

The War of 1812

The war began badly for the American land forces. Three offensive operations were planned against Canada for 1812. One would be launched from Plattsburg, New York, against Montréal; a second would consist of a movement from Detroit against British forces across the river in Upper Canada; a third would move from western New York across the Niagara River to attack the British forts located there. All were fiascos. Brigadier General William Hull, governor of the Michigan Territory (once a dashing Revolutionary War hero but now an aging and indecisive shell of his former self), was appointed Great Lakes commander. He arrived at Fort Detroit in July 1812 with a force of 1500 militiamen from Ohio and led them across the river into Canada soon afterwards. Facing him were only 750 British regulars, militiamen and

Indians, most at Fort Malden, downriver from the Detroit crossing. Instead of moving directly against Fort Malden, Hull issued a bombastic proclamation to the people of Canada asking them to join the Americans – which was answered by musket fire – and then slowly began to make his way downriver. His opponent, General Isaac Brock, crossed over the river from Canada and cut off Hull's communications with Ohio. Then Hull received word that the 60 defenders at Fort Mackinac at the head of the Lakes had meekly surrendered to a small party of British regulars and Indians and that reinforcements had arrived at Fort Malden (Hull estimated Brock's reinforcements as ten times their actual number). Accordingly, Hull retreated to Detroit, and Brock showed up across the river and began to set up artillery units preparatory to an attack.

On the morning of 16 August 1812 the British fired but one shot into the American position and Hull ordered that the American garrison surrender. He and his regulars were taken as prisoners to Montréal; the militiamen were released on parole. To make matters worse, the day before, a small American relief force from Fort Dearborn (present-day Chicago) was massacred by Indians as they moved out for Detroit, after which the Indians returned to burn the fort. Thus, with the loss of Detroit, Mackinac, and Dearborn, the entire Northwest Territory had almost at once fallen under British control. It was hardly an auspicious beginning.

The offensive across the Niagara Frontier went no better, despite the fact that the Americans numbered 6500 troops. They were divided between Major General Stephen van Rensselaer, a New York militia officer with no fighting experience but with

By 1812 the shako had replaced the top hat and officers wore bicorns.

important political connections, and Brigadier General Alexander Smyth, an Army regular. Rensselaer's forces stood at the north end of the Frontier in and around Fort Niagara. Most of Smyth's were to the south around Buffalo. Rensselaer, as senior commander, wanted to attack across the entire 40-mile front, but Smyth refused to cooperate. Facing this insubordination, Rensselaer decided to make his attack across the river below Niagara Falls and take the heights of Queenston on his own. On 13 October 1812, 600 of Rensselaer's men were ferried across the river and climbed the heights to take Queenston. The British were quick to counterattack, but the Americans held their ground in the melee that followed. Yet Rensselaer's position was precarious. Few reinforcements were coming to aid his beleaguered troops. Because most of the New York militiamen refused to leave the territorial United States, Rensselaer could induce only 1300 men to cross the river and fight beside their comrades, and Smyth ignored Rensselaer's call for help from the regulars under his command. As a result, the besieged troops on the Canadian side of the river were forced to surrender. Some 900 of them put down their arms; 350 more had been killed or wounded.

After this debacle Rensselaer resigned and Smyth assumed command. But Smyth merely marched his men back and forth along the river, allegedly to move into position for an attack but always complaining of a lack of reinforcements. Eventually the disgusted militiamen wandered away to their homes, the volunteers were dismissed, and

The War of 1812 began badly for the US. Within months Hull (*right*) had surrendered Detroit. By October an invasion of Canada, well begun with the taking of Queenston (*below*) had collapsed, with 1250 men lost. An attack on Montréal was similarly unsuccessful.

One of the few successful American generals in the war was Jacob Brown.

the regulars were ordered into winter quarters. Smyth requested leave and received it. Within three months his name had been dropped from the Army rolls.

The attack on Montréal in 1812 was similarly unsuccessful. This force, the largest of all, was under the command of Major General Henry Dearborn. Dearborn held his force of 5000 in readiness around Albany,

Another attempt to invade Canada in 1813 petered out soon after Zebulon Pike's death at York (Montréal).

waiting for Rensselaer to move on Niagara. Then he slowly made his way north to Plattsburg on Lake Champlain, beginning his advance on Montréal only in mid-November. When he was within a mile and a half of the Canadian border he was challenged by 3000 British who drove back his advanced guard. At this point the New York militia announced that it would not advance into Canada, so Dearborn, evidently relieved, marched back to Plattsburg and went into winter quarters. Thus, as 1812 came to a close, the American armies had suffered three humiliating defeats against inferior forces. They would do better in the following year.

Detroit had to be retaken, so President Madison chose Brigadier General William Henry Harrison, the hero of Tippecanoe, to carry out the task. Assembling a force of 6500 men from the western territories, Harrison began to move north in October 1812. By January 1813 an advanced detachment of 1000 had moved to Frenchtown on the Raisin River, southeast of Detroit, where it came under attack by a slightly larger force of British and their Indian allies. Over 100 Americans were killed and another 500 were captured, and the campaign was marked by the ruthless slaughter of wounded American prisoners by their Indian guards. 'Remember the Raisin' became a rallying cry in the Northwest Territory, but Harrison was forced by the winter and British control of Lake Erie to defer the Americans' thirst for revenge. Harrison built Fort Meigs and Fort Stephenson at the western end of Lake Erie and waited.

A second American force, under Dearborn, was sent to capture the British naval base at Kingston at the eastern end of Lake Ontario, near its opening into the St Law-

rence. But Dearborn, moving from Sackett's Harbor across the lake with a fleet assembled by Commodore Isaac Chauncey, changed his mind, and with a force of 1700 sailed to York (now Toronto) instead, turning over command temporarily to Brigadier General Zebulon Pike because of ill health. The troops landed near York on 27 April 1813 and proceeded to take the town from its 600 defenders. As the Americans moved through the town, a powder magazine exploded, killing many British and Americans, including General Pike. Apparently confused and with their leader dead, the American troops paused to burn and loot the provincial capital before leaving to attack British forts on the Canadian side of the Niagara River.

In the meantime, the stripped garrison at Sackett's Harbor, under Brigadier General Jacob Brown of the New York militia, was under attack by a force of 800 British regulars plus militia, which Sir George Prevost, the governor-general of Canada, had ferried from the Kingston base across the lake. The

400 American regulars and 750 militiamen fought off two frontal attacks on 26 May before launching a successful counterattack that drove the British back to their ships.

While Prevost was attacking Sackett's Harbor on the eastern end of Lake Ontario, Dearborn and Chauncey, having left York, were invading Canada at the other end of the lake. At first all went well. A successful amphibious attack, led by Colonel Winfield Scott and Commander Oliver Hazard Perry of the Navy, was carried out against Fort George and Queenston on the western shore of the Niagara River. Dearborn had 4000 men

Far right: Tecumseh died in October 1813 when Harrison defeated an Anglo-Indian force on Canada's Thames River.
Right: The Navy's Oliver Hazard Perry.
Below: In September 1813 Perry defeated a British naval squadron on Lake Erie. 'We have met the enemy and they are ours,' he reported. The Army was now free to attack Upper Canada, which it did, successfully, within the month.

and could have achieved a compelling victory after taking Fort George, but he dallied, and his advance forces were routed on two separate occasions. Settling in at Fort George, Dearborn resigned his commission because of his ill health. By December both Fort George and Fort Niagara had fallen into British hands.

Farther to the west, on Lake Erie, Oliver Hazard Perry had been given the job of seizing naval control of the lake. Accordingly, he built and manned nine ships at Presque Isle and then moved his little fleet to Put-in-Bay, near Forts Meigs and Stephenson. There, on 10 September, near the southern shore of the lake, Perry met the six-ship British squadron, and in a four-hour battle disabled two of its vessels and forced the remainder to surrender. His famous message to General Harrison was: 'We have met the enemy and they are ours.'

With Lake Erie in American hands, Harrison could now attack the British in Upper Canada. Moving on the British via Detroit and Fort Malden, Harrison compelled a small 2000-man British regular and Indian force to fall back into the interior. He caught up with them on the Thames River, where, on 5 October, the British force was completely broken by a cavalry charge by mounted Kentucky militia, and over 500 British regulars and Indians were taken prisoner. Among those killed was Tecumseh, who had guided Indian resistance for the British ever since Tippecanoe, two years before.

By these operations the Americans gained control of the Northwest forts, Lake Erie and Upper Canada, but their attempt to bring Lower Canada under American domination in the fall of 1813 was an unmitigated disaster. It was supposed to be a classic two-pronged attack. One arm, 4000 men, assembled at Plattsburg on Lake Champlain under Brigadier General Wade Hampton, was to move on Montréal from the south. The second arm, 6000 men at Sackett's Harbor, under Major General James Wilkinson, was to attack down the St Lawrence as the left wing of the attack. Neither made it. Soon after leaving Plattsburg in September Hampton ran into British resistance on the Chateaugay River and retreated all the way back to Plattsburg. Wilkinson, seeing one of his detachments mauled on the St Lawrence north of Ogdensburg, gave up his part of the operation and, like Hampton, fled to Plattsburg. Both were soon dropped from the Army rolls.

In 1813 fighting also opened in a new theater, the South. Here the main American force was the Tennessee militia under its ardent Indian-hating leader, Andrew Jackson. Two thousand in number, the Tennesseans were spoiling for action, but since they

were neither permitted by Madison to move into West Florida (claimed by the United States as part of the Louisiana Purchase) nor, still less, into Spanish Florida, as Jackson wanted, they had been left in frustration in Nachez while the regulars took West Florida. Jackson and his army finally got their call to action when the Creek Indians went on the warpath in the summer of 1813, attacked Fort Mims, in the southern Mississippi Territory, and massacred more than 500 men, women, and children. Jackson caught up with the fractious Indians at Horseshoe Bend. In his attack on the 900 Indians Jackson had 600 regulars, 2000 militia, and hundreds of friendly Indians. The battle was a rout and was followed by a massacre of the Creeks. Although this campaign had no direct effect on the war, it led to Jackson's becoming a national hero and to being appointed a major general in the regular Army and commander

Above: Macdonough's victory on Lake Champlain, 11 September 1814.
Below: The battle of Lundy's Lane, 25 July 1813, one of the war's bloodiest.

Future president Andrew Jackson won his victory at New Orleans 15 days after the formal end of the War of 1812.

of the southern theater, from which position he would lead the defense of New Orleans in the following year.

Throughout 1813 the Royal Navy continued to blockade American ports and keep the miniscule American Navy off the seas. The British Navy also roamed freely up and down Chesapeake Bay, although a British attempt to take Norfolk by amphibious assault in June ended in failure, the British on that occasion consoling themselves by crossing Hampton Roads and burning the town of Hampton. Thus at sea, as well as in the North and the South, the year 1813 ended as indecisively as it had begun.

The war plan for 1814 decided upon by Madison and his cabinet was for yet another invasion of Canada, this time from the Niagara Frontier. Placed in command there was Brigadier General Jacob Brown, who had led the successful defense of Sackett's Harbor the year before. Serving under him was Winfield Scott, now a brigadier general, who had distinguished himself at Queenston. Brown was ordered to cross the Niagara River at Buffalo and capture Fort Erie before moving northward to Lake Ontario, there to join with Commodore Chauncey's naval force and seize control of the entire Niagara peninsula. Brown crossed the river with 3500 troops on 3 July 1813, took Fort Erie, and started north. Two days later his force came face to face with the troops of Sir Gordon Drummond and General Phineas Riall at the Chippewa River. The ensuing battle was fought in classic battle line style. The well-trained Americans, under the command of Scott, won the day, leaving Brown free to move on to Queenston and the junction with Chauncey.

But Chauncey declined to reinforce Brown (and nobody in Washington ordered him to do so), so Brown pulled back to the Chippewa. Then, trying to get around to the British rear, Brown's forces again collided with those of Drummond and Riall at Lundy's Lane, and a bloody slugging match ensued on the night of 25 July, each side losing over 800 men. The Americans pulled back south to Fort Erie to regroup, but the British were the first to be reinforced and soon placed the Americans at Fort Erie under heavy siege. Reinforcements, under Major General George Izard, sent to Brown from Plattsburg, did not arrive at Niagara until 5 October. By then the American position was untenable, even with the reinforcements, so early in November, Fort Erie was abandoned, and the Americans crossed back into their own territory.

When Izard had first received orders to leave Plattsburg he had protested that this would leave the Lake Champlain route wide open to the enemy. He was correct. Three days after he left, on 1 September, a major British expedition, including a naval squadron, began moving down Lake Champlain. Commanded by General Prevost, the army consisted of 12,000 veterans of the European wars. The naval units consisted of four armed brigs and twelve gunboats. Taking advantage of Napoleon's defeat and subsequent abdication, the British were now going on the offensive in America, with the goal of winning back some of the lands surrendered in the Treaty of Paris.

Facing this massive invasion force were but 3000 regulars and militia under militia brigadier Alexander Macomb. Prevost arrived at Plattsburg on 6 September. There he decided to wait until his naval force had destroyed Commander Thomas Macdonough's American flotilla before proceeding with his attacks on the American fieldworks. By skillful maneuvering and superior naval gunnery Macdonough and his men forced two large British ships to surrender and damaged enough of the others to win complete control of the lake. Realizing that even if he took Plattsburg he could not hold it without his waterborne supply line, Prevost the next day ordered his troops to return to Canada. The most dangerous British offensive on the northern frontier had been defeated by Macdonough's two-hour naval defense on Lake Champlain. The northern frontier was safe at last. Now the war shifted to the East and South.

In August 1814 a British force of 4000 men under Major General Robert Ross sailed from Bermuda, its destination Chesapeake Bay. There they were to destroy stores and attack the cities of Washington and Baltimore. The purpose of all this was to create a diversion of attention away from Prevost, who was then making his way down Lake Champlain. Ross's force sailed up Chesapeake Bay, landed on the Patuxent River, and began a march on the capital. The government tried desperately to organize defenses. It eventually collected 5000 regulars, militiamen, and sailors and marines from the navy yard to meet the attack, but the British easily brushed aside this defensive force and went on to burn the Capitol, the White House, and other government buildings.

The invaders then returned to their ships and sailed on to Baltimore. Under a major general of the Maryland militia, Samuel Smith, 10,000 militiamen had turned out to defend the city by earthworks constructed on the land approaches, while the harbor was protected by Fort McHenry, with 1000 regulars and sailors inside. On 13 September the British attacked the city after bombarding Fort McHenry for twenty-four hours but could not break the militia's defenses. Baltimore was saved, and America gained a National Anthem, thanks to Baltimore lawyer Francis Scott Key, who watched the bombardment. The British reembarked and sailed off to the West Indies, there to plan another operation, an attack on New Orleans. Taking that city would close the Mississippi to the Americans and provide the British with a valuable bargaining chip in the peace negotiations that had already begun.

The British gathered a force of 8000 regulars and 50 warships to carry out the assault on New Orleans. Andrew Jackson, as southern theater commander, assembled a force of 5000 men to oppose them. Major General Sir Edward Pakenham had been sent to America to lead the British invasion, but the expedition left Jamaica in November, before Pakenham's arrival, and began operations on 8 December. When Pakenham arrived on the scene on Christmas Day, 1814, he discovered that his troops had already been committed, thanks to decisions made by Admiral Alexander Cochrane and some subordinate army officers. Pakenham found his troops dug in on an isthmus below New Orleans with the Mississippi River on one side and a cypress swamp on the other. Opposite were the American lines, which stretched from the river to the swamp and consisted of high earthworks behind which 4500 men waited for the British attack. Jackson also had some 20 artillery pieces, nine of which were sighted on the British from across the Mississippi.

Pakenham decided on a frontal assault of 5300 men, with a secondary movement of 600 others crossing the river. When the attack came on 8 January 1815 the British were mown down by the murderous fire from behind the American parapets. Pakenham and 2000 other British regulars – over one-third of the forces making the attack – fell under the American fusilade. So great was the carnage that the officer commanding the secondary movement called it off. The British returned to the coast and attacked Fort Bowyer at the entrance to Mobile harbor, then, on hearing of the news that a peace treaty had been signed, returned to their ships and sailed for the West Indies.

Peace negotiations had in fact been going on for months at Ghent, Belgium, with neither side in a favorable enough position to agree to a peace treaty. Finally the negotiators, on Christmas Eve, 1814, had decided to accept a simple formula that had ended the war – two weeks before the Battle of New Orleans was fought.

In the War of 1812 for a second time the Army and the militia had teamed up to fight

Top: 'War Hawk' Representative John Calhoun became War Secretary in 1817.
Right: US troops, like these dragoons, sometimes wore full dress in the field to impress Indians with whom they were negotiating treaties.
Below: Britain's brief 1814 capture of Washington had small military effect.

for the nation. And for a second time it became obvious that despite the militia's occasional sterling performances, as at the Battle of the Thames, the defense of Baltimore, and the Battle of New Orleans, America's future military security would depend almost entirely on how proficient its regular forces could become.

The Thirty Years' Interlude

In the immediate aftermath of the war there had been considerable popular support for the maintenance of a sizeable professional army, but as the years went on without a visible enemy on the horizon, Congress' enthusiasm paled, and by 1817 the Army had been cut to about 8200 men. By 1823 it was down to about 6000. Even as trouble began to brew with Mexico over Texas' independence and its possible annexation by the United States, there was no disposition to increase radically the size of the Army.

Nevertheless, within the Army a number of major changes were taking place. Among them was the increased attention given to the US Military Academy at West Point, where officer-engineers were being trained. In 1816 money was appropriated for new buildings, books, maps, and engineering instruments; and in that same year the cadets received regulation gray uniforms, honoring the regulars at the Chippewa and Lundy's Lane who had had to wear gray uniforms because they lacked the regulation blue. Perhaps, most important, in 1817 Brevet Major Sylvanus Thayer was appointed superintendent. Well schooled in modern military tactics and military education, Thayer introduced a number of reforms both in the organization of the corps of cadets and in its instruction. These innovations started the Academy on the road to becoming a first-rate military and educational institution, its officers competent not only in engineering but also in the three branches of combat arms: infantry, artillery and cavalry. By 1846 the Academy had graduated almost a thousand cadets, about half of whom stayed in the Army to form the backbone of a professional force.

Fortress Monroe, Virginia, at the mouth of

Chesapeake Bay, was established as an artillery school in 1824, the first of the Army's specialist schools. Also founded was the infantry school at Jefferson Barracks, near St Louis, in 1827. Unlike today's specialist schools, at both these schools whole units, not individuals, were trained for up to a year.

The man largely responsible for these major changes was John C Calhoun, Secretary of War from 1817 until 1825. Besides re-establishing the office of commanding general as part of his overall reorganization of the Army's high command, Calhoun, one of the nation's great secretaries of war, also argued forcefully for his concept of an 'expansible army.' Faced with a demand that the Army be cut to 6000 men, Calhoun insisted that this should be done by halving the number of enlisted men in each company, leaving the senior enlisted and officers as a nucleus upon which to rebuild a force of 19,000 officers and men in case of a national emergency. In the event, Congress cut the total number of companies and regiments instead, but Calhoun's idea later became the basis of plans for a ready reserve for the US military. Calhoun also pushed for the protection of America's seacoast, a weakness that had been manifest in the recent war against the British. By 1826 18 harbors and ports, from Maine to the Mississippi, had been fortified with 31 defense works.

While the nation met no foreign enemies during this period, persistent problems with the Indians remained, and three wars were fought against them before the lands east of the Mississippi were made safe. The first came in 1817, as the result of attacks made out of Spanish Florida by Seminoles, Creeks and runaway slaves on settlements in lower Georgia. The Spanish governmental officials in Florida had little control over the Indians, and British adventurers encouraged the raids, telling the Indians that southern Georgia still belonged to them. The American government reacted vigorously to these incursions, in what has come to be known as the First Seminole War. Major General Andrew Jackson, commanding the Southern Department, was instructed to remove the menace, even if he had to cross into Florida. Jackson was only too happy to comply. Assembling a force of 800 regulars, 1000 militia from Georgia and (later) 1000 militia volunteers from Tennessee, Jackson moved into Florida in February 1818, executed two British citizens whom he believed had incited the Indians, and shortly gained control of all central and western Florida, the Indians having melted away into the swamps in the face of this superior force. When Spain and Britain protested the incursion, the United States expressed its regrets but made it clear to Spain that it would either have to control the Indians or cede Florida to the United States. Spain chose the latter course, in return for a money payment.

The second of the Indian wars was known as the Black Hawk War. It took place on the Illinois and Wisconsin frontiers, on the upper Mississippi, and began when the Sac and Fox tribes, under Chief Black Hawk, moved back across the river to their former lands in Illinois, after having earlier been removed to Iowa. Black Hawk returned in 1832 with perhaps 500 warriors and 1000 women and children. Alarmed by the Indians' reappearance, the Illinois government collected 1000 militia to ride against Black Hawk, and the federal government ordered Colonel Henry Atkinson and his 500 regulars from Jefferson Barracks to march to the troubled area. (A third force of 1000 was sent from the East coast via the Great Lakes but arrived too late to take part in the conflict and was largely disabled by an outbreak of cholera among the troops.) Black Hawk moved north into the Wisconsin Territory, trying to escape back across the Mississippi, but the military caught up with him, first at Wisconsin Heights and then on the Bad Axe River, and destroyed his forces.

The third Indian war took place in the South. Labeled the Second Seminole War, it began in 1835 and dragged on until 1842. It was essentially a guerrilla war conducted by the Seminoles under their half-breed leader, Osceola, with the Indians operating out of bases in the swamps and forests of Florida. It

Left: A US victory at Bad Axe River, 1832, ended Black Hawk's War, one of several Indian wars between 1812-60.
Right: Drab-looking uniforms worn by US soldiers in the frustrating Second Seminole War, 1835-42. Painting by Charles McBarron.

George Catlin's portrait of Osceola, who successfully led the Seminoles until 1837.

began when the Seminoles repudiated a treaty by which they had agreed to move west of the Mississippi and attacked a detachment of Army regulars. Before it was over, the Army had to deploy 10,000 regulars and 30,000 militia to put down its evasive enemy. The Army persisted in marching columns of soldiers on suspected enemy strongholds, only to find the enemy gone when they arrived. Rather than face the Army in open combat, the Seminoles preferred to attack small detachments and outposts, then disappear from sight. As the war dragged on without the enemy being brought to bay, the army became increasingly desperate and ruthless in its treatment of the Indians, and Army leaders finally resorted to trickery by inviting Osceola and the other chiefs to a conference under a flag of truce and then taking them prisoner. Osceola died in captivity in 1838 at Fort Marion, Florida (later being strangely honored by having a county in western

Michigan named after him), but it was the relentless campaign of extermination that finally ended the Second Seminole War.

During this same thirty-years' interlude the Army led the way into the trans-Mississippi west. There it built roads, surveyed, and built fortifications in Iowa, Nebraska, and Kansas. Fort Leavenworth, Kansas, built in 1827, served as the base for expeditions by Army engineers and explorers along the Santa Fe and Oregon Trails. The Army also made treaties with the Indians and protected settlers moving into the vast new territories opened by the Oregon Trail and to California beyond. Such officers as Lieutenant John C Fremont and Colonel Stephen W Kearny earned national reputations for their part in such endeavors.

The Mexican War

Between 1820 and 1835 some 35,000 Americans poured into the Mexican territory of Texas. At first welcomed by the Mexicans, the Americans became increasingly independent and their relations with the government became strained. When Mexico for-

bade any more immigration into the territory, the Texas Americans were incensed. In March 1836 they declared their independence of Mexico. Before the year was out, under the leadership of General Sam Houston, they had bested the Mexican forces that had tried to bring them back into subjection. Texas, upon winning its independence on the battlefield, then turned to the United States and asked for admission to the Union.

Much as many Americans wanted to see their fellow countrymen brought into the Union, the uncomfortable fact existed that while the United States had recognized Texas' independence, Mexico had not. If the United States accepted the Texans' request, it would be annexing Mexican territory, according to the Mexicans. Whether or not to take the risk of war with Mexico became the subject of a ten-year battle in the halls of Congress. It was a debate that, though long, could probably have only one outcome.

In November 1844, upon receiving the news that the ardent expansionist and candidate for the Democratic party, James K Polk, had won the presidential election, President John Tyler interpreted the election results as a mandate from the people for the annexation of Texas. Accordingly, he began to push for annexation, and Congress, on 1 March 1845, by joint resolution agreed to admit Texas into the Union. Mexico broke off diplomatic relations, a clear sign of an impending clash.

Anticipating that Texas would accept Congress' invitation to join the Union, President Polk ordered Brevet Brigadier General Zachary Taylor to move his forces from Louisiana into Texas to a point 'on or near' the Rio Grande. Taylor marched to the mouth of the Nueces River and set up camp. His force of regulars, volunteers, and Texas Rangers soon rose to 4000. There he waited for six months until ordered by Washington to the Rio Grande, 100 miles down the coast. The Army was now clearly on land never claimed either by Texas or by the United States, land that in the Mexicans' eyes clearly belonged to them, whatever the legality of the Texas annexation.

Setting himself up at the mouth of the Rio Grande, across the river from the Mexican town of Matamoros, Taylor built Fort Texas. Shortly afterwards, on 25 April 1846, a Mexican army crossed the river and attacked an American detachment of dragoons, killing eleven men. Taylor informed Polk that military hostilities had begun and prepared himself for major conflict.

Leaving a small detachment at Fort Texas, Taylor pulled back 18 miles to Point Isabel, where his supply ships were waiting. On his return to Fort Texas with fresh supplies and more cannon, he was met, at Palo Alto, on 7 May, by a Mexican army of some 4000 men. With his superior six-, 12- and 18-pound artillery firing cannister and solid shot, Taylor was able to outduel his opponents' artillery in a day-long battle. The Mexicans suffered almost 700 casualties, the Americans only 56. The next day the Mexicans began a full retreat, stopping briefly to put up a delaying fight at Resaca de la Palma that cost them an-

In March 1836 the 183 Texan rebels who defended the Alamo were overwhelmed by 4000 Mexican regulars. Yet Texas won its freedom soon thereafter.

other 550 casualties. The Mexican army then hastened in headlong retreat back across the Rio Grande. The Americans could not follow since they had no pontoon bridges and Taylor had neglected to acquire bridging materials or boats. When they finally crossed on 18 May the Mexican army was gone.

In the meantime, Congress, on 13 May, declared war on Mexico and authorized the expansion of the Army to 15,540 regulars and 50,000 volunteers. The American Army of 1846 was undoubtedly far better prepared to wage this conflict than it had been in either 1775 or 1812. True, it was small – only 7885 men and 734 officers distributed among eight regiments of infantry, two of dragoons and four of artillery – but it was well trained and equipped, its officers were professional, and its long years of Indian fighting had given all ranks valuable combat experience.

It had also benefited from the evolving technology of warfare. The flintlock firearm, which had dominated the field of battle since the mid-seventeenth century, was now beginning to give way to a new innovation: the

Most contemporary prints wrongly show US soldiers in battle wearing dress, rather than campaign, uniforms.

percussion lock weapon. Flintlocks had always been subject to a certain amount of misfiring, either because of worn flints or because damp had gotten into the priming powder in the flashpan. And even at best, all flintlocks suffered from a small but annoying hangfire – the brief moment, after the trigger was pulled, that was required for the lock to fall forward onto the frizzen, for the spark to drop onto the priming powder and for the

fire from the ignited primer to flash through the vent hole and explode the propellant charge inside the barrel. It was only a brief interruption, but often it was enough to interfere with the shooter's aim, especially if his target were moving. In the new percussion system a hammer fell directly onto a waxed paper or thin-copper cap containing fulminate of mercury, the instant explosion of which set off the propellant charge. Misfires were

radically reduced, hangfire time was shortened, and the whole reloading process was considerably speeded up. By 1841 a percussion lock musket had been ordered as the standard US infantry weapon, though during the Mexican War the older Springfield Model 1835 .67-inch calibre flintlock musket was still more prevalent, thanks mainly to General Winfield Scott's continuing prejudice against the new mechanism. The cavalry, on the other hand, took to percussion enthusiastically. Between 1833 and 1843 it adopted five different versions of the new Hall carbine (the majority being .54-inch

calibre), all of them not only percussion-firing but breech-loading as well.

In the Corps of Artillery innovation was more tactical than technical. Since analyses of the recent Napoleonic wars seemed to suggest that the mobility of artillery could be a key factor in winning battles, by 1846 approximately half the cannons in the US Army were represented by light horse-drawn six-pounders. These weapons proved exceptionally useful in the Mexican War, though the Civil War would later demonstrate that they were not quite the be-all-and-end-all some of their proponents at first thought. Indeed, so well did the Artillery perform in the Mexican War that in 1847 Congress went so far as to authorize the formation of four more artillery regiments.

The Mexican War was the first war in which the Army was not plagued by shortages of uniforms. The standard dress uniforms looked much as they had in 1812, but for campaigning a somewhat simpler and more practical kit was adapted: the cotee and trousers (now both generally sky blue) were looser-fitting, and a soft, visored cap was worn in place of the unwieldy shako.

The Mexican War was also the first American war in which militia was not to play a major role, the augmentation of the small regular force being accomplished mainly by the recruitment of one-year volunteers. This system certainly had its disadvantages, but at least the volunteers were under direct Army control and could be professionally equipped, trained, and led. Both Generals Scott and Taylor insisted on giving all volunteers at least six hours of training each day before taking them on campaign.

At the beginning of the war the Americans planned a three-pronged attack on northern Mexico. One prong, under General Taylor – 'Old Rough and Ready' or 'Old Zack' – was to advance westward from Matamoros to Monterrey. A second, under Brigadier General John E Wool, would move from San Antonio west to the village of Chihuahua and then south. A third, under Colonel Stephen W Kearny, was to leave from Fort Leavenworth for Santa Fe and then March on to San Diego, on the California coast. Northern Mexico would then be in American hands. Only later was it decided that another expedition would be sent under Major General Winfield Scott, commanding general of the Army, to invade Vera Cruz and then proceed overland toward the capital at Mexico City. Meantime,

An infantry officer and a dragoon clad in the campaign uniforms worn in the Mexican War.

Future president Zachary Taylor: His campaign in Mexico was exemplary.

Several Civil War generals were Mexican veterans, among them Grant and Robert E Lee (*above*).

Polk had promoted Zachary Taylor to brevet major general and given him command of the Army in Mexico because the president feared the political ambitions of Scott, as did Taylor.

'Old Zack' made his way to Camargo, 125 miles northeast of Monterrey, to set up a base for his advance on that city. Soon he had 15,000 men assembled there, and in late August he advanced with over 6000 regulars and volunteers toward Monterrey. He reached the city on 19 September, to find it defended by 7500 Mexicans equipped with 42 artillery pieces. Taylor placed the city under siege. By 24 September the Mexican commander realized resistance was hopeless and offered to surrender the city if his troops were allowed to withdraw and if an eight-week armistice were declared. Being far from his base and having suffered the loss of 800 men to battle and sickness, Taylor agreed. But President Polk was angered by Taylor's battlefield decision and ordered that the armistice be terminated. Taylor then took Saltillo, on the main road to Mexico City. There he was joined by General Wool, who had turned south when he found that Chihuahua had been abandoned. But at this point Taylor had all of his 4000 regulars and an equal number of volunteers taken away from him: they were to join General Scott at Tampico for the invasion at Vera Cruz.

Enraged at this decision, Taylor chose to regard Scott's further order to pull back and stand on the defensive at Monterrey as 'advice.' Instead, he moved 4650 of his remaining troops south of Saltillo to Agua Nueva. Mexican General Santa Anna was then 300 miles to the south assembling a large army, but Taylor believed the Mexican leader could not march an army so far north through barren desert and would therefore move east against Scott at Vera Cruz.

Taylor realized he was wrong on the morning of 21 February 1847 when his scouts reported a great Mexican army advancing up the Saltillo road. He withdrew to the hacienda Buena Vista to await the enemy. Before the hacienda was a broad plateau; to the east was a series of mountain spurs, La Angostura being the longest and deepest; to the west was a network of gullies. Taylor had only 5000 men, many of them green volunteers; General Santa Anna had 15,000. Taylor's only apparent advantage was that his artillery was well emplaced at La Angostura.

The first day of the Battle of Buena Vista, 22 February 1847, was spent mainly in jockeying for position. The decision was reached the next day. First Santa Anna tried to break the American left wing on La Angostura, but his troops were driven off by artillery and infantry. Then he hit the plateau in the center with two divisions, and the Americans broke and ran. The battle was quickly turning into an American rout when Taylor's dragoons, the Mississippi Rifles, under Colonel Jefferson Davis, arrived on the scene and broke the Mexican cavalry charges. With reformed lines, and in the midst of a mighty thunderstorm, the Americans gradually forced the Mexicans back. Santa Anna threw fresh troops into the fray, an entire division. Again the American lines began to crack. And again the situation was saved by the Mississippi Rifles (and some troops from Indiana) galloping onto the field under the leadership of the now-wounded Davis. These mounted warriors fell upon the Mexicans and forced them to retreat, while the American artillery continued to punish them from La Angostura. That night Santa Anna began his retreat, having lost over 1500 killed and wounded, to the Americans' 800. The fighting spirit of the green volunteers, the conspicuous bravery of Zachary Taylor who stationed himself on his horse in the midst of the line, the slashing attacks by the American mounted volunteers, and punishing American artillery had won the day.

Northern Mexico was soon safely in American hands. Colonel Kearny had arrived in San Diego in December 1846 to find that the Americans in the 'Bear Flag Revolt,' the Navy's Pacific squadron, and John C Fremont's small army of 'explorers' had already wrested control of California from Mexico. And Colonel Alexander W Doniphan and his Missouri volunteers cleared the upper Rio Grande by their victory over a large Mexican force at Chihuahua shortly after Taylor's victory. Mexico City, the capital, was next.

General Scott, 'Old Fuss and Feathers,' assembled a force of over 13,000 men at Lobos island, 50 miles south of Tampico, for his attack on Vera Cruz. It was the first major joint amphibious landing in the history of the US military. Joining with a supporting naval squadron on 5 March off Vera Cruz, the unopposed landings took place on 9 March,

Most brilliant of US generals in the Mexican War was Winfield Scott. He would run for the presidency in 1852.

three miles south of the city. In four hours more than 10,000 men had been rowed ashore in surf boats, along with their artillery and stores. When it was subsequently discovered that the available artillery of mortars and howitzers was insufficient to reduce Vera Cruz and its fortress of San Juan de Ulua, six naval guns were brought ashore and manhandled into position. These breached the walls of the city and fortress, and on 27 March the city fell. Scott then moved inland toward the capital.

He soon met Santa Anna's army of 12,000 men near Cerro Gordo, on the National Highway cutting through the mountains to Mexico City. Santa Anna thought his position was unassailable, but by making their way through the rough terrain around the Mexican positions, the Americans brought their heavy artillery on to the high ground above them. The result was a complete American victory, on 18 April, that forced the Mexicans to flee back toward the capital.

The road was now open to Mexico City, but at this critical point the enlistments of seven of Scott's volunteer regiments, about 4000 men, expired, and few chose to remain on the fatiguing campaign. The loss of these volunteers, plus the ravages of death and sickness among his troops, had brought Scott's force down to less than 6000. Yet he pushed on to Puebla, took the city without resistance, and there settled down to await reinforcements and the outcome of peace negotiations then underway. The reinforcements eventually came, after ten weeks, and in the meantime the peace negotiations had broken down. It was obvious that Santa Anna, now the president of Mexico, would need

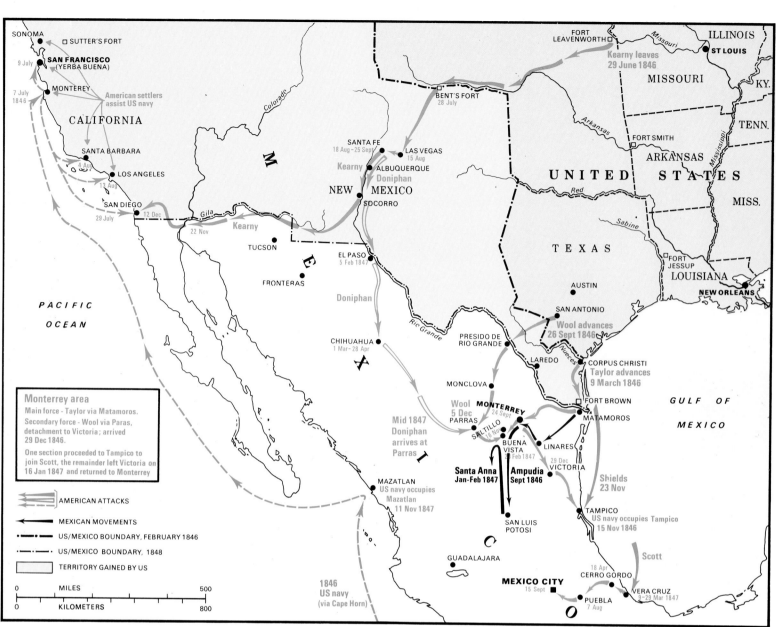

Map labels (top map):

SONOMA · SUTTER'S FORT · 9 July · SAN FRANCISCO (YERBA BUENA) · 7 July 1846 · MONTEREY · American settlers assist US navy · CALIFORNIA · SANTA BARBARA · 4 Aug · LOS ANGELES · 13 Aug · SAN DIEGO · 29 July · 12 Dec · Gila · 22 Nov · Kearny · TUCSON · FRONTERAS · PACIFIC OCEAN · Colorado · M E X I C O · SANTA FE 18 Aug – 25 Sept · LAS VEGAS 15 Aug · Kearny · Doniphan · NEW MEXICO · ALBUQUERQUE · SOCORRO · EL PASO 5 Feb 1847 · Doniphan · CHIHUAHUA 1 Mar – 28 Apr · Rio Grande · FORT LEAVENWORTH · Kearny leaves 29 June 1846 · BENT'S FORT 28 July · Missouri · Arkansas · FORT SMITH · ARKANSAS · TEXAS · Red · Sabine · AUSTIN · SAN ANTONIO · Wool advances 26 Sept 1846 · Nueces · PRESIDO DE RIO GRANDE · LAREDO · CORPUS CHRISTI Taylor advances 9 March 1846 · ILLINOIS · ST LOUIS · MISSOURI · KY. · TENN. · MISS. · FORT JESSUP · LOUISIANA · NEW ORLEANS · Mid 1847 Doniphan arrives at Parras · Wool 5 Dec PARRAS · MONCLOVA · MONTERREY 24 Sept · SALTILLO 16 Nov · BUENA VISTA 22 Feb 1847 · Santa Anna Jan-Feb 1847 · Ampudia Sept 1846 · LINARES · VICTORIA 29 Dec · FORT BROWN · MATAMOROS · GULF OF MEXICO · Shields 23 Nov · MAZATLAN US navy occupies Mazatlan 11 Nov 1847 · SAN LUIS POTOSI · GUADALAJARA · MEXICO CITY 15 Sept · PUEBLA 7 Aug · CERRO GORDO 18 Apr · VERA CRUZ 9-29 Mar 1847 · Scott · TAMPICO US navy occupies Tampico 15 Nov 1846 · 1846 US navy (via Cape Horn) · WOOL

Monterrey area

Main force - Taylor via Matamoros.
Secondary force - Wool via Paras, detachment to Victoria; arrived 29 Dec 1846.

One section proceeded to Tampico to join Scott, the remainder left Victoria on 16 Jan 1847 and returned to Monterrey

AMERICAN ATTACKS
MEXICAN MOVEMENTS
US/MEXICO BOUNDARY, FEBRUARY 1846
US/MEXICO BOUNDARY, 1848
TERRITORY GAINED BY US

MILES 0 ... 500
KILOMETERS 0 ... 800

Top: General map of the Mexican War.
Left: Scott's landing at Vera Cruz: A near-perfect amphibious operation.

greater pressure before agreeing to abandon the war.

Although he had no men to guard his supply lines stretching all the way back to Vera Cruz, Scott, with his army of 10,000 men, moved on toward Mexico City on 7 August. Within three days he was only 14 miles from the city. Deciding not to attempt to take the city from the east because of its fortifications, Scott sent his forces to the south, through difficult terrain, to flank the defenses. Although sharply challenged by the Mexicans at Contreras (they lost 700 dead and had 800 taken prisoner, to only 60 American casualties), the Americans drove on. On 20 August Santa Anna's men made another gallant defensive stand at Churubusco, losing 4000 killed or wounded, but could not withstand the frontal attack of infantry and artillery launched by the Americans. Scott offered an armistice to Santa Anna, which he accepted, but when it became obvious that the Mexicans were still in no mood to acquiesce in American terms and were using the armistice to bring reinforcements, the war was resumed.

As Scott moved inland from Vera Cruz Santa Anna tried in vain to block his way to Mexico City at Cerro Gordo.

Now with only about 8000 men to challenge Santa Anna's 15,000 in the heavily fortified city, Scott persisted in his offensive. First he took an outlying defensive position called El Molino del Rey and then moved on the Castle of Chapultepec, guarding the approaches to Mexico City. On 13 September American artillery and infantry succeeded in a well-conducted three-pronged attack on the citadel, while infantry used scaling ladders to top the walls and then push on to take the Belén and San Cosmé gates to the city itself. The next day Santa Anna surrendered. Scott had proven himself a brilliant theater commander, and he had been aided in his victories by some highly promising young Army officers – Robert E Lee, George E Meade, Pierre G T Beauregard, Joseph T Johnston and Ulysses S Grant – all West Pointers who would put their battle experience in these campaigns to good use in another war yet to come.

The war with Mexico ended on 2 February 1848 with the signing of the Treaty of Guadelupe Hidalgo. By 1 August 1848 all American troops were out of the country, and the United States had gained clear title to Texas, with the Rio Grande as its recognized southern border, and to over one million square miles of new territory, including all of present-day

Taylor partly owed his Buena Vista victory to the Kentucky Dragoons who twice broke Mexican infantry charges.

Arizona, New Mexico, Utah, Nevada, and California, and parts of Wyoming and Colorado. The cost had been high. Almost 13,000 Americans had been lost in the war, although only 1700 had died in battle or from wounds, the rest having succumbed to disease or accident. Whatever the morality of its inception, the Mexican War resulted in impressive victories for the American Army and served as a valuable classroom for the use of new mobile artillery and fluid battle tactics.

After the Mexican War the Army resumed its duties on the frontier: defending against Indian tribes, surveying trails through the mountains and across the plains, and building forts and roads. Standing at about 13,000 men, the Army returned to its peacetime duties, while developing its service schools, new weaponry, and new doctrines. But events were soon to overtake it as the nation, wracked by controversy over the expansion of slavery into the new and expanding West, drifted toward the horror of civil war – a civil war in which the Army would fight itself.

Sherman's March to the Sea, a brutal episode in America's bloodiest war.

THE CIVIL WAR: 1861-1865

Attempts to reconcile the many deep-seated differences between the North and South, both over the expansion of slavery and other economic and political issues, came to naught after the Mexican War, and the cleavage widened between the two sections of the country. The Compromise of 1850 over the admission of California into the Union resulted only in bad feelings. The Kansas-Nebraska Act of 1854, which attempted to allow the people in the territories to decide the issue of slavery themselves by 'popular sovereignty,' resulted only in bloody warfare in Kansas and further inflamed emotions on both sides of the Mason-Dixon Line. The rapid emergence of the Republican party and its fielding of a presidential candidate in 1856 was a sign of an impending split, for the new party was clearly a Northern party and a descendant of anti-slavery political groups going back two decades.

The Democratic party managed to win that year by straddling the issue of slavery and offering a 'neutral' and innocuous candidate, James Buchanan of Pennsylvania, for the presidency. But bad feelings continued to intensify during the next four years, especially after John Brown's vain, violent attempt to set up an asylum at Harper's Ferry for runaway slaves within slaveholding Virginia. Then, in 1860, the Republican party placed Abraham Lincoln of Illinois in nomination for the presidency and declared again against the extension of slavery. With Lincoln's victory in November, some Southern states, believing that their enemies had finally and decisively won control of the Federal government, began to draft ordinances of seces-

Right: Soldiers with deadly new 1855 percussion-lock musket-rifles.
Below: As Congressional compromises failed civil war became inevitable.

sion. Even before Lincoln's inauguration on 4 March 1861 seven states in the Deep South, led by South Carolina, had seceded from the Union and had formed the Confederate States of America. Two days after Lincoln's inauguration, on 6 May, the new president of the Confederacy, Jefferson Davis – an ex-West Pointer, former hero of the Mexican War, and former US Secretary of War – called for 100,000 volunteers to defend the Confederacy's existence against any attempts by the Federal government to return its citizens to loyalty to the Union.

The North seemed to have all the advantages as each side began to prepare itself for probable conflict. Its twenty-three loyal states had a population of 21 million people; the South had only 9 million, including over 3 million slaves whom the South would be loath to put under arms (although the slaves could be used as military laborers and kept in agricultural production, thereby freeing more white males for military duty). More important, the North had over 80 percent of the nation's factories and 67 percent of the nation's farms. And almost all of the South's factories were small and technologically primitive, making them very difficult to convert to modern war-making capacity. The North, on the other hand, had both highly skilled labor and the mechanical means to fight a technological war, plus far greater capacity for sustained and increasing production of the goods of war. The South never managed to gain industrial self-sufficiency during the course of the conflict, despite prodigious feats of improvisation.

Furthermore, the North had a developed and integrated transportation system, especially in railroads, which would play a vital role in transporting men and supplies both from the home front to the war zones and back and forth within the war zones themselves. The North also had a developed system of steamboats and barges as important ancillary means of transportation. All told, the North had over 20,000 miles of track, with adequate locomotives and rolling stock, and almost all of this railroad mileage was well integrated, with convenient intersections, good 'through' lines, and standard track gauges. The South, on the other hand, had but 9000 miles of track, little integration or standardization of track gauges, and virtually no capacity for replacing locomotives and rolling stock once they fell victim to deterioration or enemy action. Yet in the war to come transport would be all-important.

The North likewise enjoyed a preponderance of naval and maritime power. Virtually all of the American merchant marine belonged to Northerners, and the US Navy of 90 ships, while not adequate for the war, was easily capable of expansion. By 1864 the Union had a navy of 670 ships and 50,000 men,

The election of Lincoln in 1860 was the event that triggered civil war. By inauguration day (*below*) seven rebel states had seceded. But Lincoln was to prove more dangerous to the South in war than in peace.

this in a war in which blockade was one of the basic strategic goals to be pursued. The Confederacy had no navy and no first-rate building and repair facilities, either at the beginning or at any time during the course of the war. Captured facilities and inland production allowed the South to scrape together a force of some 130 vessels, manned by 4000 men, but as the Federal blockade became tighter, and as the Union gained control of the inland waters in the South, there was no way the small Confederate navy could loosen this nautical stranglehold.

Given this preponderance in numbers and materiel, the Lincoln administration, with the aged Winfield Scott as General in Chief, settled on a basic three-part strategy for early victory. Part one called for capturing the Confederate capital at Richmond, Virginia. The second part called for seizure of the entire route of the Mississippi River down to the Gulf of Mexico, thus cutting the South in two and denying it support from its western territories. This was to be followed by the seizure of Chattanooga, which was to be used as a base for a second bisection of the south. The third part of the strategy, the 'Anaconda Policy,' was to impose a tight blockade on the

Above: CSA president Jefferson Davis.
Below: Recruiting for the Confederate Army in Woodstock, Virginia.

entire Confederacy, from the Chesapeake Bay to the extreme southern coast of Texas, thereby denying aid from the outside and at the same time strangling Southern commerce by denying to it its world markets, especially for cotton.

That the Union, given time to gear up for the war effort, could carry out these plans was not seriously in question. The only possible doubt was whether or not it would have the will to do so if the war became protracted. That will was supplied by Abraham Lincoln, president and Commander in Chief, who never faltered in his determination to restore the Union. The unknown Lincoln, elected to the presidency in 1860, emerged as the iron-willed Lincoln of history, who provided leadership to rally the people of the Union behind him and to pay whatever price was necessary to preserve the Union. Lincoln's hope was that the wounds of war would leave no permanent scars on the body politic, so that, after the defeat of the secessionists, the nation could again be united to pursue its destiny as the 'last best hope of mankind.' In this he never faltered, and this was undoubtedly the most important ingredient in the eventual Union victory.

Yet the South, despite its inferiority in manpower and war-making capacity, had certain advantages. For one thing, the Confederacy did not have to carry the war into the North in order to win; it had only to remain on the defensive and prevent serious Northern incursions into its territory, to hold out long enough and raise the 'butcher's bill' high enough to convince the North that the war was not worth the sacrifices demanded. In this respect the Southern secessionists stood in much the same posture as had the rebels in the American Revolution. For such an essentially defensive effort the South might, with determination, adequate production, and effective military defensive tactics, hold the North at bay for a very long time – perhaps enough time.

But to do this, the South needed both effective leadership and great self-discipline. Unfortunately for the Confederacy, Jefferson Davis, for all his manful efforts to create an effective strategy for victory, his 'offensive defensive,' lacked both the personal qualities and the organizational skills to mold a government strong enough to sustain the pressure of protracted and determined Federal force. And he was continually handicapped by the independent-mindedness of the various states of the Confederacy, which displayed an understandable but fatal tendency to see the needs of the Confederacy only in their own terms. Davis, in the midst of war, was essentially trying to mold a new

Southern Union. Whether or not it could ever have been done can never be determined, but what the outcome might have been, had the South been blessed with a Lincoln at the helm instead of a Davis, will never cease to be a subject of fascinating speculation.

The Contending Armies: 1861

When the seven Southern states seceded from the Union, they seized all Federal properties within their borders except for Fort Pickens at Pensacola and Fort Sumter in Charleston harbor. Feeling that secession was perfectly constitutional and legal, they argued that these Federal properties were now within their jurisdictions and, as 'foreign' installations, could only exist at their sufferance. For the Federal government to abandon these posts voluntarily would be to give *de facto* recognition to the constitutionality of the South's claim. This Lincoln, as president and as a believer in the indissolubility of the Union, could not and would not do.

Lincoln informed the Confederate commissioners, sent to him a few days after his inauguration, that he would not re-supply the forts without proper notice to the Southern government, but there was no easy way out of his dilemma. If he re-supplied the forts, the South might see this as a provocative act, and the eight remaining slave states might join their confreres in leaving the Union. If he did not re-supply the forts and they were forced to surrender, he would be bowing to Southern pressure. He finally decided that the re-provisioning would have to take place and duly notified the governor of South Carolina on 8 April that a small expedition carrying supplies only, not men, would be sent.

With the moment of decision now upon the South, Confederate Brigadier General Pierre G T Beauregard, the local commander at Charleston, demanded that Major Robert Anderson, commanding at Fort Sumter, surrender the installation. Anderson refused. On 12 April 1861, in the early morning hours, the ring of batteries around Charleston harbor began a 34-hour bombardment of the fort. Anderson's guns fired back but could not equal the Confederate firepower. On 14 April Anderson surrendered the fort, after saluting the American flag with fifty guns. The following day Lincoln signed a proclamation declaring the seven Confederate states to be in rebellion and called for 75,000 militia from the states to suppress the rebellion. This call for troops caused the remaining eight states to begin the process of joining in secession, and the two sides lined up for all-out war.

President Davis' call, on 6 March, for 100,000 volunteers for twelve-month service hardly gave the South enough men to fight a war effectively. A law passed later in 1861 allowed Davis to accept up to 500,000 troops for enlistments lasting from one year to the duration of the war. Some 300,000 men stepped forward, but the great majority of these were twelve-monthers, meaning they could be going home in the spring of 1862. By 1862 the South had turned to conscription, with terms of three years' service, but still it had dif-

ficulty filling its ranks because of the provisions of its conscription laws. These provided too-generous exemptions for persons declared critical to the war effort at home (for example, that any white man owning 20 or more slaves did not have to serve). The Southern conscription laws also allowed a draftee to buy a substitute to serve for him, with no limit on the amount which could be paid the proxy. And they allowed for members of the state militia to be exempt; this was a privilege jealously guarded by some Southern governors, who placed more and more men in service as militia officers. (In some instances the numbers serving in the militia exceeded those serving in the Confederate ranks.)

Eventually some 900,000 Southerners probably served three years or more in the Confederate armies (the records are notoriously incomplete), but while 465,000 were on the rolls in 1863, with about half present for duty, by 1864 the recorded number was down to 200,000, with about half of this number having deserted or gone home. Thus

Though Lincoln had tried to avert war through conciliation, when the rebels attacked Fort Sumter in April 1861 there could be no turning back.

by the crucial period of the war, as the Southern cause was feeling its greatest pressure, its effective army strength stood at only about 100,000 men, few enough at the beginning of the war and now grossly inadequate when compared to Northern strength.

With only about 16,000 officers and enlisted men at the beginning of the crisis, the Union Army was likewise in no condition to begin hostilities. The majority of the Army personnel were deployed in the West, six of the seven departments of the Army being located west of the Mississippi. Only 15 companies were in the Department of the East, and these were scattered along the Canadian border and the Atlantic coast. This small force was weakened by the fact that of the active officers, numbering a little over 1000, almost 300 resigned to join the Confederates (including 184 West Point gradu-

US regulars wore blue; Confederates, gray. But many militias, like these Zouaves, were more colorfully clad. One militia wore kilts; another, Italian plumed hats.

ates, out of a total of 824, many of whom had held high commands in the regular Army).

Knowing that the regulars, plus 75,000 militia, would be completely unequal to the task ahead, Lincoln called for an increase in the regulars to 23,000 men and for an enlistment of 42,000 volunteers for three-year stints. Congress was willing to go along with the president when it reconvened in late 1861, and proceeded to authorize him to raise a force of 500,000 men for three years. Under these provisions almost 600,000 men came

forth in 1861 pledged to serve for an adequate period of time to allow them to be trained and utilized. Throughout the war the regular Army was kept intact, the Union supplementing it with volunteers at all ranks. And unlike the South, the North enacted conscription under a system whereby each state was divided into enrollment districts. If any district met its quota with volunteers (with or without cash bounties), no one would be drafted. This meant that most Union soldiers were volunteers. Less than 50,000 were drafted into Federal service, but few exemptions were allowed, although a person drafted could hire a substitute or pay the government a commutation fee of $300 to escape service. Eventually 1.5 million men served in

the Union Army on a long-term basis, and as the war went on the numbers in the Union Army continued to rise, reaching 500,000 in active service by 1864. Despite their continued high place in American myth, militia units played almost no part in the Civil War: regulars, volunteers and draftees made up the ranks of the gargantuan armies needed for this fratricidal contest.

The Union Army's volunteers were drawn from partially-trained state militia units and from enthusiastic recruits from civilian life. Since the states were the basic units from which both volunteers and draftees were drawn, the military units thus formed were state units, with prominent state politicians chosen to lead them. By law, Lincoln could

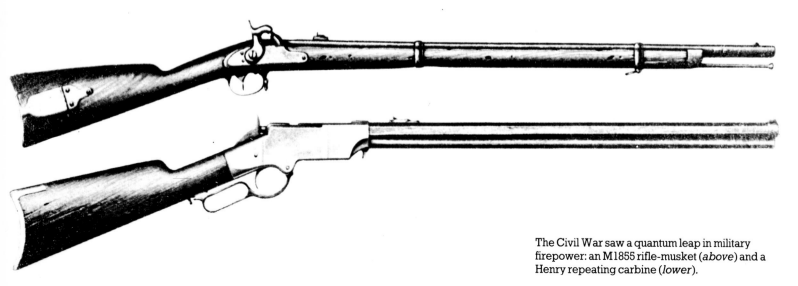

The Civil War saw a quantum leap in military firepower: an M1855 rifle-musket (*above*) and a Henry repeating carbine (*lower*).

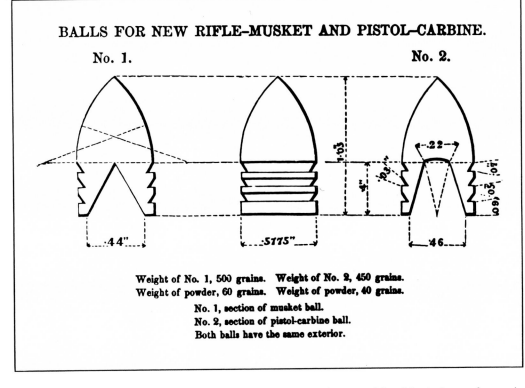

BALLS FOR NEW RIFLE-MUSKET AND PISTOL-CARBINE.

No. 1. **No. 2.**

Weight of No. 1, 500 grains.   Weight of No. 2, 450 grains.
Weight of powder, 60 grains.   Weight of powder, 40 grains.
No. 1, section of musket ball.
No. 2, section of pistol-carbine ball.
Both balls have the same exterior.

Easy to load and non-fouling, the new Minie Ball now made rifles practical as standard infantry weapons.

appoint the units' general officers, and he often chose governors or other high state officials to assure the loyalty of the states to the Union cause. Some of these politician-officers were of poor quality, while others proved to be surprisingly able. Resupply of recruits to the state-based units was carried out by the states themselves, often necessitating officers being sent back home to recruit more men for the regiments.

The state volunteer units were organized into larger theater armies based on the area in which they would be operating, e.g., the Army of the Potomac or the Army of the Tennessee. The volunteer units within the theater armies were largely made up of infantry, to which artillery and engineering units, both regular and volunteer, would be added. Special units of dragoons (mounted infantry) and Zouaves (special infantry), with distinctive and colorful uniforms and their own local-based officers, plus cavalry units, were also assigned to theater commanders.

In command over the armies thus created was the General in Chief. In fact his powers were shared with Secretary of War Edwin M Stanton and were additionally limited by the bureau chiefs (known as the General Staff), who reported to the secretary, not to him. Furthermore, Congress created its own committee to oversee the war, adding political interference into an already clumsy command system. Only in 1864 did Congress create the rank of lieutenant general and declare that this person could also be General in Chief. And only when Lincoln subsequently named Ulysses S Grant to this dual position to exercise total military control over the Army, was some measure of command unity attained. (And even then the War Department and the bureau chiefs continued

to exercise considerable independence in their functions.) It was probably only Lincoln's personality and political acumen that kept the Army's high command functioning as well as it did throughout the war. In this respect the South was less fortunate.

Both the Union and Confederate Armies used essentially similar (and often identical) weapons. While at first glance it might appear that the quality of these weapons had increased only incrementally during the fifteen years since the Mexican War, in fact the improvement had been sufficient to alter the face of war. Although hardly anyone on either side realized it at the outset, the rate of fire, range and accuracy of the new weapons had now reached such levels as to make brute firepower virtually the king of battle. In the Civil War sheer attrition would come to matter as much as – and often more than – any other tactical consideration. Combat casualties would rise to unprecedented proportions – in some instances of attacks on well prepared positions, to nearly 80 percent. Indeed, the total number of battlefield deaths, about 215,000, would be higher than in any other American war save World War II, and in proportion to total population, the

lethality of the Civil War would far exceed even that of World War II.

The technological advances that made these horrors possible were relatively simple: the widespread replacement of the musket by the rifle and of the flintlock by the percussion lock, the growing use of breech-loading and repeating weapons (mostly pistols and carbines), and the introduction of rifled artillery. Beginning in 1841 the Army's old smoothbore muskets began to be replaced by a succession of percussion rifles. When the Civil War began the latest of these was the .58-calibre US Model 1861, which had an effective range of nearly 300 yards and an extreme range of over 1500 yards. Rifles had, of course, been around for a long time, and it had always been known that they were very much more accurate than smoothbore muskets. But they had never been widely used by military forces because of their distressing tendency to develop clogged barrels after repeated firing. Then, in the 1830s, a French army captain, C E Minié, invented a type of non-fouling rifle bullet, and suddenly the military rifle became a practical proposition. Only a few years earlier, in the Mexican War, Ulysses S Grant had been able to say of smoothbore musketry: 'At the distance of a few hundred yards, a man might fire at you all day without your finding out.' By 1861 those days had gone forever.

Along with advances in accuracy and range came greater rapidity of fire. The percussion lock, now standard, was inherently faster and more reliable than the flintlock, and refinements in percussion lock design had advanced apace in the decades before the beginning of the war. The rate of fire of single-shot weapons was further increased by another innovation, breech loading, which was a much faster method of recharging a shoulder arm than muzzle loading had ever been. During the war breech-loading in rifles was confined mainly to cavalry carbines, the .54-calibre Burnside and the .52-calibre Sharps being the most widely used models. The apogee of rapid fire in percussion lock rifles was achieved when repeating carbines were introduced, by far the most famous of which were the six-shot .52-calibre Spencer and the classic 15-shot .44-calibre Henry. And as with rifles, so with pistols, the murderous new standards now being set by the fast-firing six-shot revolvers manufactur-

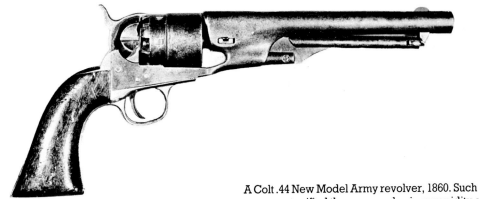

A Colt .44 New Model Army revolver, 1860. Such weapons typified the new emphasis on rapidity of fire.

The contemporary apex of rapid fire, the Gatling machine gun, was, oddly, little used in the Civil War.

ed by Remington, Starr and, above all, Samuel Colt.

Artillery was similarly transformed by technology. To be sure, probably the war's single most popular artillery piece would continue to be an old-fashioned smoothbore, the US Model 1857 'Napoleon' 12-pounder, which was both highly mobile and could still, when charged with cannister or grape, visit awesome execution on massed troops. But it is also true that by 1863 nearly half the Union Army's cannons would be new, highly accur-

ate three-inch rifled guns with an impressive effective range of 2500 yards. A simultaneous development would be a gradual increase in the use of explosive shells, in place of old-fashioned solid shot. It was doubtless fortunate for all concerned that the technique of adding shrapnel to these explosives was still in its infancy.

Although these great advances in fire-power did not much affect formations (the ideal infantry organization – seldom realized in practice – was now thought to be the three-battalion regiment, each battalion being composed of eight 100-man companies), they would significantly affect basic battlefield tactics. The special character of the new

firepower favored defense. It is estimated that during the war only one out of every eight assaults on prepared positions ever succeeded, and those that did succeed often did so at frightful cost. The Civil War would never degenerate into the kind of sanguinary stalemate that characterized World War I – weapons technology had not yet evolved so far as to preclude maneuver entirely – but we can now see in retrospect how this greatest of American wars would prefigure the grisly shape of things to come.

When the Confederate capital was moved to Richmond, Virginia, only 100 miles south of Washington, it was inevitable that the initial cockpit of war would be the Northern triangle of the Old Dominion state. For the first three years of the war, fighting raged on the Potomac-Chesapeake Bay right leg of the triangle, the Blue Ridge Mountains-Shenandoah Valley left leg, and along the base formed by the James River-Richmond axis. Only in 1865 when the legs had been crushed and the Army of Northern Virginia was held under successful siege at Petersburg, south of Richmond, would the triangle collapse and the war be won.

Initially neither side was in a hurry to engage the enemy, since most of the troops in place were green recruits badly in need of training. The Federals had some 30,000 men, under the command of Brigadier General Irwin McDowell, at Alexandria, just south of Washington, and another 15,000, under the aged Major General Robert Patterson, guarding the northern end of the Shenandoah Valley. The Confederates had an army of 22,000 troops 30 miles southwest of Wash-

A 15-inch Rodman siege gun. The size and accuracy of the artillery used in the Civil War was unprecedented.

The Battle of Bull Run (*above* and *right*), the first
big battle of the war, ended in a total rout of the
ill-led Union forces.

ington at Manassas Junction, under Brigadier
General P G T Beauregard, and another
11,000 at Winchester in the Shenandoah
Valley, under Brigadier General Joseph E
Johnston.

Bowing to public pressure for an offensive,
and perhaps believing that one great offensive victory would break the back of Southern rebellion, in June 1861 Lincoln ordered
Winfield Scott, the aging General in Chief, to
order McDowell to move into the South.
McDowell, hesitant to move until his troops
were ready, nevertheless obeyed Lincoln's
orders and prepared his plans. Assured by
Scott that Patterson would not allow
Johnston's forces to slip out of the Valley to
join Beauregard, McDowell set out on 16 July
toward Manassas, his coming well advertis-
ed to Beauregard by articles in the press.
Beauregard drew up his forces behind a
stream called Bull Run and waited. By 20 July
he was reinforced by Johnston's forces,
which had slipped away from the Valley and
traveled the intervening 50 miles by rail. This
meant about 30,000 men on each side would
be facing one another as the two untried
armies met in the initial combat of what was
to be America's bloodiest war.

Both McDowell and Beauregard, as it turned out, planned to hold in the center and
push their right flanks around the enemy. On
the morning of 21 July Beauregard's right
flank movement bogged down, but
McDowell's moved well and threatened to
win the field. Beauregard thereupon drew
his forces to the left to reinforce his left flank

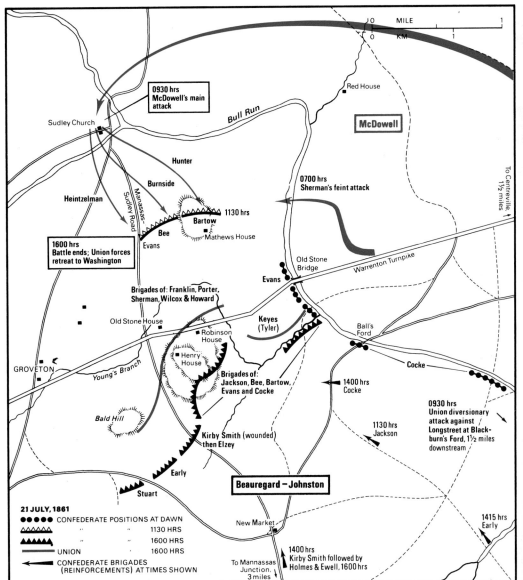

(by this time running almost north to south) with 15,000 troops, sufficient to stop the 13,000 Federals and their attacks. He then ordered a sudden counterattack that forced the Federals back across Bull Run. Their retreat soon turned into a rout, and McDowell, unable to regain control of the situation, ordered his troops to retreat all the way back to Washington. As the Confederates were unable to organize an effective pursuit, the battle simply came to an end. It was forever marked by Brigadier General Thomas Jackson's having here earned the nickname 'Stonewall' for his brigade's strong defensive stand against the Union forces.

For the remainder of the summer the two armies eyed one another south of Washington, but neither would make a move until their numbers increased. Lincoln now called upon thirty-five-year-old Major General George B McClellan to command the armies around Washington. McClellan, who also assumed the office of General in Chief on 1 November when Scott retired, would soon prove himself to be an inspiring leader and trainer of men, but one sadly lacking in the judgment and aggressiveness needed in the field commander of the now-christened 'Army of the Potomac.' Lincoln was to find the first of the 'fighting generals' he needed not in the East, but in the West.

Foreshadowing of Northern Victory: 1862

The campaign of 1862 began in the west. There Brigadier General Don Carlos Buell, USA, headquartered at Louisville on the Ohio, had a force of 50,000 men undergoing training. Farther south and west, Major General Henry W Halleck, in St Louis, had another 90,000 men under his command, including 20,000 in Kentucky under Brigadier General Ulysses S Grant and another 30,000, across the Mississippi in Missouri, under Major General Samuel Curtis. The objectives of these Western armies, as part of the overall Union strategy, were to seize the Mississippi and to capture some vital rail junctions in Tennessee, preparatory to slicing through the South toward Atlanta. Facing the Union forces were 43,000 Confederates, scattered all the way from western Virginia to Kansas and under the overall command of General Albert Sidney Johnston. Near the center, and helping to protect the valuable railroad lines, were Fort Henry, on the Tennessee River, and Fort Donelson, twelve miles away to the east on the Cumberland River, just south of the Kentucky border in northern Tennessee.

By January Halleck had approved Grant's plan to move south down the Tennessee and

Top: Ulysses S Grant, the Union's best general, was criticized for the heavy casualties he sustained.
Right: Details of the equipment and uniforms of Union and Confederate artillery.
Below: A typically lethal battle of the war was Antietam: 12,000 Union and 10,000 Confederate casualties.

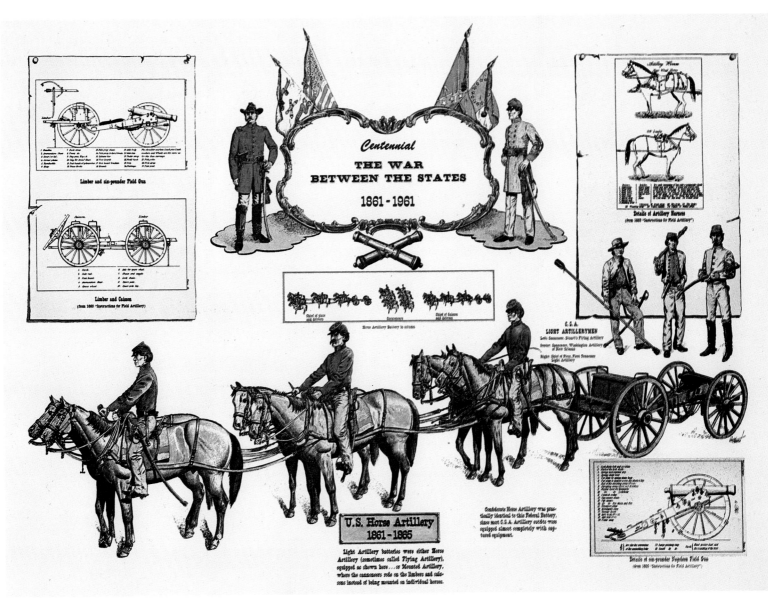

take Fort Henry. This would be done in co-operation with gunboats of the Navy, commanded by Flag Officer Andrew H Foote. Grant's 15,000 men jumped off in early February and, with the help of naval gunfire, took Fort Henry with no difficulty. Grant then plunged overland to take Fort Donelson, twelve miles away. Confederate reinforcements in the number of 12,000 were hurried to Fort Donelson by General Johnston, who concurrently pulled 14,000 more toward Nashville, farther up the Cumberland. Grant put the 100-acre fort and outer works under seige, and soon reinforcements from Halleck brought Grant's numbers to 27,000, about a 2-to-1 edge over his enemies. After an attempt to break out failed on 15 February, the Confederates surrendered unconditionally. Some 15,000 Confederates had fallen into Union hands, and the upper Cumberland and Tennessee rivers were now open to Union penetration.

Halleck, who had been placed in command of the whole Western theater by Lincoln, next sent Major General John Pope's Army of the Mississippi downriver to attack New Madrid and 'Island No. 10,' located on a crucial hairpin turn of the Mississippi, in co-

The capture of Fort Donelson on 15 February 1862 was Grant's first big victory in the West.

In April 1862 Confederate General Johnston
surprised Grant at Shiloh and came close to
defeating him.

operation with Foote's naval forces. Halleck
also decided to unite Grant's Army of the
Tennessee and Buell's Army of the Ohio at
Shiloh (Pittsburgh Landing) north of Corinth,
Mississippi, an important rail juncture, there
to begin a pursuit of Johnston's Confederate
forces south along a line inland and parallel
to the Mississippi River. Johnston, who was
aware of Halleck's plans, elected to attack
Grant at Shiloh before Buell could join him. It
took two days for Johnston's 40,000 untrained
men to move the 22 miles north to attack
Grant's army of 40,000, but, fortunately for the
Southern cause, Grant was caught completely by surprise.

Early on the morning of 6 April 1862 the
Union forces at Shiloh found themselves
under very heavy attack by Confederates
bursting out of the woods. They fell back in
disarray, but then dug in to put up a fierce
resistance. A Confederate victory seemed to
be in the making when suddenly General
Johnston fell mortally wounded. General
Beauregard, assuming command, pulled
back the Confederate attackers to re-
organize them, but that night 17,000 of Buell's
troops arrived on the scene and were ferried

across the Tennessee to bring Grant's forces
back up to 40,000. Grant counterattacked the
next morning and drove the Confederates off
the ground they had won the day before. Yet
he did not pursue when the Rebel forces
moved back to Corinth. Over 13,000 of the
63,000 Union troops involved in the Battle of
Shiloh had become casualties, and the Confederates had suffered 11,000 casualties out
of 40,000 they had committed. By far the
bloodiest battle that had ever been fought in
North America, Shiloh was but a harbinger of
things to come.

On that same day, 7 April 1862, 'Island No.
10' fell to Pope and Foote, and, with the capture of Memphis on 6 June, the central Mississippi was firmly in Union hands. In that same
month a concentration of 46 US naval vessels,
under the command of Captain David G
Farragut, appeared off the mouth of the Mississippi. It carried 18,000 troops under Major
General Benjamin F Butler. Late in the month
Farragut forced his way past two forts on the
lower river and took the vital port city of New
Orleans, before moving on to take Baton
Rouge and Natchez. With the lower Mississippi now in Union hands only the section
commanded by Vicksburg and Port Hudson
remained to deny full Federal control of the
entire vital waterway.

In the meantime, Halleck took over direct

control of the armies in the West and plod-
dingly made his way to Corinth, leaving
Beauregard time to evacuate the city before
he arrived on 30 May. Nevertheless, the
Mississippi River, and its vital shores, especially on its eastern side, were clearly coming
under Union domination in this second year
of the Civil War.

Yet the Confederates were far from done
in the West during 1862. A giant counter-
offensive was planned. It was to move out of
northern Mississippi and Tennessee to penetrate the heart of the Union-held territories
and bring neutral Kentucky into the Confederacy. Commanding would be General
Braxton Bragg, who had replaced General
Beauregard after the latter's evacuation of
Corinth. Bragg moved the bulk of his forces
from northern Mississippi by roundabout rail
connections to Chattanooga, whence, in
company with Lieutenant General Edmund
Kirby Smith, he launched a drive against the
forces of General Buell. Although this major
offensive had resulted in furious fighting at
Perryville, Kentucky, and later at Stones
River, near Murfreesboro, Tennessee, no
great uprising of Confederate sympathy had
occurred in Kentucky. Nor was Buell's army
defeated, although this army (now called the
Army of the Cumberland) had been badly
mauled and would require six months to re-

cover. Nevertheless, while the Confederates still held Chattanooga, and therefore eastern Tennessee and Georgia, the great arc of land along the Ohio River and down the Mississippi was still firmly in Union hands. Thus if the Federals could capture Chattanooga, they would have a base from which to threaten a second bisection of the Confederate homeland.

In the east the year 1862 had begun with General McClellan assiduously training the 150,000-man Army of the Potomac and resisting any pressure to go on the offensive until the troops were 'ready.' Facing him at Manassas was General Joseph E Johnston's 50,000 Confederates (although McClellan kept insisting their numbers were at least twice that many). McClellan was working on a plan that would move his entire army on naval transports to the mouth of the Rappahannock River and land at Urbanna, east of Richmond. An invasion here, argued McClellan, would pull Johnston's forces south, away from the capital, to fight on ground of McClellan's choosing, and might thereby compel the surrender of Richmond. But Lin-

coln was insistent that a covering force of 40,000 be left near Washington to protect the capital, and then in March Johnston upset McClellan's plan by pulling his army back behind the Rappahannock, where McClellan had intended to land.

Now McClellan proposed to move his army to Fortress Monroe on Hampton Roads, at the tip of the Virginia Peninsula, and then march 75 miles up the Peninsula between the York and James Rivers to assault Richmond. Thus was born the Peninsula Campaign of 1862. Preparing to launch his expedition in March, McClellan attempted to mislead Lincoln as to how many troops he was leaving behind to protect Washington, but Lincoln peremptorily removed 30,000 men, under General McDowell, from McClellan's attack force and dispatched them to Fredericksburg on the Rappahannock to cover the capital.

McClellan still had about 100,000 men,

Right: Robert E Lee, Grant's great Southern adversary.
Below: General map of the Civil War.

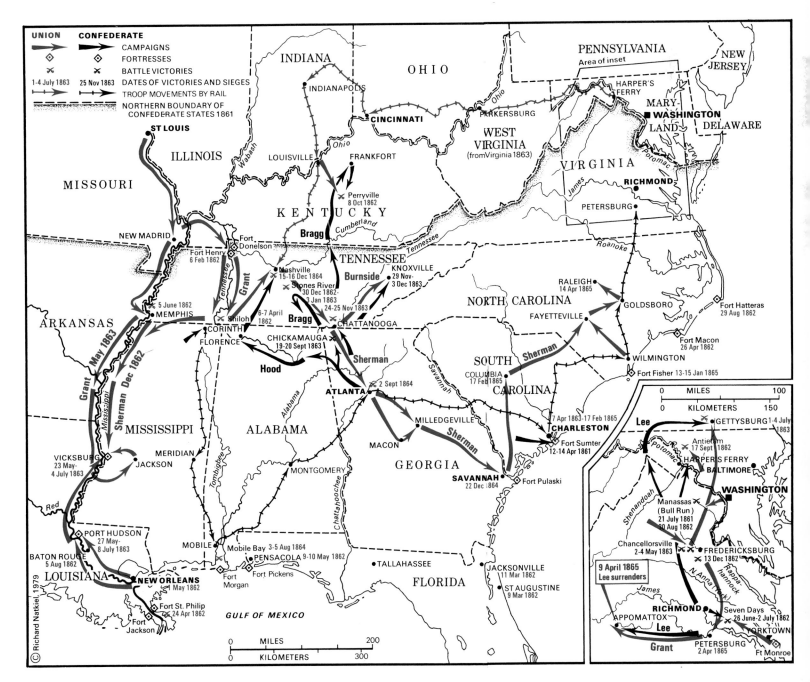

After the Battle of Fair Oaks in May 1862 Lee took over the command in Virginia from the injured Johnston.

more than enough to wage a vigorous offensive operation, but the Federal commander moved so slowly up the Peninsula that the Confederates were able to gather 70,000 troops to meet him. When he finally arrived within 20 miles of the Confederate capital in mid-May, McClellan had his forces disposed on both sides of the Chickahominy River, the northern contingent covering his communications with his base on the York River, the southern to threaten Richmond. At McClellan's pleading, Lincoln finally agreed to allow McDowell's 30,000 to move south by land and join McClellan on the Chickahominy, but the Confederate high command decided to forestall this movement by sending Stonewall Jackson and a force of 17,000 out of the Valley, on the upper left leg of the Virginia triangle, to threaten Washington as a diversion. Lincoln immediately sent three armies, under Lieutenant General John C Fremont, Major General Nathaniel P Banks, and General McDowell, to trap him west of Washington. But the Union generals were dilatory, and Jackson escaped back into the Valley, thus having successfully drawn McDowell's troops away from reinforcing McClellan.

In the meantime, on 31 May, Johnston had attacked McClellan's army at Fair Oaks and Seven Pines but could not crack their lines. As Johnston had been badly wounded in the fighting, President Davis appointed Robert E Lee to replace him. Lee and his newly-named Army of Northern Virginia at once went on a spirited offensive. Lee brought Jackson down from the Valley to reinforce himself and then struck McClellan's right wing on 25 June, setting off what has come to be known as the Seven Days' Battle (25 June-1 July 1862). Even though the attack was poorly coordinated McClellan was forced to retreat. He pulled back, not to the York River on the east, but south to the James River, where the Navy was setting up a base at Harrison's Landing. Lee followed, always shielding Richmond, but could not destroy

Lee's invasion of Maryland in 1862 was halted by the bloody battle of Antietam (Sharpsburg) in September.

McClellan's army, although taking 11,000 casualties in the attempt. The Union Army might still have moved on Richmond from this position, but Lincoln and his advisors (perhaps putting stock in McClellan's claim that Lee had 200,000 men in his army) decided to withdraw the Union army from the Peninsula and to advance on Richmond by land instead. Thus ended the Peninsula Campaign of 1862. McClellan was ordered to withdraw to join with a new united army that was being assembled just south of Washington. This force was to be commanded by General John Pope, brought from the West to rejuvenate the spirit in the Army of the Potomac.

McClellan was in no hurry to join Pope, even when it became obvious that Lee was preparing to hit Pope before McClellan's troops could arrive by water from the Peninsula. As a result, when Lee's forces attacked Pope on 29 August to begin the Second Battle of Bull Run (Second Manassas), below Washington, few of McClellan's troops had joined the hapless Pope. Despite the fact that he had 75,000 men, the Union commander engaged in fruitless piecemeal attacks on the Confederates, and when Lee, with a total of 60,000 men, suddenly assumed a determined offensive, a Union defeat soon became a Union rout. As Pope's forces struggled back into Washington, Lincoln relieved him and placed McClellan back in charge of the Eastern armies. Apparently Lincoln's theory was that if McClellan was not a fighter, he was at least a good organizer of men, and that was what was needed at the moment.

But Lee was not disposed to give Lincoln and the Federals time to recover. To shake the enemy's will, and perhaps convince Maryland to join the Confederacy, he began a move over the Potomac into Maryland, Jackson joining him after he had taken the Federal stronghold at Harper's Ferry. Now Lincoln would have to settle for McClellan to meet this new and unexpected challenge.

Yet luck seemed to be with the Unionists when a captured Confederate order revealed clearly where Lee was going and that his forces were divided, with Jackson moving toward Harper's Ferry. McClellan had only to advance rapidly across Maryland and destroy Lee's forces piecemeal before they came together, but once again he was too late and caught up with Lee at Sharpsburg, Maryland, behind Antietam Creek, only after most of Jackson's forces had joined with Lee's. Still, Lee had only 50,000 troops to McClellan's 90,000. McClellan attacked Lee, beginning early on the morning of 17 September 1862, and all day long furious fighting raged along the extended lines. Before the sun set, 12,000 Union soldiers and 10,000 Confederates had been killed or wounded; it was the bloodiest single day of the Civil War. McClellan could have used his reserves that day (which might have given him the victory), but he refused to do so. He also refused thereafter to pursue Lee, who returned in a rather leisurely fashion back across the Potomac into Virginia. Lincoln was furious: He, unlike most of his generals, realized that the destruction of the enemy's

armies, not the taking of territory, was the key to Union victory. McClellan was removed, but his replacement, Major General Ambrose E Burnside, would soon display that he, too, was hardly the aggressive and determined commander Lincoln and the Union so desperately needed.

Burnside decided on a new advance on Richmond. His plan was to move to the east and south, cross the Rappahannock at Fredericksburg, and then follow the railroad line into the Southern capital. The plan was not ill-founded, but its success depended on getting the Union army across the Rappahannock at Fredericksburg before Lee intercepted him. Burnside, with his 100,000 men, won the race to Fredericksburg but dallied in crossing. This gave Lee enough

At Antietam and many other fights Thomas 'Stonewall' Jackson proved to be Lee's most valuable lieutenant.

time to reach the city with his 70,000 men and set up strong defensive positions on the hills around the town. Now Burnside's forces would have to cross the river under fire and climb the steep embankments in order to reach the town and confront Lee. Inexplicably, Burnside launched his main attack, on 13 December, directly against Fredericksburg itself, Lee's strongest defensive position. The Union forces were mown down in a hail of Confederate fire from the hills above. Before the day was out, Burnside had suffered an appalling 15,000 casualties. He withdrew his forces from the field, leaving the Con-

76

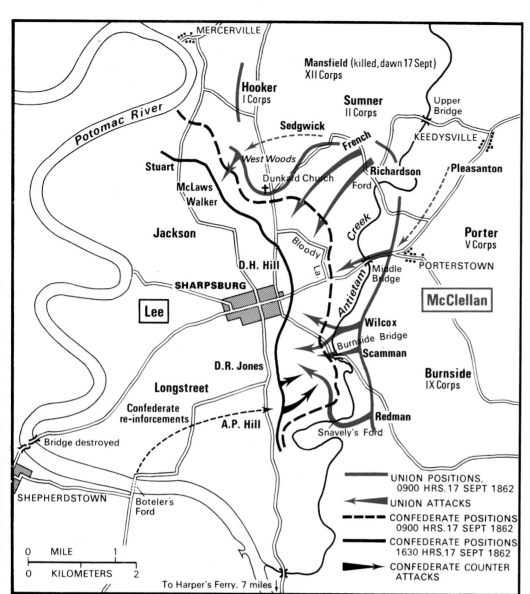

Left: Map of the Battle of Antietam.
Right: Yet another Union advance on Richmond foundered at Fredericksburg when troops were decimated crossing the Rappahannock under fire in an ill-conceived frontal attack.

federate right leg of the strategic northern Virginia triangle still intact and Richmond as safe as it had been when the year began.

Yet despite the fact that the Confederates had shown great tactical skill in reacting to Union thrusts at the heartland of the eastern theater and had scored notable victories against the enemy many times over, the Union forces were still intact and capable of replenishment. Neither had Northern will to fight been broken by dogged Southern resistance, nor had the Confederate invasion of Maryland succeeded. Furthermore, the military situation in the western theater was tilting toward eventual Union victory beyond the Appalachians. And finally, the US Navy, by neutralizing the Confederate hope for naval supremacy in Chesapeake Bay in the Battle of Hampton Roads (8-9 March 1862), and by its dogged campaign both to extend its blockade of the Confederate coast and to take key Southern port cities, was beginning to strangle the South. Thus the year 1862 had brought many victories to the Confederate cause, but foreshadowed in its events was the specter of final defeat.

The Tide Turns Against the Confederacy: 1863

As 1863 opened, General Burnside, badly shaken by his defeat at Fredericksburg the previous December, was replaced by Major General Joseph 'Fighting Joe' Hooker, a corps commander who had earned a reputation for being a fearless fighter and good organizer, as well as an inveterate braggart. Lincoln was aware of Hooker's faults but wanted a general who would at least fight. Hooker soon came up with a plan that seemed in keeping with his reputation for aggressiveness. With his army of 100,000 encamped across the Rappahannock, to the northeast of Fredericksburg, and with General Lee facing him across the river, Hooker would not repeat the suicidal frontal assault that had led to Burnside's defeat the month before. Instead, his plan called for moving three corps of his army 30 miles upriver to come in behind Lee. Two corps would remain conspicuous across the river from Fredericksburg, and two more corps would be concealed in reserve. When the enveloping right wing was in position and attacking, the troops opposite Fredericksburg would cross the Rappahannock below the city and assail Lee's front.

Hooker's campaign began in late April. The flanking army, under Hooker's personal command, made the 30-mile loop and began

Left: An 11-inch Union naval gun. The blockade came close to ruining the South.
Right: Rebel hopes of breaking the blockade with ironclads faded when USS *Monitor* defeated CSS *Virginia*.

The repulse of Pickett's charge, 3 July 1863. The Battle of Gettysburg was the turning point of the war in the East. Simultaneously Grant was winning the decisive battle in the West at Vicksburg (*inset*).

to advance on Lee from the rear, through a desolate area of scrub pine known as The Wilderness. On schedule, the corps opposite Fredericksburg crossed over and began to fight their way west toward Lee. When Lee realized what was happening, he reacted vigorously and struck hard at Hooker's force in his rear. This completely unnerved Hooker who, despite his subordinates' pleas, cancelled his offensive movement and took up a defensive position at the little town of Chancellorsville. Lee did not hesitate. Leaving a sufficient covering force at Fredericksburg, he wheeled left with 42,000 men and the cavalry of 'Stonewall' Jackson to take on Hooker and break out of the developing vise. Sensing that Hooker's extended right flank was vulnerable, Lee sent Jackson and 28,000 men to sweep around the Union right while he applied direct pressure against Hooker at Chancellorsville.

Lee was outnumbered and his forces were split, but he had surprise and audacity on his side. Hooker received reports that Confederate troops were on the move off to his right, but he assumed they were retreating from the field. That evening, 2 May, at dusk,

Chancellorsville: Lee's victory here in May set him on the road to Gettysburg. The death of Stonewall Jackson, accidentally shot by his own men, was, however, a blow to the South.

Jackson's men came charging out of the woods on the Union right and broke through the Federal lines, yet somehow the Union forces held on. At this critical moment, the impetuous Jackson, riding out to survey the battlefield in the failing light, was mistakenly shot by his own men, who mistook him for a Federal. (He died eight days later, denying Lee his greatest cavalry commander.) The Confederate attack was blunted, and by the next day it seemed that the Union forces, being superior in numbers, might still hold their own and perhaps even break out of the trap. But Hooker had lost his nerve. Two days later, on 5 May, he began to withdraw his entire army back across the Rappahannock.

Lee, although taking 13,000 casualties at Chancellorsville, had again thwarted a Federal attempt to penetrate the right side of the triangle. Hooker had taken 17,000 casualties in a losing campaign in which he even failed to field one-third of his troops. Now the initiative seemed to have passed to the South, and Lee did not intend to give Lincoln and the Union armies time to recover.

Although some other Confederate generals wanted the Army of Northern Virginia to stand on the defensive and send aid to relieve the pressure on General Joe Johnston's forces in the West, especially around Vicksburg, Mississippi, then under siege, Lee persuaded President Davis to authorize

an offensive into Pennsylvania. He argued that a major offensive into the North, coming on the heels of Chancellorsville, would break the Federal will to continue the fight. Also, it would be better for his troops to be living off the rich farmlands of Pennsylvania than off the ravaged Virginia countryside. But while Davis assented to the operation, he allowed Lee only 75,000 troops to carry it out because he did not want to leave the Virginia triangle defenseless.

Early in June 1863 Lee began his movement west into the Valley, then north across the Potomac into Pennsylvania. He sent General J E B Stuart and his cavalry out on his right flank to scout for enemy movement, but Stuart, taking advantage of latitude in his orders, attempted to ride all the way around the Federal forces paralleling Lee's line of march and thus was lost to his commander when the ensuing battle developed. Without cavalry, Lee was without his 'eyes' and could not know the location or size of the shadowing Union army. Nor could Lee know that the hesitant Hooker had just been relieved by Lincoln. To Lincoln's dismay, Hooker's response to the news that Lee was moving west and north had been to suggest that the Army of the Potomac should again move south and take Richmond. Apparently Hooker never realized that the Northern military objective had to be destruction of the Confederate

Top: George Meade, victor over Lee at the Battle of Gettysburg.
Right: Map of Gettysburg.

south from Gettysburg). He was to hit the Union left at or near the promontories called Little Round Top and Big Round Top. If these could be secured, the whole Union line running to the north would be subject to enfilading fire from Confederate guns. At the same time, General Ewell was to push his men up Culp's Hill on the north. But the attacks were slow in starting, and despite furious fighting at both ends of Cemetery Ridge, the Union lines held, although losing some ground.

Encouraged by these partial successes, Lee next decided to launch a grand assault by 15,000 men, under Major General George Pickett, the next day. They were to advance the full mile from their starting point on Seminary Ridge, crossing the open field between the forces, and swarming up Cemetery Ridge to the east. On the afternoon of 3 July, after a two-hour bombardment that had little effect on the Union lines, Pickett's men stepped out in line to cross the field. 'Pickett's Charge' began as a well-ordered advance, but it soon crumbled under the merciless barrage of artillery and rifle fire that poured

down on the Confederate forces from the ridge above. Of the 15,000 who began the advance, only 5000 reached the crest, and these were shortly driven off. As the pitiful remnants of Pickett's troops staggered back to their lines on Seminary Ridge, General Lee could only murmur over and over, 'It's all my fault.'

The next day, 4 July, the armies eyed one another across a battlefield strewn with the human and material detritus of war. At length, Lee, rightly surmising that Meade was not about to attack his positions along Seminary Ridge, began the long withdrawal out of Pennsylvania, across the Potomac and back to the safety of Virginia. Meade followed but refused to attack, much to Lincoln's annoyance.

In this, his second offensive into the North, Lee had suffered almost 25,000 casualties. The North had lost 20,000, but whereas it could replenish its losses, the South could not. From now on Lee would have to stand on the defensive, a position which, he realized, would sooner or later lead to Confederate

armies, not simply seizure of Confederate territories. In his place, Lincoln appointed Major General George G Meade, a corps commander and a determined fighter.

As Lee moved across the Potomac he spread his three corps, under Lieutenant Generals James Longstreet, Richard S Ewell, and Ambrose P Hill, over the Pennsylvania countryside. Learning late of the Union army's effective shadowing movement and that the Federals were close at hand, he ordered the three corps to meet at the country crossroads town of Gettysburg, Pennsylvania. On 30 June Lee's forces, approaching Gettysburg from the west, and Meade's advance forces, approaching from the southeast, first met west of Gettysburg. Meade knew that the Virginian would either have to fight or retreat and, concluding that this was as good a place as any for battle, rushed his forces forward to the little town.

On 1 July, the first day of battle, the Confederates, at this point superior in numbers, engaged the Federals to the west and north of Gettysburg. On the north, Ewell's troops succeeded in breaking the Federals' lines and pushed them south through the town and onto the heights of Culp's Hill and Cemetery Ridge, just outside the town. Lee's exhausted forces could not dislodge the equally exhausted Union soldiers from these heights, but the Confederates had scored a notable victory that first day. On the other hand, the Yankees still held the high ground and were bringing up reinforcements. Lee would either have to attack them in their superior defensive positions or give up the fight and retreat. He chose to attack.

The next day, 2 July 1863, the real fight began. General Longstreet was ordered to attack from Seminary Ridge (a mile from Cemetery Ridge, both running north and

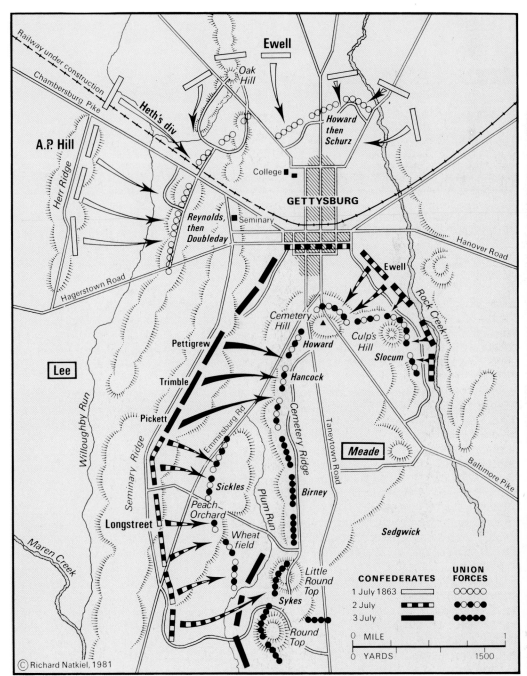

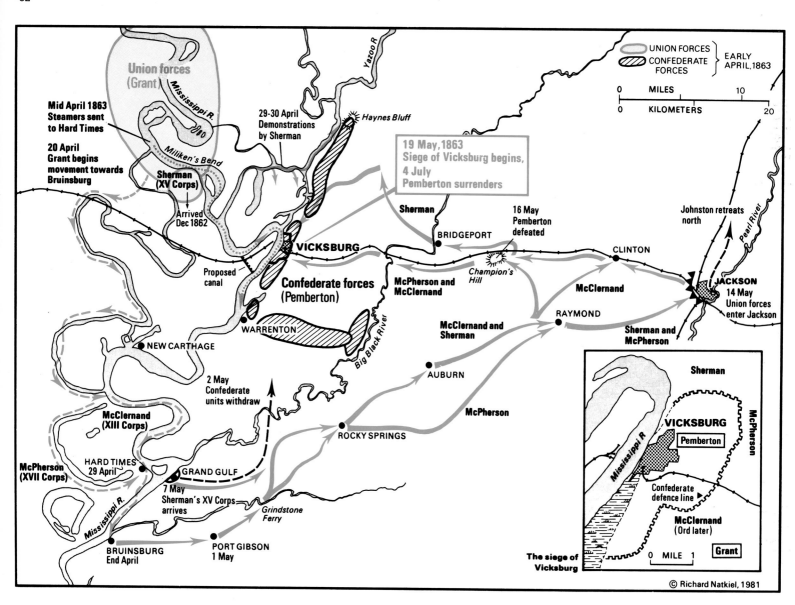

© Richard Natkiel, 1981

defeat. He had lost a crucial battle, perhaps *the* crucial battle.

While the Battles of Chancellorsville and Gettysburg were being fought, another important campaign was being conducted in the west. After the Battle of Shiloh Grant had been left with little to do by General Halleck for the latter part of 1862, but in December Halleck had finally given him permission to strike out at Vicksburg, on the Mississippi River, the last major obstacle to complete control of the Mississippi and the guardian of a corridor for supplies flowing into the Confederacy from the west. Grant first tried to take the city by marching down from Memphis toward the Alabama capital of Jackson, there to swing west against Vicksburg, while his favorite subaltern, Major General William T Sherman, advanced down the river in a simultaneous movement to hit Vicksburg as the right wing of Grant's attack. This operation failed: Sherman was repulsed, and General Joe Johnston's troops threatened Grant's supply lines so seriously that he had to retire.

Undeterred, Grant gathered his forces at Memphis and, with naval support, moved down the Mississippi in January 1863, landing on the west bank of the river in Louisiana above Vicksburg. He had with him 75,000 troops, more than all the 60,000 Confederates in Mississippi, who were divided between

Vicksburg on the river and Johnston's forces inland. But Grant knew that subduing the natural fortress of Vicksburg would be no easy matter. The ground north, south, and across from Vicksburg was so low and marshy that it was very difficult, if not impossible, to traverse. The land behind Vicksburg, to the east, was high and dry but out of the reach of the Union troops. Vicksburg itself stood as a bastion high above the river, with its artillery effectively commanding the river itself and defying any force to assault it. It seemed, in short, impregnable.

During the early months of 1863 Grant tried by various stratagems to get at the defenders of Vicksburg. An attempt was then made to cut a canal through the bends of the giant hairpin loop in the river below Vicksburg so as to allow the Navy to bypass the city safely and carry troops below the 'Gibraltar of the West.' But the canal, when finished, held too little water to float the naval vessels. An attempt to bring naval vessels through the narrow and winding river channels in the bayous north of the city likewise ended in failure.

Finally Grant hit on a plan. Commodore David Porter, the naval commander with him, would run his vessels past the batteries of Vicksburg at night, taking whatever punishment he must, while Grant's men would march through the swamps on the Louisiana

side of the river and meet Porter's ships 50 miles below the city, there to be carried over to the eastern shore. Then Grant could strike out on firm ground to attack the Confederates. While all of this was going on, Colonel Benjamin Grierson would rapidly move his cavalry south toward Jackson and continue all the way to Baton Rouge, creating as much confusion and disruption as possible while Grant played out his hand on the river.

It was a good plan, but to make it succeed would require courage, careful timing, and not a little luck. On 16 April Porter's ships ran the gauntlet of guns pounding away from the Vicksburg shore and emerged almost unscathed below the city. Within two weeks he had joined Grant's army below Grand Gulf and ferried it across the river. While Grierson's stabbed south over 600 miles in 16 days, Grant's men made the march down through the Louisiana swamps across from Vicksburg almost without incident. Then, when Grant and his 45,000 men had been ferried to the east side of the river, he moved with lightning speed, first east to Jackson, where he drove off Johnston's forces and took the city on 14 May, then west to Vicksburg, 40 miles away, in the process fighting three major battles and winning them all. The Southern defenders were now divided, with Johnston driven northeast of Jackson and the garrison at Vicksburg, under Lieutenant General John C

Pemberton, cut off. Grant's first move was to try to take the city by assault on 23 May, but, when this failed he settled down to lay classic siege to the city.

Day and night for the next six weeks the bombardment continued, as Grant moved his siege lines ever closer to the doomed city. With no hope of aid from Johnston, with supplies running out, and with civilians resorting to eating horses and mules as their only sustenance, Pemberton finally asked for terms. He surrendered the city and garrison on 4 July 1863, one day after the great Confederate defeat at Gettysburg.

While Grant was laying siege to Vicksburg, General Nathaniel Banks and 15,000 men from New Orleans had been investing Port Hudson, farther south. With the news of the fall of Vicksburg, the defenders at Port Hudson gave up. At last the vital Mississippi River was finally and firmly in Union Hands, and the South had been cut in two. Only in the center of the great arc stretching from Virginia to New Orleans was the Confederacy holding firm.

Chattanooga, Tennessee's southern border with Georgia, was the key to the center of the Southern position. From here the Confederates could strike north to fracture the Northern lines arcing above them, and as long as this vital rail center was in the South's hands no Union offensive could be

mounted into the lower South. The North was determined to take Chattanooga in this third year of the war.

Commanding the Union forces in the region was Major General William S Rosecrans. Remembering the carnage of Stones River, he dawdled, called for reinforcements at every turn, and made it clear that he was loath to make a serious effort to take Chattanooga from General Braxton Bragg and his Confederates. Finally Rosecrans had to be issued direct orders to move. He arrived at the southern Tennessee town in early September, just as Major General Ambrose Burnside occupied Knoxville to the northeast. General Bragg had pulled out of the town by the time Rosecrans got there, but he had only moved south a few miles into Georgia. There he set himself up in superb defensive positions and was soon reinforced by Longstreet's corps of 15,000 men from Virginia.

Rosecrans rushed into the mountains south of Chattanooga in pursuit of Bragg, only to find himself confronted by superior forces. He drew his men up behind Chickamauga Creek (in Indian language, 'River of Death') to await the southern attack he knew was coming. It began on 19 and 20 September as Bragg, now with 70,000 men against Rosecrans' 60,000, assaulted the Federals' lines. On the second day of the fight, Rosecrans,

Top left: Map of the Vicksburg Campaign.
Above: The Union offensive into the Deep South was halted in September 1863 at Chickamauga Creek by CSA General Braxton Bragg.

acting on misleading information, shifted a division from the center of his line and opened his entire position to Confederate penetration. It collapsed completely, with only the left wing, the US 19th Infantry, under Major General George H Thomas, the 'Rock of Chickamauga,' avoiding the general retreat that carried Rosecrans and his troops all the way back to Chattanooga. Thomas pulled out only when ordered to do so late the second day.

Chickamauga was a great but costly victory for the Confederates. They lost 18,000 men, an astonishing 25 percent of their forces, but the Union Army was now under siege in Chattanooga, and the South rejoiced. Yet a battle is not a campaign, and when General Grant arrived to relieve the distraught Rosecrans, 20,000 Union troops, under General Hooker, were brought in from the East, supply routes were reopened, and the situation began to change.

Grant was not a man content to sit on the defensive when offensive operations were possible; and his army had now grown to 60,000 men. The Confederate command outside Chattanooga was, on the other hand, in

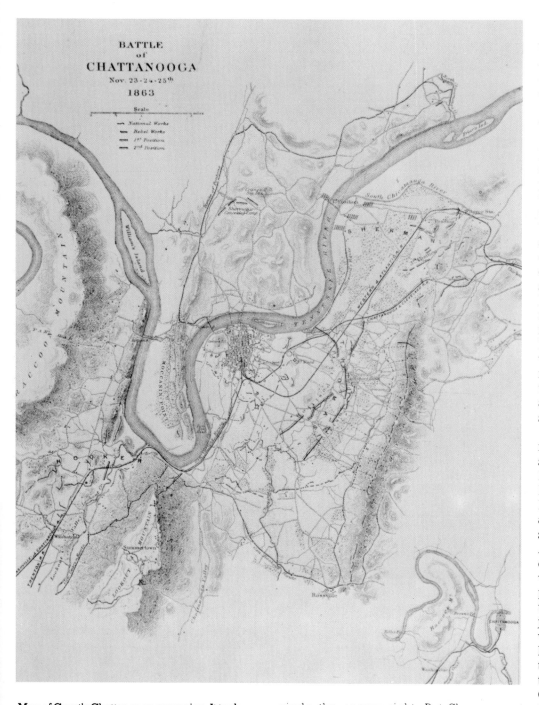

**BATTLE
of
CHATTANOOGA
Nov. 23-24-25th
1863**

Map of Grant's Chattanooga campaign. It took Grant most of November 1863 to undo the Chickamauga disaster.

Bragg was soon relieved by General Joe Johnston, but the damage had been done. The Union now had firm control of Chattanooga and central Tennessee. The door to the lower South had been kicked open, and the Yankees were about to walk in.

Victory: 1864-1865

In Ulysses S Grant Lincoln had finally found a general who would fight. In March 1864 he promoted him to lieutenant general and soon thereafter appointed him to be General in Chief, replacing Halleck, who stayed on in Washington giving the armies valuable aid as a logistical coordinator. Brought east to command the Union armies, Grant remained out of Washington as much as possible by staying with General Meade's Army of the Potomac. He hoped thereby to avoid political intrigues and to take both the pulse of his own forces and those of his brilliant enemy, Robert E Lee. Grant soon thereafter came up with the plan that, with some changes demanded by Lincoln, eventually would bring the Confederates to their knees, but only after another sixteen months of hard, sanguinary battle.

Grant's plan called for three offensive movements. Meade's Army of the Potomac, stationed north of the Rapidan River near Fredericksburg, would push south toward Richmond with the objective of destroying Lee's Army of Northern Virginia. A second army under General Sherman would drive southeast from Chattanooga, first to seize Atlanta and then to strike south from that key city. A third army, under General Banks, would move up the Red River, take Shreveport and then perhaps enter Texas to warn off the French forces of Napoleon III, who had just taken control of troubled Mexico. Banks would then move back east from New Orleans to take Mobile, Alabama, and from there march north toward Mongomery and the South's heartland. This third part of the Grant strategy failed, thanks in large measure to the dilatory Banks (Mobile was eventually taken by the US Navy), but its failure had only a limited effect on the outcome of the war. The real decision of arms was reached by Grant's advance on Richmond and Sherman's march toward Atlanta and the sea.

In 1864 the Virginia triangle was finally and definitively penetrated by the Union army. Meade had 120,000 men facing Lee's 63,000 across the Rapidan and was preparing to force him out of The Wilderness and into open combat. In addition, Grant had another 33,000 men, in Major General Benjamin F Butler's Army of the James, ready to move up that river from the east to take Richmond and the vital rail center at Petersburg, south of the capital. Still another force of 23,000 Federals was in the Valley on the left leg of the triangle guarding Grant's right flank as he carried out his grand maneuver south.

As Grant, with Meade's Army of the Potomac, moved out on 4 May 1864 the General in Chief began to slide the entire Army to the left in order to gain a direct rail connection with Washington and to establish supply

disarray, with feuding between Bragg and his generals (who thought Bragg a coward and a fool for not pursuing Rosecrans into Chattanooga after Chickamauga). President Davis had to visit the scene personally in order to try to restore harmony. The unfortunate result of his intervention was that Davis left Bragg in command but allowed the unhappy Longstreet to leave on an ill-conceived expedition to take Knoxville. This left Bragg with only 40,000 men to face the rising tide of Grant's strength.

Grant took his time. First he cleared dominating Lookout Mountain of the enemy, while simultaneously clearing his supply lines. Then, on 25 November, he moved against the main enemy line on Missionary Ridge. His plan was for General Thomas to make a demonstration in strength before the center of the Confederate line while Sherman made a wide flanking movement to en-

circle the enemy right. But Sherman got bogged down, so Grant ordered Thomas' troops to seize the rifle pits at the bottom of Missionary Ridge and await further orders. The Confederates in these rifle pits had been ordered to hold their places as long as possible and then to retreat up the hill to the safety of the main Confederate line of infantry and artillery at the top.

The men of Thomas' Army of the Cumberland, still smarting from criticism of their recent retreat back into Chattanooga, overran the rifle pits and then kept going right on up the hill. Even the officers got caught up in the enthusiasm of the moment and clambered up the hill with them. The Confederate infantry and artillery at the top of the hill had not been told that their skirmishers below were supposed to scamper up the hill to safety. Now they assumed that a general retreat was taking place, and they abandoned the center of Missionary Ridge to the exuberant Federals. This cracked the entire Confederate line. Bragg was obliged to retreat all the way back to Dalton, Georgia.

depots on the Chesapeake and its tributaries along the Virginia coast. Attempting to thwart Grant's lateral movement, Lee launched an attack on the Unionists on 5 May. For two days the two armies fought a series of bloody battles in The Wilderness west of Chancellorsville. The butcher's bill was staggering, but unlike previous Union commanders in the East, Grant refused to pull back, even when temporarily bested. As his southeast slide continued, the local focus of attention devolved upon the vital crossroads at Spotsylvania. Lee got there first and set up an entrenched roadblock to stop Grant. In preparation for this encounter Grant dispatched Major General Philip H Sheridan and his cavalry corps south toward Richmond to meet and destroy Lieutenant General J E B Stuart's harassing cavalry forces. In a 16-day series of running engagements that culminated in a decisive battle at Yellow Tavern, Sheridan did just that, destroying any offensive power Stuart's cavalry might have contributed to Lee's strategic defense, Stuart himself falling mortally wounded in the fray.

Grant now threw his troops against Lee's log entrenchments at Spotsylvania. For four days, beginning on 9 May, both sides took heavy casualties in a grim battle of attrition. Frustrated but hardly checked, Grant broke off the engagement on 20 May and continued his advance to the southeast. Lee raced south

to meet him and dug in on the North Anna River, but Grant ignored the challenge and, continuing his slide south toward Richmond, was soon northeast of the Confederate capital. Lee followed and finally the two armies faced each other again at Cold Harbor, on an 8-mile front on Richmond's outer defenses. Grant attacked on 3 June and was again unable to break the determined Southern resistance. Since beginning his campaign a month before, Grant had suffered 55,000 casualties (to the South's 32,000), but still he persisted. Again he slipped south, now to the James River, which he crossed by a 2100-foot pontoon bridge, and established a supply base connected by rail and water to his reinforcements at City Point. By 18 June he was in position to begin siege operations against Petersburg, south of Richmond. Lee's defensive perimeter now ran from north of Richmond in a loop around the eastern part of the city and south to below Petersburg. If this line was penetrated, especially at Petersburg (the vital rail center that controlled resupply to both Richmond and Lee's army), Lee would be doomed.

To break this pressure and lift the siege, Lee, in early July, sent Major General Jubal A Early and his cavalry corps up the Shenandoah Valley to menace Washington and draw off strength from Grant's investing army. This type of distraction had worked

well in 1862, but it did not work now. Both Lincoln and Grant refused to panic, and few troops were sent north to protect the capital, even though Early reached the northern outskirts of Washington before being driven off. Grant, however, was determined that such raids up the Valley should not be allowed to continue. Accordingly, he unified the capital's defenses under General Sheridan and ordered him and his army to pursue Early to the death. For the rest of 1864 Sheridan did just that, defeating Early at Winchester, Fisher's Hill, and Cedar Valley and finally putting the whole Valley to the torch to prevent Early and his men from using its resources. These 'scorched earth' tactics were effective: Never again would the Valley route be used by Confederate armies as their grand highway into the North.

While all of this was occurring in Virginia, the Union forces in Tennessee, anchored at Chattanooga and Nashville, prepared to move into Georgia. At Chattanooga General Sherman had 100,000 troops to confront General Joe Johnston's 65,000. As he moved out, on 4 May, the same day Grant was beginning his advance in the East, Sherman's

The Battle of Lookout Mountain, one of several in Grant's Chattanooga campaign that prepared the way for the decision at Missionary Ridge and the invasion of the Deep South.

valuable base in case Hood should attempt to double back and capture it. Then Sherman, with 62,000 men, began his famous 'march to the sea' at Savannah, where he was to link up with US Navy units and be transported north to join Grant outside of Richmond. Before leaving Atlanta, Sherman ordered all vital buildings burned and all railroads destroyed. This was merely a foretaste of the havoc he would create on his unopposed march to Savannah. The material destruction along his line of march was great, but the psychological destruction of Southern morale was greater. This was what Sherman wanted, for he realized that the ultimate enemy was Southern will, and he was determined to break it by bringing the war home to the middle South. Cutting himself off from resupply, he drove for the sea, leaving a shambles of Southern hopes for victory in his wake. He arrived at Savannah on the 10th of December; on 21 December the Confederates abandoned the city.

The South had only one more card to play. If General Hood could move north from Florence, Alabama, and seize Nashville, he might then be able to join Lee around Richmond and fight off the encircling Federal armies. But Hood was slow in making his move, allowing Thomas at Nashville to be reinforced and permitting the 30,000 men Sherman had sent back to get between Hood's troops and Nashville. The forces of Major General John M Schofield, head of the contingent hurrying back to Nashville, met

Left: William T Sherman, whose march to the sea cut the South in two.
Right: Grant in the Wilderness, the beginning of the final Union drive to capture Richmond and end the South's will to resist.
Below: Joseph E Johnston, one of the greatest Confederate generals.

targets were both Atlanta and Johnston's army. Sherman and Johnston were equally fond of maneuver and constantly tried to out-flank one another as Sherman slowly pushed south, the only major battle being fought at Kennesaw Mountain, northwest of Atlanta, in late May. After 74 days of almost constant skirmishing, Johnston had held Sherman to only 100 miles of conquest. Johnston's army was still intact, and Atlanta was still in Southern hands. But this was not good enough for President Jefferson Davis, who relieved Johnston and replaced him with Lieutenant General John B Hood.

Unlike the judicious Johnston, Hood was willing to attack the tenacious Sherman head-on, but his offensives outside of Atlanta only slowed the Union juggernaut, and Federal forces soon began to encircle the city. Hood was forced to pull back, and on 1 September 1864 Union forces began to move into the city. The capture of Atlanta, along with Rear Admiral David G Farragut's dramatic seizure of Mobile Bay the previous month, gave Lincoln all the popularity he needed to assure his re-election in November.

Sherman sent 30,000 men north to General Thomas at Nashville in order to protect that

Hood's army at Franklin, Tennessee, on 30 November 1864. Hood launched a frontal attack by 18,000 of his veterans on the Federals' entrenched positions. By nightfall Hood had suffered 6000 casualties, including 11 of his general officers, and Schofield was safely behind Thomas' lines in Nashville. Hood was now too weak either to attack or to try to break through to the north. His army was demoralized, and his situation was precarious.

This opportunity was not lost on Thomas. After making thorough preparations, on 15

Left, top to bottom: The battles of Richmond, Kennesaw Mountain and Spotsylvania.
Below right: Grant's victory at Petersburg doomed Richmond and the Southern cause.

December he launched a devastating three-pronged cavalry and infantry attack on Hood south of Nashville. By the second day of battle Hood's army had been reduced to a remnant and had begun a disorganized flight 200 miles south to Tupelo, Mississippi. It would never again be a fighting unit.

The new year dawned with the ports of Wilmington, North Carolina, and Charleston, South Carolina, falling to Army-Navy expeditions in January and February. Sherman, now ordered to move north by land rather than by sea, began to march toward Richmond, sweeping away the disintegrating Southern defensive forces as he made his way through the Carolinas toward juncture with Grant and Meade at Petersburg.

Around the periphery of the Richmond and Petersburg defenses the pressure on Lee and the Confederates began to mount. When the Federals broke the last rail line to the South and safety on 2 April, Lee realized he had to make a break for freedom. He struck out west along the Danville Railroad hoping somehow to join up with Johnston's forces farther south. But Grant's troops shadowed him as he moved, and Sheridan raced ahead to cut off his escape. Sheridan intercepted Lee and his forces at the little crossroads of Appomattox Court House, Virginia, on 6 April. Lee now realized that escape was impossible. It was time to speak of surrender.

Three days later, on 9 April 1865, Robert E Lee and Ulysses S Grant sat down in the drawing room of the comfortable home of Wilbur McLean in Appomattox and worked out the terms. Grant graciously accepted Lee's surrender of the Army of Northern Virginia, allowed his 28,000 prisoners to go home on parole with their horses and mules, gave them rations, and strictly forbade his soldiers from raising any cheers or firing weapons in celebration of their victory.

Five days later Abraham Lincoln, the nation's great war leader, lay dead, the victim of an assassin's bullet. Within two weeks the gallant Joseph E Johnston had surrendered his army to Sherman. By the end of May the last straggling trans-Mississippi Confederate units had given up. The Civil War was over, secession had failed, and the most frightful carnage in the nation's history had ended in an overwhelming Union victory.

West Pointers on summer encampment, 1890. The traditional gray uniform of the cadets was adopted in 1816, when the Army was short of blue cloth.

SERVING A CHANGING NATION: 1865-1898

The martial spirit and pride in military might that the Civil War had generated in the popular imagination was symbolized by the grand parade of Sherman and Meade's infantry and cavalry units up Pennsylvania Avenue in Washington. The parade lasted for two days; but America's love affair with the military was not destined to last. Although 52,000 men under General Sheridan were dispatched to the Texas-Mexican border to convince Napoleon III that his adventure in colony-making in Mexico would not be allowed by the United States (the French emperor withdrew his army from the country and left his puppet emperor, Maximilian of Austria, to face a firing squad of Mexican nationalists in 1867), and although Army units remained in the South on garrison duty, the volunteer army that had won the war was discharged, leaving only the regulars to carry on.

By late 1865 only 11,000 men (mostly United States Black troops) were still in uniform. General in Chief Grant wanted 80,000

In the Reconstruction Period the Army was used to protect the voting rights of the newly-enfranchised black citizens of the Southern states.

regulars retained in the postwar Army, but the number was soon reduced by a budget-minded Congress and a peace-minded public to 54,000 in 1867, then 37,000 in 1869, and finally 27,000 in 1876.

Most Americans assumed that martial law and the Army's physical presence in the South would end with the war, but politics and Southern recalcitrance dictated otherwise. Southern resistance to accepting the outcome of the war and to the newly-mandated place of the ex-slaves in Southern society resulted in such violent opposition as to require the constant intervention of the Army to assure local peace and to guarantee civil rights to the Freedmen. The Army had assumed control of the seceded states as they had been conquered during the war and had aided the ex-slaves in many ways during the conflict. The civilian Freedmen's Bureau, created in 1865, was a legal extension of that work, an experiment in educational, vocational, and social aid to the blacks unprecedented in American history.

The work of the Freedmen's Bureau was fiercely resisted by ex-Confederates, both through the courts and through direct violence toward its personnel and those

The violence of Southern resistance to Reconstruction was expressed in the rise of the Ku Klux Klan.

they were trying to help. This resistance was unintentionally encouraged by the lenient reconstruction policies of President Andrew Johnson who, following Lincoln's ideas on postwar reconciliation, quickly declared the Southern states reconstructed in 1865, after they had fulfilled minimal conditions, and made it known that he wanted to remove the Army as soon as possible. But to the victorious Republican party, as well as to many Army personnel and to Secretary of War Edwin M Stanton, early removal of the Army seemed almost a guarantee that there would be a quick return to the prewar Southern way of life with many of the same persons in power. The tremendous sacrifices of the war would then have been in vain.

This difference of opinion over treatment of the vanquished South set off a political and legal dispute, with Johnson (and many Democrats) on one side and the Radical Republican-dominated Congress and the Army high command on the other. The result was Republican-inspired federal legislation in the form of the First Reconstruction Acts of 1867. These disbanded Southern militia units (often used to resist Federal reconstruction policies) and divided the South into five military districts in which martial law superseded civil law. With the Army ruling over civil affairs (usually with great reluctance), most of the Southern states were re-admitted into the Union. But as Army rule became increasingly tainted by civilian opportunists (called 'carpetbaggers' and 'scalawags') and by alleged corruption on the part of Blacks elected to office, Southern resistance waxed.

Reacting to the Northern-based Union League's attempts to ensure the voting rights of Black voters and to the Freedmen's Bureau-backed state governments' efforts to use loyal militia units to make sure both that newly-enfranchised blacks could vote and

that ineligible ex-Confederates could not, Southern die-hards soon formed activist resistance societies such as the Ku Klux Klan and the Knights of the White Camellia. These para-military units regularly beat, murdered, hanged, and raped blacks, as well as those who sympathized with them. Such terrorism led to increasing demands that the Army put down the lawless white Southern elements, even though by 1868 only 17,000 men were on duty in the former Confederate states. As directed by the Enforcement Acts of the 1870s, and especially the Ku Klux Klan Act, the Army tried manfully to stem the violence, but its numbers were simply too few to deal effectively with the problem. If the KKK gradually lost effectiveness in the South, it was more because of public revulsion from its indiscriminate violence than because of any measures taken by the Army. The Army was always hobbled in carrying out Federal policy in the South both by Northern indifference to what was happening there and by incessant demands to cut Federal expenses. Even after the influence of the KKK began to wane, the Army could do little to curb the activities of its successors, espousers of more selective violence, such as the White League and the Red Shirts.

The policy of Reconstruction finally collapsed with the disputed election of 1876, in which the Democratic candidate for president, Samuel J Tilden of New York, won the popular vote for the office over the Republican candidate, Rutherford B Hayes of Ohio, but not the electoral vote. Since the returns from four states were in dispute, the Republicans, anxious to hold on to the White House at any price, made a deal with the Southern Democrats to allow Hayes the electoral vote in return for an end to Reconstruction. This 'Compromise of 1877' led directly to the 'redemption' of the South, to the return of the Blacks to subjugation, and to the removal of the Army from its onerous duties as enforcer of political and social policies in the postwar South.

While almost one-third of the Army regulars had been stationed in the old Confederacy, the rest had been scattered all about the nation. Some were on coastal fortification duty and others were patrolling the border with Mexico, and about 9000 were stationed on the Great Plains. Although immediately after the war veterans made up the bulk of the regular forces, by the 1870s their places were largely being taken by immigrants or other persons unable to find employment. Morale and professionalism suffered accordingly. In some years desertions ran as high as one-third of the enlisted men on the rolls.

Over this mixed assemblage existed a command structure that was rife with acrimony. The line officers in the field quarreled incessantly with the staff officers who ran the various bureaus and whose duty it was to supply the more than 100 posts around the country. Both William T Sherman, General in Chief from 1869 to 1883, and Philip Sheridan, who held the office from 1884 until his death in 1888, knew of the problems created by the increasing bureaucratization and independence of the Army's staff section, but neither had the political power or the administrative ability to set matters right.

The resulting lack of coordinated and effective planning was exemplified by the Army's slowness to adopt the new and improved weaponry available in other Western countries in the late 19th century. The standard infantry weapon during the Civil War had been the muzzle-loading rifle, and after the war the Army had been content merely to convert its old muzzle-loaders into breech-loaders. Finally, recognizing the need for a more modern weapon, an Army board in 1872 recommended the single-shot 'trap-door' Springfield, so named because its breech snapped upwards like a trap door. This .45-caliber rifle still fired a black powder cartridge, despite the fact that rifles firing cartridges with smokeless powder were than available. Yet the 1873 Springfield remained the standard infantry weapon for twenty years. Not until 1893 did the Army adopt the five-shot, .30-caliber Danish Krag-Jörgensen rifle that fired smokeless powder, and not until 1897 had the 'Krag' been issued to all of the regulars. The Army was also dilatory in adopting machine guns, such as the famous Gatling Gun, and failed to see it as useful for infantry warfare. (It was viewed only as an adjunct to artillery or as useful for protecting bridges.) New breech-loading

Edwin M Stanton, Lincoln's Secretary of War, remained in office until 1868. Andrew Johnson was nearly impeached for firing Stanton, whose high-handed actions angered the president.

Technical improvements in weaponry continued throughout the remainder of the century.
Left: A Remington Army revolver of 1874.
Below: A US infantryman with a Krag bolt-action breech-loading rifle of 1896.

rifled artillery pieces were also slow in being adopted, and, even then, black powder was still used. Indeed, the Army was even slow to change its uniforms. It was not until 1898 that khaki began to replace the blues the Army had worn on campaign ever since 1800.

But if the Army was slow in reacting to the command and equipment changes taking place in the world's other armies during these years, it nevertheless made considerable progress in its training methods. West Point, of course, still continued to turn out professional young officers (the Corps of Engineers relinquished control of the Military Academy in 1866, and thereafter its curriculum was broadened somewhat), and under Sherman and Sheridan several postgraduate professional schools for Army personnel were either revived or created. In 1868 the Artillery School at Fort Monroe was reopened (it had been closed in 1860); a Signal Corps School was opened that same year; in 1881 the School of Application for Infantry and Cavalry was opened at Fort Leavenworth (its name was changed to the General Service and Staff College in 1901); and the Army Medical School was opened in 1883. Also very important in developing a professional officer corps was the founding in 1878 of the Military Service Institution, a professional society interested in the dissemination of military knowledge through its bimonthly *Journal.*

These same years also produced one of the most important reformers in Army history, General Emory Upton. Upton, an 1861 West Point graduate who had served under Sherman during the Civil War, was appointed commandant of cadets at the Military Academy in 1870 and served there for five years. He had earlier published *Infantry Tactics* (1867), immediately adopted by the Army as a standard text for its regulars and militia. After his West Point tour, Upton was sent on a world mission to study military systems and returned to write his greatest book, *The Military Policy of the United States.* It was not published until 1904 but was widely circulated in manuscript form before his death in 1881. *Military Policy* had a profound impact on Army thinking. It also provided

The nation's yearning for post-war reconciliation is suggested in this somewhat sentimental tobacco advertisement.

Frederic Remington

valuable ammunition against politician and ex-general John A Logman's arguments in his *Volunteer Soldier in America* (1887), which asserted that the military should be based on a strong militia and that the military academies should be closed.

Upton argued that America could no longer afford to remain unprepared in peacetime and then try quickly to gear up for war, as it had done in the past. He also asserted that the Army's command system was antiquated and that the secretary of war, the line officers, and the bureau chiefs in command should be replaced with a general staff similar to that used by the Prussians. (Though never adopted, this idea, even today, has many adherents.) He argued further that volunteers and militia, being inadequately trained and led, could no longer constitute the backbone of the Army at war and that a compact and 'expansible' professional Army was the answer, since it would provide for 100,000 properly trained and led troops for combat, the militia being only a force of last resort. Thus the regular Army, with national volunteers and draftees to supplement it, could adequately fill the bill for manpower in a 'modern' war.

Upton's ideas clearly called for a larger standing army under the control of professional soldiers, but these ideas, plus the increased cost of such a system, collided

directly both with American tradition and the parsimony of Congress. As a result, few of Upton's proposals were acted upon, yet his ideas would become increasingly influential as the decades passed.

Greater professionalism was also aided by legislation. In 1882 retirement was made mandatory for officers at age 64. Promotion by examination only, for all ranks above major, came about after 1890. Regular efficiency reports on all Army officers were required by the mid-1890s. By these changes the stultifying promotion-by-seniority-only logjam was broken, and the way was opened for talented young officers to move up more quickly to command positions.

Curbing Domestic Violence

While these attempts at reform were taking place, the Army continued to be called upon to play a role in curbing America's domestic troubles. Faced with what they considered intolerable working conditions, American industrial workers began to organize into unions after the Civil War. In 1877 a great wave of railroad strikes swept across the nation, and President Hayes called upon the Army and Marines to protect Federal property endangered by the actions of the strikers. The regulars operated in small detachments and exhibited strong discipline

and great restraint in putting down these strikes, winning considerable praise for their behavior.

Best known of the labor incidents in which the Army became involved was the so-called Pullman Strike of 1894. Originating in the model factory town of Pullman, Illinois, it quickly spread to many parts of the country. The most direct confrontation between the Army and the railroad strikers came in nearby Chicago. Although Illinois Governor John Peter Altgeld had protested the sending in of Army troops, President Grover Cleveland insisted on using them to assure the unimpeded passage of the US mails, and the courts sustained him. Major General Nelson A Miles, who commanded the 2000 Federal troops in Chicago and who had cautioned against using them in this situation, at first unwisely intermingled his troops with policemen and Federal marshals, but then, under orders, consolidated them for greater control. Army troops fired on a mob in only one instance, this in Hammond, Indiana, where they killed one rioter when they were about to be overwhelmed by a crowd of strikers. In retrospect, the Army's role in the Pullman strike appears commendably restrained, yet inevitably this single death occasioned some harsh criticism from labor's supporters. And it also threw into sharp relief the underlying question of whether the Army

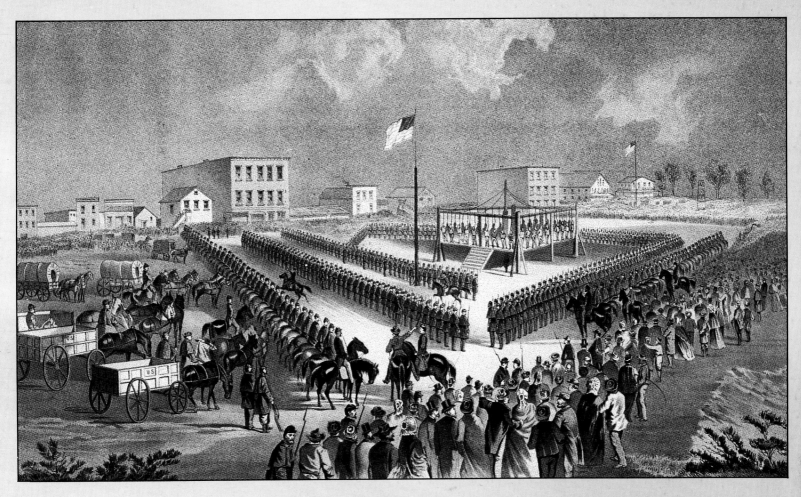

Top: This hanging of the leaders of a bloody Sioux uprising in 1862 was a foretaste of Indian troubles to come.
Below: US troops protecting a train in the Pullman strike of 1894.

The use of Army troops to intervene in labor disputes did little to enhance the Army's popularity.

really was the proper instrument for maintaining public order in such situations.

The wave of strikes also led to a revival of militia units on the state level, for by the 1870s governors and legislators began to see a volunteer militia under state control as an answer to their need for more policing power. State after state began to re-form its militia in the 1870s, almost uniformly under the name 'National Guard.' By 1879 a National Guard Association had come into being, and between 1881 and 1892 every state revised its laws to provide for a regularly organized volunteer militia free of Federal control. By the 1890s the Guard had a total enrollment of over 100,000 men, far more than the regular

The Wagon Box Fight near Fort Phil Kearney in 1867 was an early post-war encounter between Army and Sioux.

Army. Drawn largely from the middle class, it was a growing force that the Army, itself facing slim budgets and niggardly congressional support, had to reckon with. Although the Guard was used primarily for breaking strikes, being called out over 350 times by governors between 1877 and 1903 to handle such situations, its local prestige grew apace. The problems raised by such a military force, independent of the Army's training and control, would emerge clearly in the early 20th century as the National Guard demanded a larger and larger role in the nation's defense structure.

The Indian Wars

West of the Mississippi lived about two million whites and roughly 270,000 Indians. Of these Indians, perhaps 100,000 were willing to fight the white man rather than accept being confined to reservations. Called upon to police the Indian lands extending from the Canadian border to Mexico were about 9000

Army troopers scattered in posts on the northern and southern Plains. Their task was made more difficult and dangerous by the fact that the Plains Indians were both mobile, usually being mounted for combat on small but sturdy ponies, and carried rifles in addition to their traditional weapons of bows and arrows and lances. In effect, they were light cavalry, and they displayed great bravery and endurance in war.

But while individualism gave the Indian warriors many advantages in combat where courage and stealth were important qualities, it also meant that alliances with other tribes were very difficult to create or sustain for long periods of time. To this disadvantage were added the facts that the white man had greater technological advantages in weapons and materiel, greater numbers, and greater political unity. Still, before the Indians had been pacified and removed from the path of frontier development, they had engaged the Army in over 950 combat actions and had inflicted 2000 casualties while suffering 6000 deaths of their own.

The Army's campaign to pacify the Indians was as thankless as it was difficult. The soldiers were always caught between the demands of the humanitarians, who condemned the Army for every Indian death, and of the frontiersmen, who only wanted the Indians removed quickly, at whatever cost in blood, and who would threaten political retribution whenever the Indians were off their reservations or engaging in warlike acts. Most individual Army officers were probably ambivalent toward their assigned duty, hating the Indian's methods of warfare and use of torture, yet admiring them as brave and resourceful warriors fighting for their homes and way of life. But government policy was clear: The Indians had to be removed from their traditional lands and confined to reservations: if they strayed, they had to be forced back; if they resisted, they had to be treated as enemies and warred upon.

In campaigning against the Indians the Army soon discovered four complementary and effective methods of dealing with their adversaries: well-planned campaigns; the use of converging columns to force the Indians to stand and fight; the destruction of the Indian's camps, food, shelter, and livestock; and the use of friendly Indians both as scouts and as regular military forces. Effective as these methods were, the Indian 'wars' nevertheless lasted from 1866 until 1890 and cost much blood and treasure.

The tribes of the southern Plains were the first to resist the flood of white settlers and the first to feel the power of the US Army. The warlike Cheyennes, Arapahoes, Kiowas, and Comanches were determined and skilled fighters, but they found it impossible to unite against the whites facing them. They were further weakened by internal dissension because many among them were willing to come to terms with the whites and accept reservation life. But by their campaigns of terror on the encroaching settlements on the southern Plains, the Indians finally convinced the government, in 1874, that the Army had to

tacked by 1500 Sioux and Cheyenne warriors just north of the Montana border along Rosebud Creek. The ensuing six-hour fight has been named the Battle of the Rosebud. Crook's forces were saved time and again by his Crow and Shoshone allies, but were so badly mauled that Crook decided to turn back. Not knowing of Crook's defeat on the Rosebud, the other two columns moved on, intending to catch the Sioux in the Little Bighorn Valley, 50 miles to the north. Custer was ordered to move up the Rosebud River, cross over to the Little Bighorn, and descend along it. Meanwhile, Terry and Gibbon, having joined their forces, would move south up the Bighorn to its mouth, thus trapping the Indians as Custer drove them north. Custer came upon the Sioux encampment on Sunday, 25 June, a day before Gibbon and Terry could get into position, but apparently did not realize either the number of Indians gathered there or their determination to fight. He split his command of 600 riders into three columns. The largest column, about 230 men, was kept under his personal command.

Beginning the attack, one column under Captain Frederick W Benteen was sent off to the left to prevent the Indians' flight in that direction. A second column under Major Marcus A Reno was sent forward to attack the Indian encampment directly. Reno met fierce resistance and had to be reinforced by Benteen and the pack train from the rear. (Custer had refused to bring a Gatling Gun and its supporting platoon along because it would have limited his mobility.) The survivors of these two columns held out until two days later when the forces under Terry and Gibbon arrived on the scene. In the meantime, Custer's own column, moving to the

Perhaps the two most famous foes of the Indian Wars: Sitting Bull, *left*, and George A Custer, *below*. Their 10-year antagonism would culminate on the slopes of the Little Big Horn, in the most famous battle of the Indian Wars.

be used to return them to their reservations. The result was the year-long Red River War in which 3000 Army troops, moving in converging columns, ran down the Indians and forced them onto reservations in the Indian Territory in present-day Oklahoma.

More difficult was the Army's campaign against the Sioux confederation of 30,000 people roaming the northern Plains from the Dakotas to Wyoming. These Indians were angered by incursions into their treaty territory by miners seeking gold in the Black Hills, after its discovery there in 1875. They resented the government's apparent unwillingness to keep its own treaty promises of keeping whites out of their territory, and accordingly, under the leadership of Red Cloud, they left their reservation and migrated to Montana, joining up with the 'hunting bands' of Sitting Bull and defying governmental demands that they return to their Indian Agency homes.

To return the Sioux and their allies to their reservations, Lieutenant General Philip Sheridan, commanding the Division of the Missouri, planned an expedition of converging columns to corner the Indians and force their return to captivity. One column of 1000 men and 250 Crow and Shoshone allies, under Brigadier General George Crook, was to march north from Fort Fetterman in Wyoming. A second column, of 450 men and 25 Crow allies, under Colonel John Gibbon, was dispatched from Fort Shaw and Fort Ellis in northern and central Montana to march southeast against the Sioux encampment in southeast Montana. A third column, under Brigadier General Alfred H Terry, was to move westward from Fort Abraham Lincoln in the Dakota territory. In Terry's forces were 925 soldiers, including the 7th Cavalry Regiment, under Colonel George Armstrong Custer, and 40 Indian scouts. What the Army commanders did not realize was that they faced at least 2000 warriors (some estimate 4000) led by Red Cloud, Sitting Bull, and the Sioux's greatest war captain, Crazy Horse, all determined to fight rather than be herded back to reservation life.

On 17 June 1876 Crook's column was at-

Bured of the Dead
at the Battle of Wounded Knee
Copy Righted Jan 1st 1891 by
NorthWestern Photo Co
Chadron Neb

right and blocked by the terrain from seeing the number of Indians he was facing, was suddenly encircled by thousands of Sioux under Crazy Horse, and in a two-hour fight was wiped out to the last man. The Battle of the Little Bighorn, in which over 50 percent of the 7th Cavalry was killed, became celebrated as the greatest Indian victory in American history.

After the battle, as the news of the 'massacre' on the Little Bighorn stunned the nation in the midst of its Centennial celebration, public indignation was whipped to a frenzy by the survivors' stories of Sioux 'atrocities' in distant Montana Territory. The Army poured troops into the territory, and a winter campaign was mounted under the leadership of General Crook and Colonel Nelson A Miles. It broke the back of Indian resistance, aided by the fact that the Indians had dispersed after the Little Bighorn battle to celebrate, hunt, and resume their way of life. By the spring of 1877 almost all the Sioux, including the great warriors Sitting Bull and Crazy Horse, had surrendered and had been herded onto reservations.

Other campaigns against non-Plains Indians continued during these years: the Modoc War of 1872-1873; the Nez Percé War of 1877 in the Northwest; and the Bannock, Sheepeater and Ute Wars in Idaho and Colorado in 1878-1879. The last major campaign was carried out by the Army against

the Apaches in the Southwest. Widely and rightly regarded as exceptionally fierce warriors, and led by their great chief Cochise, the Apaches had finally agreed to cease resistance and accept reservation life in 1872, but some elements of the tribe, led by Geronimo, refused to surrender and continued to kill and loot. Assigned to bring Geronimo and his renegade Apaches to bay, General Crook enlisted friendly Apaches to aid him, dispensed with wagons in favor of mule trains to follow the Indians wherever they went in the mountains and deserts, and determined to pursue Geronimo and his warriors and give them no rest until he subdued them (once even crossing the border into Mexico in hot pursuit of his quarry). His strategy worked, and, although Crook was not in the territory when the event occurred, Geronimo and his men finally surrendered in 1886.

The surrender of Geronimo marked the end of regular warfare against the Indians, although isolated actions occurred for a few years thereafter. The final flareup between the Indians and the Army occurred in 1890 when a group of Sioux on a reservation in South Dakota, intoxicated by the preachings of the new Ghost Dance religion that promised a resurgence of Indian glory (and that the Indians would be immune to the white man's bullets), left their reservation. They were intercepted by a body of soldiers at Wounded

Above: Burying the dead at Wounded Knee, 1890. This was the last major battle (massacre?) of the Plains wars.
Right: Otto Becker's famous American icon, *Custer's Last Stand.*
Below: Geronimo, right, and three of his Chiricahua Apache band, 1886. The Apache wars lasted from 1861-1900 and were of unparalleled savagery.

Knee Creek and told to relinquish their weapons. Fighting broke out when an Indian's rifle discharged as it was being wrested from him by two soldiers. Before the subsequent melee was over, 200 Indians had been killed or wounded (including many women and children), and 62 soldiers had become casualties. Thereafter the Sioux returned to their reservations. The Battle of Wounded Knee was perhaps a grimly fitting end to a bitter and tragic chapter of American history.

The Army's campaigns against the Indians, like its other occupations during the thirty years that followed the Civil War, were essentially domestic and aimed at maintaining internal order. It had not been called upon to perform its most essential function: waging war with foreign enemies. Yet events in the Caribbean, in Mexico, in Europe, and on the American political scene were shortly to catapult the Army onto foreign shores and to give it a major role in America's emergence to world power.

WARRIORS ON A WORLD STAGE: 1898-1919

Moving to the front, France, 1918.

While America's internal frontier was expanding to the Pacific Ocean, her economic expansion beyond the nation's borders was also inexorably drawing her into an orbit of much wider responsibilities in hemispheric and world affairs. Commerce was rapidly increasing both with Central and South America and with the Orient, as well as with most European nations. In the wake of this economic expansion came political, social and humanitarian concerns in areas of the world previously regarded as peripheral to the nation's interests. Such concerns were not totally disinterested, considering American economic investments throughout the world, and were at times predicated on a belief in American superiority to others, but whatever their genesis, they inevitably impelled the United States toward a policy of increasing foreign intervention, and one of the chief instruments of intervention became the US Army.

War with Spain

Since the 1820s the nations of Latin America had been engaged one by one in throwing off the yoke of Spanish domination. By 1896 only Cuba and Puerto Rico remained Spanish colonies in the New World, and the peoples on both islands felt the passion for political freedom already won by their hemispheric brothers. The Cuban people had attempted rebellion unsuccessfully in the 1860s and 1870s, and in 1895 they rose again to try to throw off Spanish rule.

From the beginning, the Cuban revolutionaries worked to get the USA involved in their new rebellion. Without American aid the revolution could not succeed against superior Spanish military power. Accordingly, the Cuban revolutionary *junta* (council) established an office in New York City to promote the Cuban cause, to raise money and volunteers in America, and to issue propaganda designed to implicate the United States in the island's struggle.

Spain's behavior aided the rebel's cause. Spanish attempts to put down the rebellion in 1896 were extremely harsh, and Spanish cruelties in Cuba were prominently reported in America's major 'yellow press' newspapers, currently engaged in a circulation war and trying to out-sensationalize one another. Feeling the pressure of popular enthusiasm for the Cuban cause, Congress adopted a resolution in 1896 saying that the United States should recognize the belligerency of Cuba (thereby granting her *de facto* recognition as a separate power and denying that the conflict was a civil war and, as such, solely a Spanish affair). But President Grover Cleveland disregarded this congressional initiative, as did his successor, William McKinley. Neither wanted war with Spain over the issue of Cuban independence.

Yet events moved beyond McKinley's

power to control them. He had refused to make too much of the insulting contents of a letter from the Spanish minister in Washington, Enrique Dupey de Lôme, to a friend in Havana. (The letter had been stolen from the post offfice in Havana and printed in William Randolph Hearst's *New York Journal*, despite the illegality of its receipt and printing.) But the American people reacted with great anger to this defamation, and their anger turned to fury when the battleship *Maine* blew up in the harbor at Havana on 15 February 1898, with the loss of the lives of 260 American sailors.

The American press was immediately filled with insinuations that the Spanish had deliberately blown up the *Maine*. An American investigating commission reported that the ship had been rocked by an external explosion from a 'submarine mine' placed against the hull outside the ship's powder magazines, but it could not say who had done

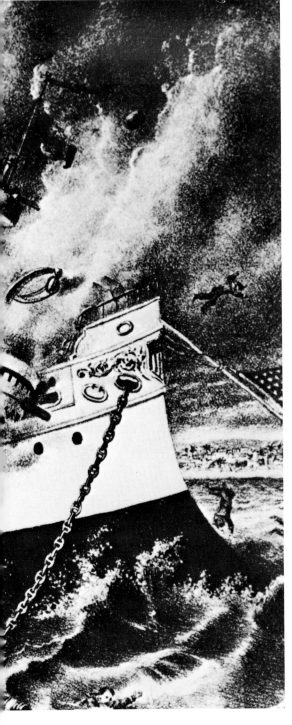

Top: Regulation uniforms for infantry and artillery, 1899. In fact, troops wore casual non-standard kits while on active campaign.
Left: The explosion of USS *Maine* in Havana harbor, 15 February 1898, was widely blamed in the US on Spanish sabotage.

the deed. A Spanish investigating team reported that the explosion was internal. The *Maine* had not been blown up, they argued, but had blown itself up, perhaps from a coal gas explosion (a very real possibility, as naval records now make clear).

Whatever had happened to the *Maine*, McKinley was now obliged to put more pressure on Spain to resolve her troubles in Cuba and offered to mediate between Spain and her rebellious colony. He wanted to avoid war if at all possible, but he could not convince Congress to cease beating the war drums. On 11 April 1898 the president finally sent an ambiguous war message to Congress, and on 20 April the bellicose Congress passed a resolution declaring Cuba free and authorizing the president to use the Army and Navy to enforce its declaration. Armed with this legislative authority, McKinley

ordered a naval blockade of Cuba. Spain reacted with a declaration of war on the United States. The United States reciprocated, and the Spanish-American War, the 'splendid little war,' as Secretary of State John Hay would later call it, was on.

While the Navy, having been in the process of rebuilding and expanding since the 1880s, was basically prepared for war, the Army was not. It did not even have a mobilization plan. Spread out over the West in small garrison units and inexperienced in tropical warfare, amphibious operations, or combined operations with the Navy, the 26,000 officers and men of the regular Army were hardly in a position even to train new recruits adequately for war, much less to carry out major operations in the Caribbean themselves. The Army's feverish attempt to prepare for conflict were further confused by the question of the readiness and participation of the various state Guard units, since it was not at all clear whether these units were forbidden by law from operating outside the continental United States.

The wartime Army, as authorized by Congress, consisted of both regular and volun-

The sunken *Maine* became a symbol for anti-Spanish 'war hawks' in the US.

teer soldiers. Guard units as such were not called up, but if enough men of a Guard unit enlisted as volunteers the Army kept them together as a special unit. During the course of the short war the regulars were expanded to 59,000 (of 65,000 authorized) and volunteers totalled 216,000, including 10,000 special volunteers dubbed 'Immunes' (men allegedly possessing immunity from tropical diseases). Lacking coordination by a general staff and with no mobilization plans, the regu-

For the war with Spain the Army was expanded by 216,000 volunteers.

lar Army's attempts to train the volunteers pouring into newly-built camps in the South ran into grave difficulties. Shortages of basic training equipment, poor sanitary facilities, inadequate food supplies, and shortages in weaponry led inevitably to inadequate preparation for combat.

Major General Nelson A Miles, Commanding General of the Army, wanted to assemble and train a special force of 80,000 at Chickamauga Park, Georgia. This force was to land in Cuba in October, after the unhealthy rainy season had passed, there to work with the Navy and the Cuban rebels to defeat the Spanish. But Secretary of War Russell M Alger, backed by a groundswell of public opinion that demanded immediate

action, overruled him and ordered that expeditionary forces be sent to Southern ports to prepare for an immediate attack on Cuba, even though no strategic plan of operations against the Spanish had yet been developed.

While the Army was still wallowing in confusion, the Navy won the first decisive victory of the war half a world away in the Philippines. Responding to orders from Acting Secretary of the Navy Theodore Roosevelt to prepare for operations in the Far East in case of war with Spain, Commodore George Dewey of the Asiatic Squadron had his vessels and men ready to go when war was declared. Sailing out of Hong Kong upon receipt of orders on 24 April 1898, Dewey's fleet steamed into Manila Bay, in the Philippines, on the night of 30 April and the next morning destroyed the entire Spanish fleet anchored there. In a matter of five hours Spanish naval power in the Pacific had ceased to exist, and the harbor of Manila was safely in American hands. Since Dewey's 1700 men were too few to take the capital city of Manila, they settled down to wait for the Army to arrive from the West Coast, meantime trying to discourage the British, French, and German naval units now arriving in Manila Bay from making any claims to sovereignty in the Philippines.

By late July 15,000 Army regulars and volunteers under the command of Major General Wesley Merritt had arrived in the Manila area. Constituted as the VIII Corps, Merritt's forces soon found that they would probably have less trouble with the Spanish

Right: Inadequately prepared Tampa, Florida, was designated the staging area for the Cuban invasion.
Below right: While the Army was still assembling, the Navy, on 1 May 1898, won a great victory at Manila Bay.

army garrison in the Philippines, whose commander was perfectly willing to surrender to overwhelming force as long as Spanish honor could be upheld, than with the guerrilla forces of Emilio Aquinaldo, who had been fighting the Spanish and who assumed that American help had been sent to drive out the Spanish in order to give the Filipinos their independence. That was not, in fact, the intention of the McKinley administration, which feared that if the Filipinos were granted their independence they would be too weak to sustain it against pressure from various European powers.

The peaceful surrender of the Spanish garrison at Manila was worked out in a carefully-planned scenario designed to salvage Spanish honor. The US Navy would place Manila under fire but would hit nothing in the city; the Spanish Army would 'defend' Manila

The most famous volunteer of the war was Teddy Roosevelt, seen here with some of his 'Rough Riders.'

against the American troops but promised not to hit any of them. The plan almost failed because of lack of cooperation by Aquinaldo's forces, but Manila finally fell to Merritt's VIII Corps on 13 August 1898, with almost no casualties on either side, and the next day the formal surrender of the city was accepted. This was two days after an armistice ending hostilities had been signed between Spain and the United States, giving Spain the argument at the peace conference in Paris that the United States had no claim to the Philippines, since its capital had not been taken when the armistice was agreed upon. But this claim was brushed aside, and the ensuing Treaty of Paris transferred sovereignty of the Philippine archipelago from Spain to the United States. The United States had thus become a Far Eastern power almost by accident. It was, however, an accident that would have important historic consequences.

While these momentous events were taking place in the western Pacific, the Army

was engaged in making the United States a major Caribbean power, as well. Under orders from the secretary of war who, as we have seen, wanted immediate action, the Army began planning for an expedition from Tampa to land somewhere in the vicinity of Havana, on the north side of the island. With considerable difficulty, the Army began to move men, equipment, horses, weapons, and food to that totally inadequate port city on the Gulf of Mexico. But then it was decided that no expedition could be launched until the Spanish fleet, which had sailed from Europe under the command of Admiral Pascual Cervera, could be located and destroyed by the US Navy.

Not until May was word received that the admiral had evaded the Navy's blockading vessels and had slipped into Santiago harbor, on the southern shore of the island. Since the ship channel there was narrow and the harbor was both mined and guarded by forts, the Navy now had to call upon the Army to destroy the forts from the land side and then

A Gatling gun in action at El Caney, 1 July 1898. In this opening battle of the Cuban campaign Spanish troops resisted more fiercely than expected.

to come around behind the city of Santiago de Cuba, at the head of Santiago Bay, and Force Cervera out of the harbor.

The War Department reacted to the Navy's request for aid at Santiago by embarking V Corps, under Major General William R Shafter, from Tampa with all possible dispatch, which in this case meant two weeks. Although V Corps was probably the best-prepared of all units, the port of embarkation at Tampa was a shambles, thanks to bad planning, inadequate rail and loading facilities, and lack of priorities for loading the available vessels according to combat needs at the point of debarkation. Nevertheless, Shafter's force of 17,000 men finally sailed out on 14 June 1898 and arrived off Santiago six days later. Amphibious landings were made at Siboney and Daiquiri, east of Santiago, beginning on 22 June. Fortunately for the Americans, their landings were unopposed, even though the Spanish had 36,000 troops in the Santiago area.

From their landing sites the American forces marched west to San Juan Heights, guarding Santiago from the east. Pausing to bring up supplies, Shafter laid out his plans. Brigadier General Jacob F Kent's infantry division was to attack the Heights on the left, while Brigadier General Joseph Wheeler's dismounted cavalry made a grand frontal assault. In the meantime Brigadier General Henry Lawton's infantry was to seize the town of El Caney, two miles to the north, then turn south-westward to support Wheeler's right

flank. When the attack was made on 1 July it was marked by Wheeler's and Kent's infantry receiving minimal field artillery support, and none was requested from the Navy. Lawton was delayed at El Caney and joined the main units only after the battle was over. Nevertheless, while black troopers from the 10th and 19th Cavalry Regiments joined Colonel Theodore Roosevelt's volunteer Rough Riders in storming nearby Kettle Hill, Kent's infantry eventually charged up San Juan Hill and broke the Spanish defenses.

Despite the American victories of 1 July, Shafter wanted to withdraw to higher ground both to save his troops from enemy fire emanating from the Santiago defenses and from the effects of the tropical diseases that were decimating his troops. Alger denied his request. With the Army reluctant to move forward and the Navy unwilling to enter Santiago Bay to destroy Cervera's fleet, strategic decision-making seemed at an impasse. Then Cervera, under orders to escape if Santiago appeared to be in danger of falling, on 3 July began an ill-fated dash for freedom out of Santiago Bay. Within two hours his entire fleet, four cruisers and two destroyers, had been either put out of commission or sunk by US naval gunfire.

With the American Army approaching from the land and the American Navy now able to sail into Santiago Bay, the Spanish military leaders agreed to quit, and on 16 July surrendered the 23,000 troops in the Santiago area without further fighting. This was a wel-

come relief for the American troops, who were being rapidly debilitated by malaria, typhoid, and yellow fever. During the course of the Cuban fighting 5462 Americans died. Of these, only 379 were battle casualties the remainder being victims of disease. The magnitude of this health problem led directly both to the Medical Corps' successful project to find the causes of yellow fever and to the Army's long-term concern with tropical medicine.

While Shafter and V Corps were gaining victory around Santiago, General Miles was preparing to seize Puerto Rico. Sailing from Guantanamo Bay, Cuba (seized earlier from the Spaniards by US Marines), Miles landed on 25 July at Guanica with 3000 troops. He met so little opposition that by 13 August he had captured the entire island, much to the delight of the Puerto Ricans, who welcomed the American troops with open arms.

Since 24 April Spain had lost two battle fleets, 23,000 troops, Santiago, Manila, and Puerto Rico. Now Spain felt that it was time to stop fighting and attempt to regain at the bargaining table what was being lost on the battlefields. In this she was disappointed. In the Far East the United States took from Spain both the Philippines and Guam in the Marianas. In the Caribbean the United States

took Puerto Rico and insisted that Cuba be given her independence (although the United States would control Cuban foreign affairs until 1934). The ensuing Treaty of Paris ratified these American gains and calamitous Spanish losses. For America it had indeed been a 'splendid little war.'

But if Spain was forced to acquiesce, Emilio Aquinaldo and his Filipino insurgents were by no means ready to accept the decisions of Paris regarding their country. They had fought for Philippine independence, not for American domination. Clashing first with Army units outside Manila in February 1899, the 40,000 rebels on the main island of Luzon forced the army to carry out extensive campaigns against them. The Filipinos made good use of their knowledge of the jungle, and even though they were handicapped by primitive weapons, their hit-and-run raids were very successful. By the summer of 1899 over 35,000 Army troops were engaged in

Left: Contrary to what many people believe, the taking of San Juan Hill was *not* the war's decisive battle.
Left below: The US naval victory at Santiago led to Spain's surrender.
Below: After defeating Spain in the Philippines, the US was obliged to go on fighting Filipino insurgents.

battles against the Filipinos, and not until fall was the insurgents' power broken on Luzon. Fighting on the other islands did not finally come to an end until 1902.

Even while this unfortunate conflict between the Filipinos and the Army was taking place, the American government was taking steps to introduce governmental, medical, educational and economic reforms that would revolutionize life in the islands. Self-government was gradually introduced, and within two decades the archipelago was well along the road to the full independence that was finally granted at the end of World War II. Thus the Philippines and the United States began their formal association in mutual warfare and ended it in friendship and respect.

The Boxer Rebellion

A clear sign of America's new interest in the Far East was Secretary of State John Hay's announcement, in September 1899, of an 'Open Door' policy, whereby the United States sought to guarantee equal trading rights in China for the occidental powers and Japan. Hay subsequently insisted publicly that all the major powers interested in securing privileges in China had agreed that China's territorial integrity would be respected, that is, that China would not be dis-

membered by the great powers. Yet though the United States perceived that her own interests would be best served by upholding China's national integrity, events would soon force the Americans to behave in a contrary way and resort to armed intervention.

Resentful of Western incursions upon their sovereignty (Britain, Russia, France, Portugal, Japan, and Germany had all made claims to parts of China), nationalistic Chinese calling themselves the Fists of Righteous Harmony, with the tacit approval of the Manchu Dowager Empress, Tzu Hsi, began attacks on all foreigners. Leaving a trail of the blood of foreign missionaries and their Christian converts, the 'Boxers,' as the Westerners called them, soon swept the countryside of 'foreign devils' and placed the foreign legations in the capital of Peking under siege. Defending the 500 foreigners and 3000 Chinese Christians in the Legation Quarter were only about 450 troops assigned to the foreign legations. The call for outside help went out as 140,000 angry Boxers and Chinese imperial troops began to attack the legations' defenses.

Although the United States reiterated its determination not to assist in the dismemberment of China under the pretext of protecting the foreign nationals, it nevertheless dispatched naval units and Marines to assist in

BATTLE OF PACEO (MANILA) FEBY 4 & 5 1899.

The 1903 Springfield rifle replaced the Krag. As late as World War II it was still the preferred sniper's gun.
Right: Poor sanitation caused more US Army deaths in Cuba, the Philippines and China than did enemy action.
Below: Boxers and Marines battle in Peking during the 1900 Rebellion.

taking the port city of Tientsin and attempting to break through to Peking. When this small expedition of 2000 men failed (the Chinese stopped the relief force before Peking and cut them off from the rear) the western powers realized that a more sizeable expedition was necessary. Accordingly, President McKinley dispatched the 9th Infantry, the 14th Infantry, and some artillery units from the Philippines to China, while other units were transported directly from the United States. Eventually some 2500 soldiers and Marines, under Major General Adna R Chaffee, were assembled and took part in the re-seizure of Tientsin on 14 July 1900.

These American soldiers represented about 10 percent of a 25,000-man army of British, French, Russian, German, Austrian, Italian, and Japanese troops. This 'International Relief Force' began the 80-mile march on Peking in early August to lift the Boxers' siege and rescue the nationals in the legation compound. American soldiers, especially the 14th Infantry and the 5th Artillery, played key roles in the fighting in and around Peking, and by 15 August the expeditionary forces had seized the heart of the capital and relieved the beleaguered foreign nationals and Chinese Christians from their 55-day siege. The Boxers had been decisively defeated, though mopping-up operations in the provinces continued for months.

American troops played little part in these latter operations, since McKinley was anxious to get the soldiers back to the Philippines. Nor were many Americans involved in the international army of occupation that stayed in north China until the Boxer Protocol had been signed and outside forces were withdrawn in September 1901. Nevertheless, under the Protocol signed by the Dowager Empress, all the powers were allowed to maintain a fortified legation area in Peking,

and a small American contingent remained in China until 1938 carrying out these duties. The victorious powers also imposed a reparations agreement on China that cost the weakened country $333 million. Of this total the United States received only $25 million and used the money solely to educate Chinese youths both in China and in the United States.

The Boxer Expedition was hardly a major chapter in the history of the nation or of the Army, but it clearly revealed the new role the United States was undertaking in the world, since for the first time the nation had taken part in an international military operation beyond its borders. If America's armed forces were to be committed internationally, they would have to be changed and modernized in order to fulfill their new responsibilities.

Modernization and Reorganization

If the Spanish-American War had reassured the Navy about its combat-readiness, the war had certainly not done the same for the Army. Among the many deficiencies the war had revealed were several that related to weaponry. Accordingly, in 1903 the Army began to replace its old Krag rifles with the improved bolt-action Springfield M1903 rifle, a .30-calibre five-round weapon capable of high-velocity sustained fire. In 1911 it also replaced the .38-calibre revolver as the standard sidearm with the efficient and brutally powerful .45-calibre seven-round Colt automatic pistol. The Army also adopted the M1902 3-inch gun as its standard field artillery piece, and it upgraded its coastal defense forces not only with improved installations but also by equipping its fortifications with new 16-inch rifled guns for greater range and accuracy. By this time, and none too soon, the Army was well along in replacing black powder with smokeless for all its weapons.

The Army also moved toward use of the airplane, first by establishing an Aeronautical Division within the Signal Corps in 1908 and then, in 1914, by establishing a separate Aviation Section in the Signal Corps. Even so, thanks to Congressional parsimony, by the time the Army entered World War I in 1917 it still lagged far behind the other belligerents in planes, pilots, organization, and combat doctrine.

The Army was also slow in adopting a modern machine gun to replace the Gatling. John Moses Browning had patented a recoil-operated machine gun as early as 1901 and formally offered it to the Army in 1910. But the Army, not realizing the supreme importance

Left: The Army was still being called into labor disputes, as at this IWW-led 1912 strike in Lawrence, Mass.
Below: Five years after this Wright Brothers' biplane first flew the US Army's Signal Corps established its new Aeronautical Division. In 1909 it acquired 'Aeroplane No 1'.

of this new class of weapon, took no action. In fact, the Army was not to get a modern machine gun until 1917, well after its crucial role in battle had been made manifest to all.

Perhaps more important to the modernization of the Army during this period was the work of fundamental reorganization of the service's high command structure. This was begun by Secretary of War Elihu Root after a special commission under Grenville M Dodge had revealed glaring deficiencies in administration and supply in the late war with Spain. Immediately upon being appointed to his post in 1899, Root began to move with determination toward basic reform in the Army's command structure. The heart of the 'Root reforms' was attained in 1903, when Congress approved creation of the office of a Chief of Staff who was to be responsible to the president, through the Secretary of War, for all Army functions. The position of Commanding General, with its built-in and necessary separation from the Secretary of War, was discarded. Previously the Commanding General had been responsible for the troops, while the Secretary of War had been responsible for administration of the Army. Now the

Guernsey Moore

The Army dress uniform, as shown on a *Harper's Weekly* cover of 1909. Képis had by now given way to visored caps.

administrative bureau chiefs would no longer be independent of the chief field officer in the Army. An important adjunct to the Chief of Staff's powers was the creation of a General Staff for overall planning, although just how influential this body might be would become clear only after the energetic Major General Leonard Wood was appointed Chief of Staff in 1912.

Reform also came to the Army with the establishment of more special schools for further and more effective training of officers. Included were the Army War College (1900) and a General Staff and Service College at Leavenworth, Kansas (1901), as well as schools in coast artillery, cavalry and field artillery, medicine, engineering, and signals.

Secretary Root also tried to dispel some of the confusion about the roles of the Army, the

National Guard and the volunteers. Spurred by military reformers, Congress in 1903 passed the Dick Act which authorized two separate militia groups. The organized militia (National Guard), under both state and federal controls, would receive federal funds by accepting Army standards for officers and enlisted men, organizing along Army lines, meeting for drill at least twice a month, and prescribing summer camp for its enrollees. In emergencies the Guard could be called up for nine months' service, although the geographic limitation – that Guard units could not serve outside the United States – remained. The reserve, or unorganized mili-

tia, consisted of all males ages 18 to 45 who were not enrolled but could be called for federal or state service when needed.

Subsequent legislation in 1908 and 1914 allowed the president to assign units of the Guard to foreign service and to appoint all Guard officers while the Guard was in federal service. Army reformers then turned to the idea of organized reserves as a workable alternative to the Guard, and the Reserve Act of 1912 allowed regulars to move into federal reserve units to shorten their terms of active service. To be sure, this alternative held little attraction at the time, although it would later become an important component of the Army, and in 1914 only 16 enlisted men were in the federal reserve. Thus, although significant steps had been taken, the essential problem of how to create an adequate reserve force to supplement the 75,000 regular Army officers and enlisted men in case of war emergencies still remained.

Latin American Interventions

Ever since the end of the Spanish-American War the Army's involvement in hemispheric affairs had been growing. It had taken the lead in Cuba in re-establishing government and in eradicating disease before its occupation duties ended in 1902. It subsequently returned to Cuba between 1906 and 1909, in the form of the 5000-man 'Army of Cuban Pacification,' to re-establish law and order when rebellion again swept the island. For the same reason it returned to the island in both 1912 and 1917.

The Army also took over the construction of the Panama Canal in 1907, under the inspired leadership of Colonel W Goethals. This came about as the result of a successful

Left: Francisco 'Pancho' Villa, the Mexican rebel leader who goaded the US into sending the Army into Mexico.
Above: Villa's pursuer, Gen. John J Pershing. To the right, General Leonard Wood, the first great Army Chief of Staff.
Far right: Pershing's personal aide in 1916 was George S Patton.

Panamanian revolution against Colombia in 1903 and a subsequent treaty with the United States which allowed the nation a ten-mile wide strip of land and the right to build the long-sought-after canal from the Atlantic to the Pacific Oceans. The new interoceanic canal was opened in 1914, a standing tribute to the Army Corps of Engineers.

Less glorious, but important for field experience, was the Army's role in the United States' difficulties with Mexico between 1911 and 1916. As revolutionary movements rocked northern Mexico in 1911, President William Howard Taft ordered the Army to assemble three brigades at San Antonio, Texas, in case trouble spilled across the border. The Army discovered to its horror that it took six months to assemble 13,000 officers and men at that location. This assemblage was not called into action, but the difficulties in mobilization compelled the Army to make a number of changes in its plans for bringing its troops together.

Then, in 1914, President Woodrow Wilson attempted to aid the enemies of the government in Mexico City by allowing them to buy arms in the United States. When this led to a minor incident at the Gulf port of Tampico, Wilson imposed a naval blockade on part of the Mexican coast. When a German freighter subsequently approached the port of Veracruz with ammunition destined for the

government of President Victoriano Huerta, Wilson ordered that the port be seized. In April 1914 8000 US soldiers and Marines carried out his orders and captured Veracruz. The major Latin American powers of Argentina, Brazil, and Chile stepped in to mediate the dispute, and the troops were withdrawn.

Two years later, in order to goad the United States into invading Mexico again so that he could 'save' the country and seize power, Francisco ('Pancho') Villa, a rebel opposing the government of President Venustiano Carranza, conducted a series of raids across the border into New Mexico and Texas. President Wilson duly ordered the Army, under Brigadier General John J ('Black Jack') Pershing, into Mexico in March 1916 to 'assist' the Mexican government in running down Villa. This Army of 10,000 men never caught up with Villa, but it became embroiled in a number of clashes with Carranza's Mexican army instead. With the Army unable to catch Villa and the clashes with the Mexican army becoming a sizeable embarrassment to the United States, Wilson finally ordered the Army out of Mexico early 1917. If the 'punitive expedition' in Mexico had added no laurels to the reputation either of the nation or the Army, at least it revealed some serious weaknesses in the Army's capacity to wage war. And it was important for the Army to understand these weaknesses, for it would shortly be called upon to wage a very large war indeed.

World War I

World War I was at first only Europe's war. It was begun in 1914 almost exclusively for the narrow national interests of the major powers involved: Britain, France, Germany, Austria-Hungary, and Russia. None was solely guilty of starting the war; none was innocent of provocative acts or of accepting the war as a means of striking out at its national competitors for territory, trade, and economic dominance. But all the well-developed war plans of the major combatants promising quick victory proved to be faulty in execution. The war settled down into a bloody stalemate on France's eastern border (the 'Western Front') and on Germany's and Austria-Hungary's borders with Russia (the 'Eastern Front'). Neither the Central Powers (Germany, Austria-Hungary and Turkey) nor the

America's reluctance to be drawn into the war in Europe is well expressed in this 1915 political cartoon. Yet well before 1917 the nation had begun to shift over to a war footing.

Allies (Great Britain, France, Russia, and – later – Italy) were strong enough to win. But neither side was weak enough to lose. All sides had underestimated the effectiveness of the machine gun as a defensive weapon capable of neutralizing infantry power as no weapon had ever done before, and hundreds of thousands of young men were uselessly fed into the maw of death.

Unable to force a decision on the Western Front, Britain sought to bring Germany to her knees by imposing a stringent naval blockade. Germany was determined to break the blockade and, in turn, to cut Britain off from outside aid by using the only weapon available to her, the U-boat. When use of the U-boat led the German navy into a number of sinkings of neutral vessels, and of the British liner *Lusitania* in May 1915, the outcry from America was so great that Germany promised to curb her submarine warfare. But in early 1917, with every indication present that Russia would soon be forced out of the war by internal revolution against Czar Nicholas II (thus collapsing the Eastern Front), and with low morale and even mutinies in the French and British armies working in its favor, the German government decided that the time was ripe for breaking the stalemate on the Western Front both by massive attacks there and by cutting off Britain completely from outside aid. This meant a resumption of unrestricted submarine warfare by Germany and probably open intervention by the United States. But Kaiser Wilhelm II and his advisors were willing to take the risk, believing that the issue would be settled in their favor before the United States could send enough troops to Europe to save their French

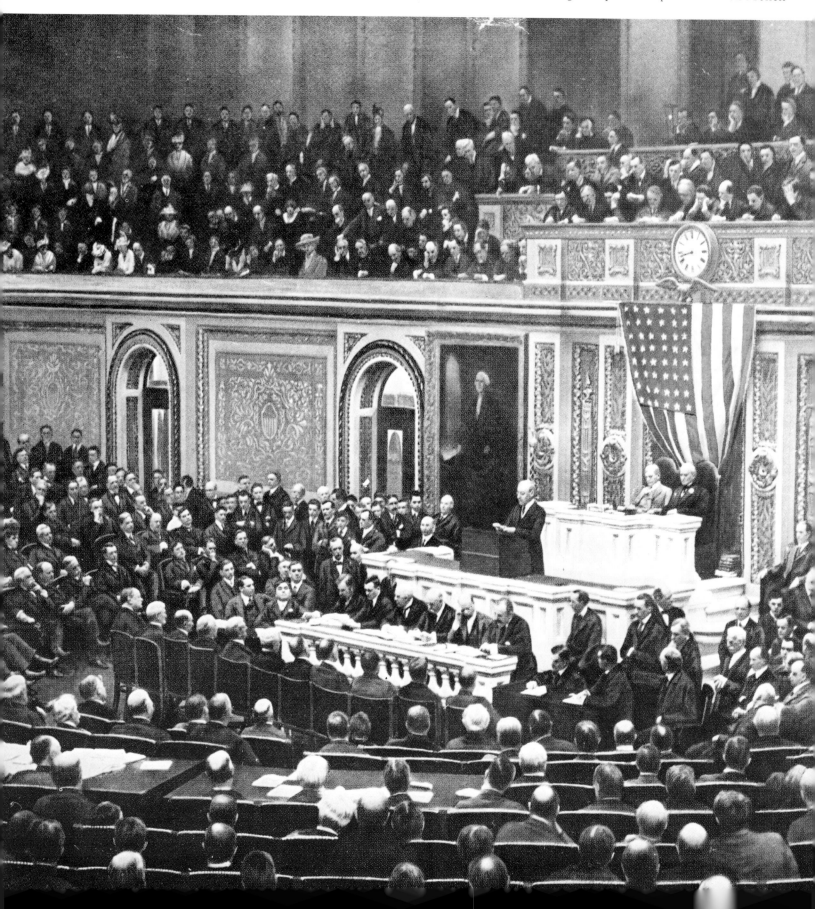

and British allies. In February 1917 Germany made its declaration of unrestricted submarine warfare, and on 6 April the United States went to war against Germany.

But even while avoiding involvement in the European war for three years, the United States had taken important steps toward in-

Right: Once America entered the war, bellicose patriotism ran high.
Below: A wave of German torpedoings of US ships in 1917 caused Congress finally to declare war on 2 April.

ARE YOU 100% AMERICAN? PROVE IT! BUY U.S. GOVERNMENT BONDS THIRD LIBERTY LOAN

U.S. TREASURY WILL PAY INTEREST EVERY SIX MONTHS

volvement in future conflicts. Of special significance was the National Defense Act of 1916, an ambiguous legislative and political compromise that nonetheless was a crucial step in the US Army's preparation for World War I. Rejecting the 'expansible' army concept of a regular nucleus expandable with volunteers, the legislation of 1916 called for strengthening the regular Army within five years to 175,000 men, with 300,000 the goal in wartime. It also provided for a federally-funded and federally-organized National Guard of 400,000 men under both state and federal controls and subject to call by the commander in chief. Additionally, it provided for an officer reserve corps and another for enlisted men, and for a volunteer army in case of war. Finally, the Reserve Officers' Training Corps (ROTC) program, an extension of the Gettysburg and Plattsburg training programs, in which businessmen and college students had participated in officer training programs on a voluntary basis, was also established by the act. In sum, this act not only provided the basic framework for military recruitment and organization during World War I, but also formed the framework for Army forces during the remainder of the century. Regulars, Guardsmen, reservists, and volunteers (including draftees) would henceforth be part of the Army in wartime, whatever the encumbrances of the system.

When the USA entered the war in April 1917 the Army was hardly ready for instant action. Including those Guardsmen in federal service on the Mexican border, it numbered slightly more than 200,000, with another 100,000 Guardsmen still in state service. A small and under-trained contingent, the 1st Infantry Division, under the commander of the American Expeditionary Force, General Pershing, was sent to France in June as a token of American support for her allies, while at home the Army was frantically attempting to expand to necessary strength and to train recruits to battlefield standards. Manpower came from the Guard and the reserves, from volunteers, and from draftees called up under the Selective Service Act of May 1917. Unlike its Civil War predecessors, this draft law made no provisions for substitutes and bounties and mandated that those drafted would serve the duration of the war. Administration of the draft, and the onerous job of calling up individuals for service or granting them occupational exemptions, was vested in local citizen boards. Men

Above: Map of Belleau Wood.
Left and below: Two examples of the foreign equipment used by America in the war: a Renault FT-17 tank and the SPAD 13 fighter plane flown by Eddie Rickenbacker.

Authors of the 1918 German offensive: Field
Marshal von Hindenburg (*left*) and General
Ludendorff.

between the ages of 21 and 30 (later 18 and
45) were subject to this 'selective service.'
The act also increased the regular Army
strength to 286,000, National Guard strength
to 450,000, and volunteer strength to a million.
These numbers were steadily raised as the
necessities of war dictated, and before the
war ended the Army's peak strength rose to
3.6 million men in 62 divisions.

Training for this rapidly-expanding force
through the year and a half of war was a major
problem, with inadequate facilities and too
few training personnel. Shortages of
weapons forced the Army to supplement its
Springfields with British Lee-Enfield rifles; to
accept the Allies' machine guns because the
Browning machine gun only reached full
production in mid-1918; to use upwards of
2200 British and French artillery pieces,
since only 100 of American manufacture
were available for the battlefields; and to
employ French tanks and Allied planes
almost exclusively. Indeed, some of this
foreign equipment would continue in service
in the US Army for several years after the end
of the fighting in Europe.

The wartime emergency also forced a
change in the army's organization, resulting
in the further subjugation of the bureau chiefs
to the Chief of Staff. Largely responsible for
these changes were Secretary of War New-
ton D Baker and General Peyton C March,
Chief of Staff after March 1918. Armed with
the legislative authority and with the backing
of Baker, March insisted that all bureau

chiefs were subordinate to the General Staff
and could report to the Secretary of War only
through him. March also reorganized and
strengthened the personnel and organization
of the General Staff so that at long last it
became what Elihu Root had envisioned, a
true general staff with real authority over the
Army. Unfortunately for the war effort,
General Pershing had been sent to Europe
with what he understood to be almost total
authority over his troops, and he steadfastly
resisted March's authority. Only when Persh-

ing returned to take over March's position
after the war would 'Black Jack' acquiesce in
final authority being given to the Chief of
Staff.

As General Pershing led his troops to
France he was ever mindful of fact that he
had been ordered to maintain his troops as a
'separate and distinct component' of Allied
forces, and he insisted on this to his British
and French counterparts, General Sir Douglas Haig and General Henri Philippe Pétain.
He also insisted that his troops undergo
further training before being committed to
battle. Accordingly, he chose as the American sector of the Western Front the area of
Lorraine between the Argonne Forest and
the Vosges Mountains southeast of Paris. This
was to the right of the French sector in the
middle, the British occupying the northern-
most sector of the long line. In this 'quiet' area,
Pershing could complete the training of his
men without too much danger of a German
attack from across the line, even though the
enemy commanded the St. Mihiel salient
protruding into the American positions.

Pershing demanded a training period of at
least six months, much to the consternation of
the British and French, who wanted the
American troops in the line as soon as possible. As Pershing saw it, his men had to be
proficient not only in trench warfare, with
such weapons as the machine gun, the hand
grenade, and the mortar, but also had to
master the use of the rifle and bayonet in
preparation for the day when the American
'doughboys' would go on the offensive.

Recognizing that the British and French
armies, as well as their own, were approaching exhaustion in early 1918 and that the US
Army might well swing the balance against

Pershing decorating Colonel Douglas MacArthur
for bravery on the Chateau Thierry front.
MacArthur was then the commander of the
famous 42nd, or 'Rainbow,' Division.

them when it got to full strength on the Western Front, the German army commanders, Generals Paul von Hindenburg and Erich von Ludendorff, decided that they had to strike a fatal blow at their enemies before it was too late. Accordingly, they prepared a massive 3.5 million-man offensive against the British and French on the Western Front. The attack was launched on 21 March 1918 along a 50-mile front against the British on the north, and in the ensuing battle the Germans severely strained, but could not break, the Allied line, despite giving and receiving horrible casualty totals. Ludendorff struck again in April, establishing a salient against the British in Flanders, on the Lys River. Before his final blow at the British in Belgium, Ludendorff planned a diversionary attack on the French northeast of Paris in an area known as the Chemin des Dames. To his own surprise, his 27 May attack knifed through the French lines, and within three days he was at the Marne River at Chateau-Thierry, less than 50 miles from Paris, the deepest penetration since August 1914.

Rushed to the aid of the French were two divisions of American soldiers and Marines, sent by Pershing at the request of Marshal Ferdinand Foch and placed in the line to stop the German offensive. Here at Chateau-Thierry, the green American troops showed

great coolness under fire and played a major part in stopping the Germans. (One officer who particularly distinguished himself was Colonel Douglas MacArthur of the 42nd, or Rainbow, Division.) The Americans then went on the offensive in Belleau Wood and acquitted themselves equally well. When Ludendorff made his last offensive efforts to break the Allied lines in June and July, American troops again played a stellar role in stopping him. By that time, ten American divisions were on the line, with 250,000 arriving each month, and the British and French positions were still intact. Ludendorff had lost his race to defeat the enemy before American numbers began to play their role on the Western Front.

Having stopped the German drive, the Allies quickly went over to the offensive. Indeed, planning was underway even before the German offensives had been halted. The result was one of the most dramatic turnarounds in military history. Within days the defender became the attacker. Foch, as overall Allied commander, had two grand objectives: to eliminate the three salients (against the British on the north, the French in the middle, and the Americans in the south) and then drive on the Germans so rapidly that they would have to flee back into Germany, abandoning their supplies and thus

finding themselves in no position to continue the war into 1919.

His first attack – to clear the Marne salient – was made by the French, aided by eight American divisions. Begun on 18 July, this so-called Aisne-Marne Offensive had completely obliterated the Marne salient by 6 August. The second offensive, in the north, the Somme offensive against the Amiens salient, was a French-British affair aided by one American division. It, too, was also a smashing success, with the British using 400 tanks in the first massed tank offensive in military history. The third offensive was carried out by the Americans against the St. Mihiel salient in the south, beginning on 12 September. Some 550,000 troops, aided by 260 tanks under Lieutenant Colonel George S Patton, Jr and 1500 planes controlled by Colonel William ('Billy') Mitchell, pushed east to destroy this salient in four days. The Americans were then directed to move north, keeping the Meuse River on their right and the rugged Argonne Forest on their left. Their new objective was to capture the rail junction of Aulnoye and Mézières so as to cut off the German retreat, while the British moved south toward the Americans in a giant

The Chateau Thierry battles included episodes of fierce street fighting.

Far larger than any previous battle in US history was the great 47-day fight for the Argonne Forest.

pincer movement to trap the Germans and the French put pressure on the center of the line. A total of 220 Allied divisions took part in this triple offensive.

The plan called for the Americans to make a giant shift, from facing east for the St. Mihiel offensive to turning north for the 'Meuse-Argonne offensive,' in a space of only ten days. They had to be in position at Verdun, 50 miles away, when the offensive began on 26 September. This shifting of 600,000 men, with all their supplies and equipment, was carried out successfully, thanks in large measure to Colonel George C Marshall of Pershing's staff, and the offensive jumped off on time. In the drive across the 24-mile front (which was gradually expanded to 90 miles as the troops penetrated the German defenses) the Americans eventually used 1.25 million troops (larger than any single American Army in any previous war) on a front far wider than had ever been attempted in any previous American conflict. The rugged hand-to-hand battle through the dense woods and choked streams of the Argonne went on for 47 days before the three German defensive lines were penetrated.

Although the American offensive was slowed by rain, mud, and logistical jams and foul-ups, once the Argonne Forest was cleared on 10 October the Americans continued to drive towards the Meuse River crossings and the key villages with their valuable railheads. The fighting here produced a national hero, in the person of Pfc Alvin C York, who killed 25 Germans and captured 132 more in a single engagement. By 5 November the Americans had crossed the Meuse, the villages of Aulnoye and Mézières having fallen to the British and the French in the meantime, and were speeding toward Sedan on the French-German border.

By now the entire German defensive position along the Western Front was collapsing. Faced with revolution both at home and in the military, the German government of Kaiser Wilhelm fell, and the new republican government asked for surrender terms. On 11 November 1918, at 1100 (in the eleventh month, on the eleventh day, at the eleventh hour), the war ended. The US Army, along with the Navy and Marines, had played a significant part in the Allied victory. After much fumbling during the early months of the war, the Americans had fought with determination, skill, and great courage and made of their Army a world-class war machine.

Compared to British losses of 947,000 men, French losses of 1.4 million, Russian losses of 1.7 million, German losses of 1.8 million and Austria-Hungarian losses of 1.2 million, the American casualty list of 50,280 killed and 200,000 wounded had not been great. But

The surrender of the German fleet in 1918, as seen from a US ship. World War I forever ended Germany's hopes of becoming a great naval power.

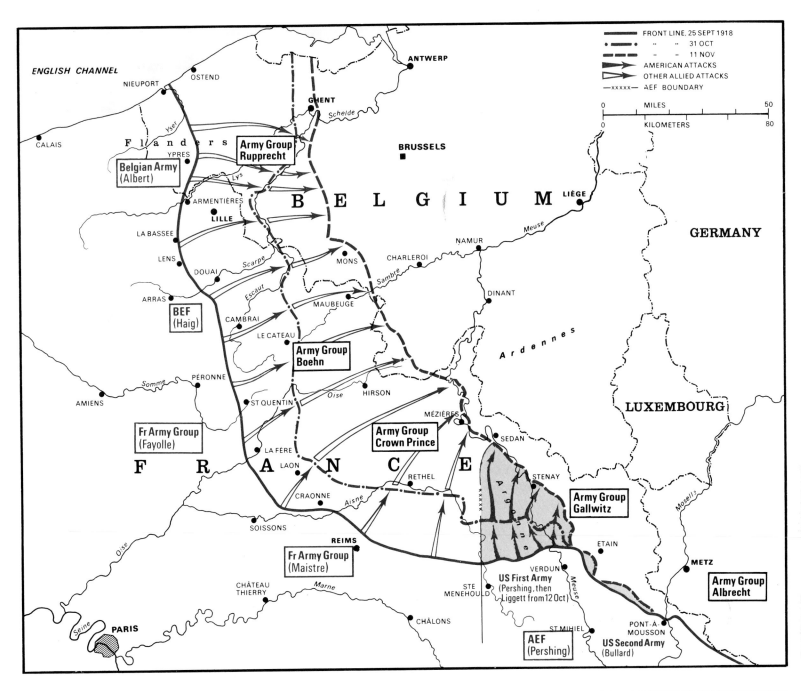

FRONT LINE, 25 SEPT 1918
                  "   "   31 OCT
                  "   "   11 NOV
AMERICAN ATTACKS
OTHER ALLIED ATTACKS
—xxxxx— AEF BOUNDARY

Above: Map of the last allied offensive in 1918. The US Army had captured St Mihiel on 12 September. By 10 October they were through the Argonne and a month later were over the Meuse.
Right: A US machine gun emplacement. The weapon is a French Hotchkiss 8mm, typical of the foreign equipment in US service.

American intervention had nevertheless been crucial to victory.

For the first time the American military had been called upon to play a major role in a great war fought far beyond its borders. If its military success was subsequently squandered by diplomatic failure, the laurels the Army won on the battlefields of France were honestly gained, and the lessons it learned about modern technological warfare – including the use of automatic weapons, armor, artillery, and the airplane – would shape its development in the decades to come. The US Army had come a long way since 1898 and its clumsy attempts to fight a war against weakened Spain. Within two more decades it would face a vastly greater challenge, this time on a planetary scale.

A famous image of World War II: St Paul's during the Blitz.

WORLD WAR II IN EUROPE: 1939-1945

With the Armistice of November 1918 the demand to 'bring the boys home' was felt in all parts of the nation. Demobilization began almost immediately, despite the Army's fervent but futile plea for a regular force of 600,000 men and a three-month universal military training (UMT) program to assure an adequate strength in the event of future war. But with the defeat of Germany, and no perceived threat from any other front, such requests were futile. America, in the words of President Warren Harding, who succeeded Woodrow Wilson, wanted 'normalcy,' not involvements. Within a year after the end of the war over three million men had been demobilized, and the Army stood at only 19,000 officers and 205,000 enlisted men. It was a regular volunteer force again.

Some of the US troops in Europe at the end of the war were kept on for occupation duty in Germany and Austria, but the last of these had been withdrawn by January 1923. Meanwhile, American troops had joined with those of other nations in trying to aid pro-Allied and anti-Bolshevik 'White' forces in Russia during the civil war that broke out after the fall of the Romanov dynasty and the subsequent seizure of power by Nikolai Lenin's Bolsheviks in November 1917. At Murmansk-Archangel, in northern Russia, 5000 American soldiers under British command joined other Allied troops in aiding the White Armies against the Red armies between August 1918 and June 1919. A second American-Allied force moved into Russia's Far Eastern regions via Vladivostock in August 1918 and remained

until April 1920. Here the 10,000 American servicemen and their Allied counterparts, like their comrades in northern Russia, were unsuccessful in helping to defeat the Red Armies, brilliantly led by Leon Trotsky. More substantial Allied intervention on behalf of the anti-Bolsheviks might have led to the Communists' defeat, but the exhausted Western forces, reflecting the war-weary spirit of the time, had little stomach for further

fighting anywhere after the bloodletting of the Western Front. Peace seemed more important than principle, and the boys came home, leaving Russia to her fate.

The Peacetime Army

A fundamental reorganization of the Army in the aftermath of the war was embodied in the National Defense Act of 1920, adopted by

Congress after months of careful study and necessary compromise. The act established the Army of the United States as the basic land component of the nation's military forces, this Army to consist of three elements: the regular Army, the National Guard, and the officer and enlisted reserve forces. This scheme would assure a small professional force of regulars for emergencies and for on-line training of the other components, plus a massive force ready for call-up in the event of greater conflicts. The regular Army was authorized an enlisted strength of 280,000 men and an officer strength of 17,000, although the actual numbers in any year would be regulated by the appropriations of Congress. The Guard units were allowed a strength of 436,000, although they averaged only about 180,000 active Guardsmen during the interwar years. Few men enlisted in the reserves at the non-commissioned ranks, but some 100,000 officers were enrolled as reserve officers, most coming from ROTC or CMTC (Citizens' Military Training Camp) programs (the latter consisting of four years

US military posture in the immediate post-war years was confused. Despite continuing foreign commitments, as in Russia (*below*), the Army was cut drastically and had a hard time in attracting recruits (*right*). At the same time, prophets such as General Billy Mitchell (*top left*), advocate of airpower, were vainly warning of basic changes in military technology. Mitchell's famous court martial did not, however, result solely from an opposition to his ideas. His conduct probably was, as charged, insubordinate.

of summer camp training for prospective officers).

Practice was less impressive than theory. Thanks to limited funds, the regular Army numbered only 12,000 officers and 125,000 enlisted men by 1922; it remained at about that level until the possibility of conflict in the late 1930s forced an expansion in the size of the Army. But the Army did undertake some useful reorganization during this period. In addition to its existing major branches of infantry and artillery, it added three new branches: the Air Service, the Chemical Warfare Service, and the Finance Department, though the embryonic tank corps that had evolved during World War I was absorbed by the infantry. The position of Chief of Staff was strengthened when Pershing came to that office in 1921, and the General Staff was reorganized by him into five divisions: personnel, intelligence, training and operations, supply, and war plans (the last-named for long-range strategic planning). Training

continued in the service's 31 special branch schools, while the command and General Staff School at Leavenworth (the old General Staff and Service College, renamed in 1928), the new Army War College, and the Army Industrial College provided capstone training for the Army's highest officers.

The creation of the Air Corps was particularly significant. Its foremost champion was Brigadier General William ('Billy') Mitchell. Mitchell, along with General Sir Hugh Trenchard of the Royal Air Force and Italy's General Guilio Douhet, was an untiring exponent of air power, believing that it alone would win or lose future wars. Mitchell attempted to prove this thesis by challenging the Navy to test the resistance of ships to aerial bombardment. The Navy had already been quietly examining this question, but now it was forced by Mitchell's open garnering of publicity to allow the Army Air Service to join in the testing. In celebrated bombing experiments in 1921 off the Virginia Capes,

Rapid progress in tank design between the wars fostered development of anti-tank guns: here, a wartime 57mm gun.

Mitchell's Air Service pilots dropped bombs on an old German battleship, the *Ostfriesland*, and sank it. While this success was by no means a valid indication of a naval vessel's ability to withstand aerial bombardment (the *Ostfriesland* was at anchor and unmanned), Mitchell made the most of the Air Service's 'victory' over the surface navy in his comments to the press.

Mitchell's penchant for notoriety hardened the opposition within the military to his extreme position. Chief of Staff Pershing named Major General Mason M Patrick as head of the Air Service in order to curb Mitchell's runaway enthusiasm. Patrick and many others in the Army were air power devotees, but they hardly agreed with Mitchell that an independent air service was necessary or that air power had made all other military power obsolete. Patrick was perfectly willing to accept the Air Service's subordination to ground commanders, but Mitchell was not, and he said so publicly. The result was Mitchell's court martial for insubordination; when convicted, he resigned from the Army in 1926.

In the meantime, however, a special board, appointed by President Calvin Coolidge and chaired by Dwight D Morrow, upheld continued development of air power. In 1926 the Air Corps Act gave the Army Air Corps full and equal status with the other branches of the Army and equal access to the Chief of Staff. It also provided for 17,000 officers and men and 1800 airplanes. Army air power was off and winging by 1927 and continued to develop and expand in the crucial 1930s.

The Army's development of armored fight-

The Army's first 'modern' bomber, the 213 mph all-metal Martin B-10, joined the Air Corps in 1934.

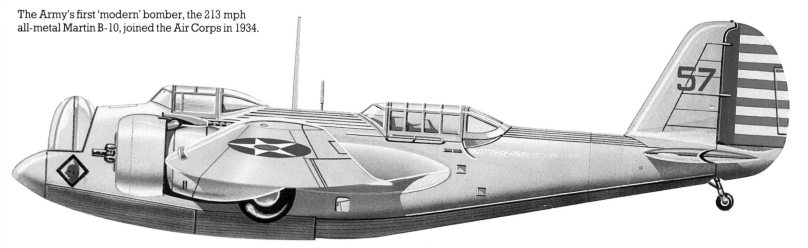

George Patton called the 1935 Garand semi-automatic rifle 'the greatest battle implement ever devised.'

ing vehicles during these same years was considerably less successful. By 1920 the Tank Corps of 5000 vehicles and 20,000 men of World War I had almost disappeared, with only 2600 men and some 700 tanks in the Army's arsenal. In the ensuing years the Tank Corps was, as we have seen, disbanded, and armored units were used only for support of infantry. Steps were taken to mechanize the Army's various ground forces in the 1930s, but little money was made available for the creation of special armored units. As a result, on the eve of World War II the US Army lagged behind its major European counterparts not only in the quantity of armor available, but also in the quality of its design. In 1940, for example, the principle US battle tank, the M3 Grant, still carried its main offensive armament in its hull, rather than in an independently traversable turret. Throughout the war the US armor strove mightily to make up for the developmental deficiencies of the 1930s, but the main wartime American tank, the M4 Sherman, never was the equal of the German Panthers and Tigers.

In other categories of weapons, the army fared better during the decade before the war. In 1936 the old Springfield rifle began to be replaced by the excellent .30-calibre gas-operated semi-automatic Garand M1. Since the end of World War I the standard automatic squad weapon had been the .30-calibre Browning Automatic Rifle, but by the early 1930s this somewhat unwieldy gun was being supplemented by the famous .45-calibre Thompson sub-machine gun, the 'Chicago piano' of gangster legend, with its impressive cycling rate of 800 rounds per minute. At about the same time the Army began receiving what were to be its standard mortars, the 81 mm M1 and the 60 mm M2. And at the end of the decade the Army added to its inventory several artillery pieces that would play significant roles in the coming war: the 37 mm M3 anti-tank gun (later to be supplanted by the more powerful 57 mm M1 AT gun, as well as by Bazookas and recoilless rifles); that all-purpose workhorse, the 105 mm M3 howitzer; and, for heavy support, the 155 mm Long Tom and the massive 8-inch howitzer.

The Air Corps made equally good technical progress. As early as 1934 it was receiving deliveries of a bomber as advanced as any in the world, the Martin B-10, an all-metal twin-engine monoplane with retractable landing gear. Two years later it got its first versions of the Boeing B-17, the 'Flying Fortress,' destined to become the most famous American heavy bomber of World War II. By 1937 it had begun to equip its fighter squadrons with aircraft of 'modern' design (ie. fast all-metal cantilever monoplanes with enclosed cockpits and retractable landing gear), and by the end of the decade it had acquired several types whose names would shortly become known throughout the world – among them, the Curtiss P-40 Tomahawk, the Bell P-39 Airacobra, and the Lockheed P-38 Lightning.

Indeed, the major problems of the interwar Army always had less to do with quality than with quantity. For most of the period it remained a small force, incapable of playing any major role in the nation's foreign affairs. To be sure, Congress in 1935 authorized the Army to increase its regular enlisted strength

An M3 Grant medium tank. Pre-war US tank designs lagged behind those of Germany, Russia, England and France.

to 165,000 and in subsequent years progressively loosened its purse strings for the purchase of new equipment. Yet it was not until after war had actually broken out in Europe, in September 1939, that the government took steps to increase the Army's strength significantly above the 1935 levels, and it was not until 1940 that conscription was begun. As events were to prove, these actions were taken only just in time.

The Road to War

Neither during the self-indulgent 'Roaring Twenties' nor in the grim depression-ridden years of the early 1930s had the American people given much serious attention to the possibility of the nation's becoming involved in another war. Yet there was no want of ominous portents. Mussolini's militant Fascisti had seized power in Italy in 1922. Japan's government was falling increasingly under the influence of a military clique that made no secret of its expansionist ambitions. And, most menacing of all, in 1933 the sinister Adolf Hitler became the absolute leader of Germany.

In 1935 Hitler proceeded to remilitarize the Rhineland, despite the provisions of the Versailles treaty. The French and British were hesitant and unwilling to challenge him. That same year Mussolini's Italian Army invaded the east African nation of Ethiopia,

easily routing its primitive defenders and meeting with no firm or meaningful resistance from the League of Nations or from the nations which had signed the Kellogg-Briand Pact of 1927 outlawing warfare forever. In 1937 Japan invaded China, serving notice that it would use military force to establish a Japanese Far Eastern empire. In 1938 Hitler carried out his annexation of Austria (a move outlawed by Versailles) in the face of only muted protest from the European democracies. In that same year he demanded and got the Sudetenland from Czechoslovakia, Britain and France acceding, despite the vehement objection of the Czechs over losing their only natural defense against expansionistic Germany. Then, despite, his promises not to do so, in March 1939 he seized the remainder of Czechoslovakia. It finally became clear to Europe's statesmen that Hitler could never be trusted, nor could he be restrained either by reason or diplomacy.

The most serious check to Hitler's ambitions, and hence the best hope of peace, lay in the fact that he still had the Soviet Union to challenge him in the east, for reigning over Russia was Joseph Stalin, the self-proclaimed implacable enemy of Nazism. Yet in August 1939 Germany and Russia signed a friendship pact providing for the division of Poland and for the Soviet right to expand into Finland and the Baltic countries. On 1 September 1939 the German armies invaded Poland. At

long last the European democracies, allied to Poland, decided to go to war to stop Hitler and his Axis partners.

However strong the desires of the American people to isolate themselves from Europe's war, advances in military technology alone meant that isolation was now increasingly difficult to maintain. If any nation in the Western Hemisphere allowed an aggressor airbases or submarine bases from which to operate, or if he seized them by force, not only America's vital Panama Canal but also the continental United States itself would be within enemy striking range. When President Roosevelt, in late 1939, approved the military's strategic hemispheric defense plan called RAINBOW (each nation was give a color and each possible combination of enemies and allies was studied for possible American military reaction), America had already abandoned in fact the idea of 'fortress America,' whether it realized it or not.

When the European war began, on 1 September 1939, Roosevelt issued a declaration of American neutrality, as well as a declaration of limited national emergency. The latter allowed him to raise the numbers in the regular Army to 227,000 and in the Guard units to 235,000 to help ensure America's neutrality. But as the nation watched Hitler's war against his neighbors succeed beyond anyone's expectations, official neutrality became increasingly compromised. The government

sought to aid embattled England and France, and neutrality legislation was amended to permit them to buy munitions in America. These purchases were initially on a 'cash and carry' basis, but American loans were soon forthcoming, in the form of the Lend-Lease program of March 1941, that kept the nation's European friends afloat. Roosevelt went one step further in September 1940 by trading fifty old American four-stack destroyers to the British in return for long-term leases on eight British bases, one in Newfoundland and seven in the Caribbean. This gave England anti-submarine weapons she desperately needed and furnished Roosevelt with the argument that he was putting the US in a stronger defensive posture in the Americas. Less openly (as a matter of fact, very secretly), Roosevelt not only extended American naval patrols ever farther out into the Atlantic, but also ordered the Navy to surreptitiously aid the British in their war against German U-boats. America was in an undeclared naval war in the North Atlantic months before the official outbreak of hostilities in 1941.

As America inched closer and closer to all-out war, the US Army found itself mobilizing and reorganizing in order to meet the challenges facing it. Thanks to larger Congressional appropriations for manpower; to the calling up of the National Guard and reserves to federal service in 1941; and to the

Above: By the late 1930s the Air Corps' best fighter was the Curtiss P-40.
Right: General Hideki Tojo, leader of the aggressive military faction that came to power in Japan in the 1930s.

passage of the Selective Service and Training Act of 1940, the nation's first peacetime draft legislation, by mid-1941 the Army had 1.5 million officers and men in its ranks. The Army Air Forces was expanding rapidly, an Armored Force was belatedly created, and the other combat arms command (infantry, field artillery, coast artillery, cavalry, and antiaircraft and tank destroyers) were likewise expanding and being trained under the leadership of Chief of Staff General George C Marshall. By late 1941 the Army had 27 infantry, five armored, and two cavalry divisions, plus 35 air groups.

Meantime, the scope and fury of the war in Europe grew apace. Hitler moved through Norway, Denmark, and the Low Countries in the spring of 1940, after a six-month winter lull, and drove the French out of the war within six weeks. The small British force in France was salvaged to fight again by the 'miracle' evacuation from the beaches of Dunkirk. Now Britain was Hitler's target, but his attempt to defeat the island nation through air power (the Battle of Britain, August-September 1940) ended in failure, forcing the German dictator to abandon his plans for in-

vasion. Unable to win in the West, in June 1941 Hitler turned east and attacked his 'ally,' the Soviet Union. The magnitude of his early successes in this vast campaign suggested that he might yet be able to realize his dream of becoming the master of Europe, and perhaps of the world.

America Goes to War

On 7 December 1941 a great Japanese naval armada launched a surprise air attack on the American naval base at Pearl Harbor, while other Japanese forces struck at the Philippines, Guam in the Marianas, and Wake Island in the central Pacific. An American public, aroused as never before in its history, vowed in the aftermatch of Pearl Harbor to bring the Japanese down and to avenge the American soldiers, sailors and Marines in the far-off Pacific who had been the initial victims of Japanese treachery. Hitler sensed this was a good time to declar war on the United States. Preoccupied with Japan, it might now be unable to continue sending war materials to the British and Russians. He was convinced, as was Kaiser Wilhelm in 1914, that he could conquer Europe before the United States could react with sufficient strength. He accordingly declared war on the United States and was followed by Mussolini.

World War II had now entered a new and fatal phase for the Axis powers. Admiral Isoroku Yamamoto, Japan's naval chief, had warned his countrymen against bringing America into the war because of her moral, industrial and military potential. He had told his fellow military chieftains that they might well run wild for six months to a year, but when America awoke and recovered from the initial attacks on her, the Axis could not win. Yamamoto was an accurate prophet. The USA rose up in wrath to strike down the enemies of freedom with a power unprece-dented in world history and joined with her allies to reverse the tide of war and bring the Axis enemies to their knees.

During World War II, 16.3 million Americans served in the nation's armed forces. Of these, 11.2 million served in the Army, 4.1 million in the Navy, 669,000 in the Marine Corps, and 330,000 in women's auxiliary corps. When the war ended in August 1945, 12 million men and women were in uniform. Most of these were brought into the military through the draft, since formal volunteering ended by law in 1942. Under the selective service legislation of World War II all males aged 18 to 64 were required to register; the operative upper age limit was initially 44, then it was dropped to 38. Locally-adminis-tered draft boards registered 36 million males. Of these, 10 million were drafted for service. Approximately one-sixth of America's males were in uniform during the course of the war. Deferments for occupational skills were given generously because the war effort required the efforts of efficient workers in the factories and on the farms in unprecedented numbers. During the course of the war the nation's civilian and military workforce jumped from 60 million to 75 million (the total population was 130 million), with the industrial work force rising by 10 million men and women.

During the war, American industry produced for American and Allied fighting men 1200 combatant naval vessels, 82,000 landing craft, 96,000 bombers 88,000 fighters, 23,000 transport planes, 2600 cargo ships, 700 tanker ships, 86,000 tanks, 120,000 artillery pieces, 2.4 million trucks and jeeps, and 14 million shoulder weapons. Of these, 37,000 tanks, 792,000 trucks, 43,000 aircraft, and 1.8 million rifles were sent to America's allies. As the United States scored feats of productivity to arm itself and its war companions, it truly became the 'Arsenal of Democracy.'

When World War II broke out in 1939 many Americans hoped the US would be able to stay at peace. But Franklin Roosevelt (*top*) understood the aims of Adolf Hitler (*right*) better and tried to prepare the country for an almost certain US involvement. Any hopes that Hitler might be stopped by Anglo-French armies were dashed by the fall of France in 1940 (*below*).

be brought over to the Allied side; and Greece had to be retained to deny Hitler the oil of the oil fields in Rumania and the Persian Gulf countries. If the Axis powers conquered Egypt and the Persian Gulf, Britain would be staring at defeat. The Mediterranean had to be kept out of Hitler's and Mussolini's hands, but the question of how to do so was still moot.

When Prime Minister Winston Churchill and the British war chieftains met in Washington with President Roosevelt and the American military leaders in December 1941, the whole strategic situation was examined in detail. The leaders agreed that the European theater of war had primacy for the time being; that the U-boats had to be defeated to assure that valuable supplies could get through to Britain; and that somehow, some-

Left: The US was in an undeclared war with German U-Boats by 1941.
Below: Adm. Isoroku Yamamoto, author of the Pearl Harbor raid that at last brought America into the war.

Phase I: North Africa

American war efforts in North Africa and the Mediterranean, which began in November 1942 with American landings in North Africa as part of Operation TORCH, represented the result of long American-British debate and compromise over the most effective joint strategy to be followed in defeating Hitler and his Axis allies. Prior to 1938 American military planners had been primarily concerned with fighting Japan and had assumed that the nation would go on the offensive in the Pacific and on the defensive in the Atlantic in any future war. In 1938 this scenario began to change, as the danger of Hitler to America's European friends became more visible. By 1940 a plan called RAINBOW 5, which envisioned a war of the United States, Britain and France against Germany, Italy and Japan, had emerged as accepted grand strategy. It called for defense of the Western Hemisphere, a strategic defensive in the Pacific until the European Axis powers were defeated, and a projection of American armed force on to Africa or the European continent. Roosevelt, as Commander in Chief, had approved of RAINBOW 5 by early 1941, and staff talks between American and British commanders were underway.

In planning its grand strategy against Germany, Britain had first thought in terms of using its seapower to blockade the Continent, as it had done so effectively in World War I, and of using strategic airpower to cause Germany's political and economic collapse. By the end of 1940 it was clear that such ideas were mere wishful thinking, and British planners were looking in other directions. While they were convinced by 1941 that an invasion of the Continent would eventually be needed to defeat the Germans, the Mediterranean theater of operations was given more immediate priority. Egypt had to be retained as a staging area for the Empire's resources; there was a possibility that French leaders in Syria, Lebanon, and Algeria could

where, an Anglo-American offensive against German land forces had to be mounted. But the Allies could not agree on where or when the offensive should take place. The more impetuous Americans wanted to strike directly at Hitler by invading the Continent as soon as possible. The British wanted first to put pressure on the periphery, build up for an invasion, and then hit the Germans only when Allied preponderance of men and materiel gave them a fair chance of success.

Undeterred by British arguments, American military planners continued to push for a direct blow at Nazi Germany, and by March 1942 they had developed several bold plans, one for a massive cross-channel invasion in the spring of 1943 and another for an earlier and smaller invasion to be launched in September 1942 if Russia were about to be defeated on the Eastern Front or if Germany were crumbling internally. But the British still were reluctant to endorse the American plans fully because, they insisted, the Mediterranean had to be protected. Any of these plans would draw too many men away from the Mediterranean theater. By mid-1942 the British had rejected any landings on the Continent during that year, at least. The war in North Africa was now going very badly for the British Eighth Army, so any invasion of the Continent was out of the question.

But President Roosevelt was determined that the Americans had to get into European action in 1942. He had promised this to Soviet Foreign Minister Vyacheslav Molotov. The German offensive in Russia was enjoying great success and pressure had to be taken off the Russian defenders. Also, the American public was demanding action. Accordingly, he sent his personal delegate, Harry Hopkins, along with General Marshall and Admiral Ernest J King, Chief of Naval Operations, to London with orders to come up with some agreement for a joint offensive in the European theater in 1942. He was willing to accept a peripheral Mediterranean invasion if necessary. Churchill, in response, resurrected a British plan for an invasion in North Africa called GYMNAST, and Roosevelt bought the idea, much to the consternation of American military planners. One of them, Major General Dwight D Eisenhower, said the day of this decision 'could well go down as the blackest day in history.'

Thus was born Operation TORCH (ex-GYMNAST), an invasion of North Africa to be carried out in November 1942. It was intended to open the Mediterranean for the Allies; give them bases for bombing German-controlled areas in southern Europe; distract the Germans away from the hard-pressed Russians; and perhaps lead to the invasion of Sicily and Italy and the collapse of Hitler's southern front. Eisenhower, named to command the operation, set D-Day for 8 November. The US Army, which had been rapidly building its strength for eleven months since Pearl Harbor, was going into action at last.

The American-British invasion of North Africa came at a crucial time in the Mediterranean war. The British had long been fight-

ing in the North African desert, that flat, almost trackless 150-mile-wide wasteland stretching 400 miles from Alamein in Egypt to Derna in Libya. In 1940, after some initial setbacks, they had succeeded in routing the Italian forces in North Africa, but this victory had only prompted a German riposte, and early in 1941 General Erwin Rommel and his crack armored troops, the Afrika Korps, began to arrive in North Africa. By late April 1941 they had driven the British army all the way back across the coast, encircling and bypassing the British garrison at the port of Tobruk in Libya, as they pushed to the Egyptian border. In June and again in November 1941 furious battles took place as the British tried to relieve Tobruk. The battles exhausted Rommel's forces, and in December he

Throughout World War II the Army's Chief of Staff would be the brilliant and respected George C Marshall.

was forced to retreat to El Agheila. But the British were too exhausted to chase and destroy him, and, after resting and being reinforced, in the first six months of 1942 Rommel fought his way back across the desert, chased the British to El Alamein, 60 miles west of Alexandria in Egypt, and this time took the port of Tobruk by siege. Rommel then attacked the British lines in July 1942 and was beaten back in the First Battle of El Alamein. The Eighth Army stopped Rommel's second offensive on 13-17 July. It was the farthest Rommel would go: Now was the time for the British to counterattack.

When General Sir Claude Auchinleck refused to press hard against Rommel until his troops had been rested, Churchill relieved him, and Lieutenant-General Bernard Law Montgomery was brought in to lead the Eighth Army (Churchill's first choice being killed in a airplane crash). At El Alamein Rommel was at the end of a tenuous 1400-mile supply line and wanted to pull back, but Hitler insisted that he 'defend every inch of ground.' So as Montgomery built up his men and supplies, Rommel could neither match him nor retreat, the result being the Afrika Korps' defeat at Alam Halfa and (Second) El Alamein in late 1942. Rommel was then forced to retreat all the way back across Libya to the Mareth Line in southern Tunisia, and, as he fled, the Americans and British launched Operation TORCH in his rear. Rommel was at the Mareth Line and dug in, but now an army was advancing from the west, and the Germans were in a trap.

As we have seen, TORCH was a strategic compromise between the British and American high commands. Once decided upon, however, plans had moved forward quickly. The objectives of the invasion forces were to gain a foothold on the North African coastal plain over a 900-mile front; to seize Casablanca, Oran, and Algiers, the three largest ports in Morocco and Algeria; and then to speed to the east to take northern Tunisia. This would trap the German and Italian forces in North Africa and take them out of the war.

The invasion of North Africa aimed to cut off the eastward escape route of German General Erwin Rommel (*left*). The invaders were ferried to North Africa by a huge naval armada (*below*) divided into three separate task forces, each destined for a different landing spot.

The invasion force, called Western Naval Task Force, was scheduled to land in the vicinity of Casablanca, in Morocco, and was under the command of Major General George S Patton, Jr. It assembled in Hampton Roads, Virginia, and sailed on 23 October 1942 with 35,000 men. The Center Task Force, containing 39,000 American and British soldiers, sailed from Scotland. In command of these landing forces was Major General Lloyd R Fredendall, US Army. They were to land east and west of Oran in Algiers and take the city. Eastern Task Force also sailed from the British Isles. It had 33,000 men and was under the command of Major General Charles W Ryder of the US Army. Its destination was Algiers. Once the landings

had taken place, all Allied troops in Algiers would become the British First Army, under Lieutenant General Kenneth Anderson, and would race for northern Tunisia.

One of the great unanswered questions before the landings was whether or not the French troops, now under collaborationist Vichy command, would fight the Allied invaders. Attempts were made to dissuade them from doing so through contacts with General Henri Giraud and Admiral Jean Francois Darlan, commanding French forces in North Africa. The meetings were only partially successful, resulting in spirited French defense in Algiers and Morocco before Admiral Darlan agreed to switch sides and bring his 200,000 French troops over to the

Top: Oran/Mers-el-Kebir was one of the three main Allied landing points.
Below: The North African landings.

Allies. It also resulted in Darlan's being assassinated by a compatriot for dealing with the invading Allies.

The landings in North Africa went well for the Americans and British. In Algeria the French around Algiers laid down their arms on 8 November, the day of the invasion, and Oran fell two days later after stern resistance. The city of Casablanca and its surrounding area was in American hands by 11 November, although the landing of men and supplies from ship to shore was so clumsily managed that the Americans were fortunate

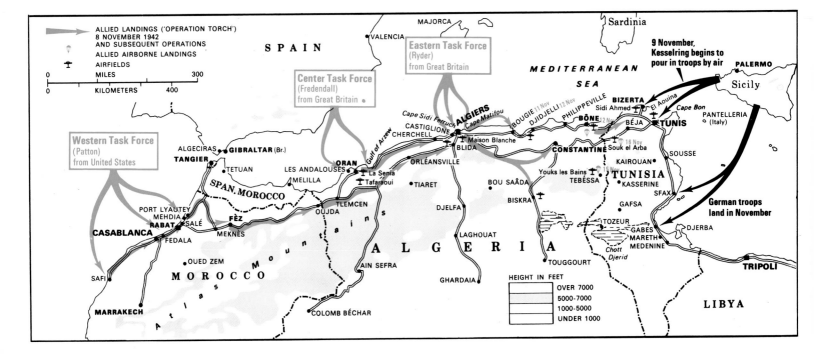

Both General Patton (*left*) and General Eisenhower saw their first major actions of World War II in the 1943 Tunisian Campaign.

the French were not able to put up a fight.

Unfortunately, the chase to the east by First Army to capture the Germans in Tunisia soon bogged down, and Field-Marshal Albert Kesselring, commanding the southern Wehrmacht from Italy, was able to reinforce his troops in northern Tunisia. The Allies had only two weeks to cover the 450 miles to the key coastal cities of Tunis and Bizerta before winter rains and mud set in. Thanks to massive logistical problems and the superiority of German tanks, especially the Panzer IV, over Allied armor, Anderson was forced to call a halt in early December far short of his goal. As the Allies made efforts to reinforce First Army in Tunisia, the Germans dug in to stop them. They also still held the Mareth Line in the south, and here Montgomery refused to force his Eighth Army against the Germans until he had overwhelming superiority in numbers.

In February 1943, taking advantage of poor disposal of troops along the American lines outside Tunis and Bizerta, Rommel and General Juergen von Armin of V Army launched an attack through the center of the Allied north-south line. Their intention was to break through to the sea and isolate and destroy the leading elements of First Army, thus breaking the encirclement of Tunis and Bizerta. Their Valentine's Day attack almost succeeded, the American and British soldiers being bloodied in the Battle of Kasserine Pass. Fortunately for the Allied troops, von Armin refused to support the operation fully and Rommel lost his nerve. Otherwise the German counterattack might well have led to a disastrous Allied defeat. Even so, the green US 2nd Army Corps lost 6500 men killed, wounded or captured in the battle; another 4000 British soldiers who came to their aid were also lost. It was a baptism of fire the survivors would never forget, but one that led the Army to engage in more extensive training for its troops before further engagements with their determined enemy.

In the aftermath of Kasserine Pass Rommel was removed by Hitler, and George Patton took over 2nd Corps. Under the leadership of General Sir Harold Alexander, the Allies subsequently went on the offensive again. As First Army began a determined push from the west, Eighth Army flanked the Germans at the Mareth Line. Together they began to push the Germans and their Italian allies ever north and west toward the shores of the Mediterranean. Despite dogged defenses by the German forces (Hitler ordered that there would be no retreat), the Allies continued to press on and also began to cut the Axis lines of air and sea supply from Sicily and Italy. On 7 May 1943 the British moved into Tunis and the Americans entered Bizerta. One week later the last German and

The tough veterans of Rommel's Afrika Korps nearly defeated US and British troops at the Kasserine Pass.

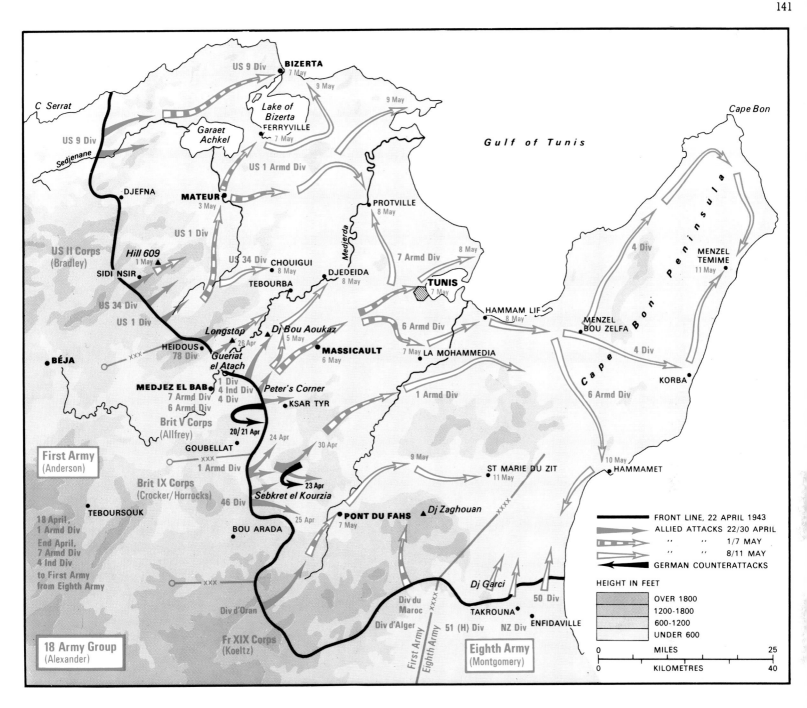

Top: The final stages of the Tunisian campaign.
Below: US paratroopers preparing for the invasion of Sicily. The surround on the USAAF insignia seen on the truck would soon be changed from yellow to red and then, finally, to blue.

Italian forces had surrendered. The battle for North Africa was over, but not before the Axis saw 40,000 killed, wounded or missing and 275,000 captured in the Tunisian campaign alone. Allied casualties stood at 66,000. Operation TORCH and the taking of North Africa had been a very expensive undertaking, but many military lessons had been learned, and, most important, the British and Americans now threatened Hitler's southern flank.

Phase II: Sicily and Italy

While the fighting was still raging in North Africa, in January 1943 Roosevelt, Churchill and the American and British Combined Chiefs of Staff met in Casablanca to discuss grand strategy. As before, the American mili-

A big Landing Ship Tank (LST) is in the foreground of this photograph of invasion craft heading for Salerno.

tary leaders wanted an invasion of France, and, as before, the British wanted to operate on the periphery until Allied forces were ready for such a large undertaking. The result was a compromise: Sicily would be invaded. The seizure of Sicily would make the Allies' Mediterranean supply lines more secure, divert Germans from the Russian front, and put pressure on Italy, already reeling from its North African losses, to drop out of the war. Accordingly, plans were drawn up for the invasion.

The British Eighth Army, under Lieutenant General Montgomery, would attack on the southeast corner of Sicily, south of Syracuse, and drive to the north. The American Seventh Army, under General Patton, would land on Sicily's southern coast to protect the Eighth Army's flank and rear, a secondary role the fiery Patton hardly appreciated. Facing the Allies would be nine Italian divisions of dubious quality and two crack German divisions of 30,000 men, the Hermann Goering armored divisions and the 15th Panzer Grenadiers of mechanized infantry. D-Day was set for 10 July 1943.

Operation HUSKY, the invasion of Sicily, was to be the largest amphibious operation in history to date. Some 80,000 troops with 7000 vehicles, 600 tanks and 900 artillery pieces would be landed in 48 hours. Seven Allied divisions would make up the assault waves. HUSKY would also include the first large-scale Allied airborne operation of the war, with 4600 men making their air assaults via planes and gliders.

The airborne troops were to land in the dark three hours before the dawn invasion. The paratroop phase of the operation was a near fiasco. The 3400 American paratroopers under Colonel James M Gavin, were scattered all over southeast Sicily, thanks to inadequate aircrew training and to American naval crews shooting at their own planes.

And almost half the British gliders scheduled to land near a key bridge south of Syracuse were released early and fell into the sea, although the bridge was taken and held by 87 brave men until relief arrived. Tragedy occurred again the following night when, the two major amphibious landings having been made with little opposition, 144 American planes carrying in 2000 American paratroopers were fired upon by nervous gunners, despite being in a 'safe' corridor and displaying proper recognition lights. In this blunder off Gela, 23 planes were shot down and 27 were damaged, and a total of 229 paratroopers lost their lives.

It was hardly an auspicious start for the invasion, but Allied power was preponderant, and the Germans and Italians were forced to withdraw gradually to the northern coast of the island, despite being reinforced by 50,000 additional German soldiers. Even so, the Axis forces had slowed Montgomery's drive up the Sicilian east coast to a crawl, and Patton could only sit on his left and protect his flank. Finally, Patton convinced Alexander that the Seventh Army should be unleashed, to drive for Palermo, on Sicily's northwest corner. Patton moved with lightning speed across Sicily, only to find that the Germans had pulled out of Palermo for Messina, at the other (northeast) corner of the island. Patton and the Seventh set out in pursuit, and, although slowed by terrain and determined German resistance, arrived in Messina to

Mark W Clark, who commanded the 5th Army in Sicily and Italy, was one of the more controversial US generals.

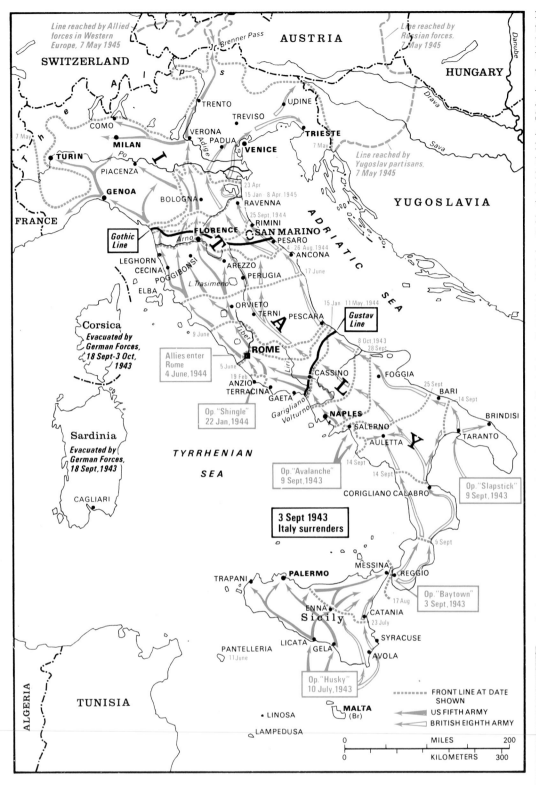

north. Meanwhile the British 19th Corps and the US 6th Corps, together constituting the Fifth Army, under Lieutenant General Mark W Clark, USA, prepared for the main invasion at Salerno, 25 miles south of Naples. As the 70,000-man force of Operation AVALANCHE hit the beaches of Salerno on 9 September 1943, backed by 82 British and American naval vessels, it ran into fierce resistance from the four German divisions that were waiting for the invasion. Only after four days of bitter fighting on the Salerno beachhead did Field-Marshal Kesselring withdraw his forces north of Naples to a line running across the entire Italian peninsula. On this 'Gustav Line' Kesselring gave the Allies the first of many lessons in brilliant flexible defensive maneuvers. Throughout the remainder of the year Kesselring's X Army held firm, only giving up territory at horrible cost to the Allies, who were also battered by one of the worst Italian winters in decades.

The linchpin of the Gustav Line (or 'Winter Line') was the area of Cassino, crowned by the Benedictine abbey called Monte Cassino, whose history went back to the 6th century and time of St. Benedict himself. Frustrated by the bloody stalemate and convinced that the Germans were using Monte Cassino as an artillery spotting post, General Sir Harold Alexander finally gave the order to bomb it out of existence. In one of the most controversial actions of the war (the Germans, in fact, were not using it as an observation post) the bombing took place on 15 February 1944. Some 660 tons of bombs and artillery ordinance leveled the famed religious house. But even as it lay in ruins, the

Left: Map of the Italian campaign.
Below: German paratroopers such as these defended Monte Cassino.

complete the conquest of Sicily on 17 August, two hours ahead of the British. Montgomery was furious at having been thus upstaged, but of somewhat greater importance was the fact that 45,000 Germans and over 70,000 Italians had gotten away across the narrow Strait of Messina to fight again. Even so, 157,000 of their comrades had been killed or captured in the campaign in Sicily, and American casualties had been only 19,000. In many ways Sicily had proved to be a cakewalk. Italy would be another story.

While the campaign for Sicily was underway, Mussolini was deposed (in July 1943) to placate the war-weary Italian people. King Victor Emmanuel II appointed Field Marshal Pietro Badoglio in his place. Badoglio pledged to continue the war, but it was widely and

correctly assumed he would try to end Italy's involvement as soon as possible. Hitler, dismayed by this turn of events, ordered the rescue of the imprisoned Mussolini and set him up as a puppet ruler in northern Italy, while at the same time directing the German armies to stand by to take over in Italy. When, therefore, Badoglio announced the signing of surrender terms on the eve of the Allied invasion of the country, the Germans immediately moved eight divisions into central and southern Italy, disarmed the Italians, and prepared to fight off the invaders.

The British Eighth Army crossed the Straits of Messina from Sicily on 3 September 1943 in a diversionary and largely useless invasion, there to move up to the instep of Italy to join with the main assault force further to the

Germans fought on along the Gustav Line, and it was not until three months later that Monte Cassino fell into Allied hands and the Gustav Line was decisively conquered.

In the meantime, the Allies tried to end-run the Gustav Line, in Operation SHINGLE, by invading along the coast north of the line at Anzio. Some 40,000 soldiers of the US 6th Corps, including the British 1st Division and the American 3rd Division, invaded on 22 January 1944 in a hastily-mounted operation. The initial landings went well, but on 16 February Kesselring's improvised XIV Army counterattacked with 125,000 men and

Twelfth Air Force B-25s pass a fiery Mt Vesuvius as they head for their target, Monte Cassino. The bombing of Monte Cassino's old abbey proved militarily useless.

almost drove the 100,000 Allied soldiers into the sea. For three months the Germans held the British and American forces on a narrow beachhead, subjecting them to day and night shelling and nightly air raids. The Allies suffered 59,000 casualties at Anzio, one-third of them from disease, exhaustion and neurosis, before they finally broke out on 23 May. Even then, an opportunity for ending the stalemated war in Italy was lost when General Clark, instead of moving east to trap the German X Army behind Cassino, decided instead to take the capital of Rome for its propaganda value. Kesselring got his troops out, and the long Italian war continued to drag on.

The Allies finally broke Kesselring's Gothic Line north of Florence in September 1944, but the onset of winter weather meant

that German resistance in Italy would continue into the next year. Only in the spring of 1945 was the Allied movement into northern Italy continued, and only after weeks of heavy fighting did the Germans finally surrender. The end came on 2 May 1945.

The Italian campaign was one of the longest and costliest of the European war. It lasted for twenty months and caused tens of thousands of casualties. It was beyond doubt the most frustrating campaign of World War II and did not end until the fall of Germany itself. Whatever the strategic wisdom of Salerno, Anzio, the bombing of Monte Cassino, and the long, slogging fight up the Italian peninsula, it had at least tied down part of Hitler's Wehrmacht while the long-awaited cross-channel invasion was launched in June 1944. But few veterans of the Italian campaign

would remember things that way. Their memories were of death, disease, cold, and German resistance that, until the last, seemed as though it would never end.

Phase III: The Normandy Invasion and Breakout

During the weeks preceding the invasion of Sicily, at the Trident Conference in Washington, the American military planners finally got their go-ahead for an invasion of the Continent when Roosevelt and Churchill agreed on a landing to be carried out in 1944 Operation BOLERO, the build-up phase for the cross-channel invasion, had been underway since April 1942. Now with OVERLORD agreed upon, preparations began in earnest, and by the summer of 1944 1.5 million Ameri-

From Italy the 12th Air Force could raid many European targets. This B-26 lost an engine to flak over Toulon.

can soldiers and airmen, plus 500 million tons of supplies and equipment, had been landed in Britain to supplement the 1.75 million British and 175,000 Commonwealth troops already assembled there. Planning for the invasion was vested first in COSSAC (Chief of Staff to Supreme Allied Commander), then in SHAEF (Supreme Head of the Allied Expeditionary Force), when General Eisenhower was appointed Supreme Commander in January 1944. Montgomery had coveted the job, but the political leaders agreed that the top position had to go to an American. Thus Montgomery was to command Allied ground forces under Eisenhower during the invasion.

Many months of preparation went into the massive operation. After extensive study and debate it was decided to land on the coast of Normandy, directly south of England, instead of in the Pas-de-Calais area on the Belgian border. Normandy was close to fighter bases in southern England, would be easier to supply and reinforce, had suitable beaches for landings, contained the potentially useful port of Cherbourg, and was manned by fewer German defenders than the Pas-de-Calais. But even as the decision for Normandy was made and preparations began, some American and British bomber chiefs were voicing opposition to OVERLORD itself. They argued that the whole invasion was a gigantic mistake because strategic bombing could take out German cities and war potential in time, making invasion unnecessary. As of early 1944, however, there was insufficient evidence to support their contention, so Operation OVERLORD was on. The troops were being assembled. Special armored equipment, such as sea-going

Sherman tanks with canvas flotation collars to enable them to 'swim' to the beaches, Shermans with chain flails on front-mounted drums to clear mine fields, and Churchill tanks with 290 mm mortars to be used against pillboxes had been developed. And in order to provide safe anchorages for supply vessels after the initial landings, floating piers, caissons, and blockships had been readied.

To convince the Germans that the main invasion would take place in the Pas-de-Calais area, Operation FORTITUDE was brought into play. It called for the creation of a fictitious army of 50 divisions and a million men, complete with camps and equipment, under Lieutenant General George Patton, in Kent. It also included extensive bombing of

the Pas-de-Calais area, at a 2-to-1 ratio over bombings of Normandy, in the weeks preceding D-Day. On the night before D-Day motor launches would set out for France towing balloons with reflectors that gave off images of ships on radar. Royal Air Force bombers would drop aluminum foil strips to simulate airplanes on radar scopes, and dummy paratroopers would be dropped all over the area. In the event, FORTITUDE fooled the Germans completely, holding them in place for the 'real' invasion in the Pas-de-Calais while the American and British troops gained a foothold on the Normandy beaches.

Although the German defenses along Hitler's 'Atlantic Wall' were the most formidable man-made barrier in the West, and

although Field-Marshal Gerd von Rundstedt had 15,000 strong points manned by 300,000 troops along the Wall, the German chain of command was weak. German air power was controlled solely by Air Marshal Hermann Goering, who was back in Germany, and four of the seven armored divisions in the Atlantic defenses were assigned directly to Wehrmacht headquarters, i.e., to Hitler himself, rather than to General Erwin Rommel, commander of Army Group B in the invasion area. Thus when crucial decisions had to be made

Right: A 5th Army tank destroyer, a form of self-propelled artillery used to fight German panzers. *Below:* By September 1944 US troops in Italy had only reached the Arno. Still ahead lay the final German defenses, the formidable Gothic Line.

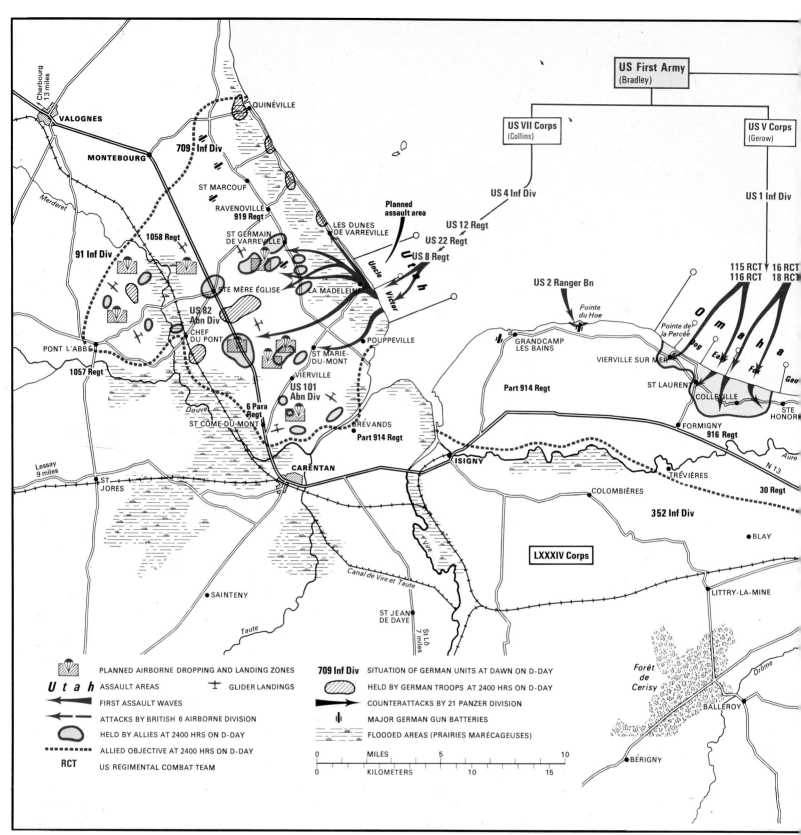

PLANNED AIRBORNE DROPPING AND LANDING ZONES

Utah ASSAULT AREAS   ✝ GLIDER LANDINGS

FIRST ASSAULT WAVES

ATTACKS BY BRITISH 6 AIRBORNE DIVISION

HELD BY ALLIES AT 2400 HRS ON D-DAY

ALLIED OBJECTIVE AT 2400 HRS ON D-DAY

RCT US REGIMENTAL COMBAT TEAM

709 Inf Div SITUATION OF GERMAN UNITS AT DAWN ON D-DAY

HELD BY GERMAN TROOPS AT 2400 HRS ON D-DAY

COUNTERATTACKS BY 21 PANZER DIVISION

MAJOR GERMAN GUN BATTERIES

FLOODED AREAS (PRAIRIES MARÉCAGEUSES)

on the battlefield, they could not always be carried out. Had German reaction been more rapid and effective, and had Hitler not been convinced until it was too late that the real invasion site was the Pas-de-Calais area, OVERLORD might not have succeeded.

Although several times delayed because of bad weather, D-Day was finally set for 6 June 1944 by Eisenhower, and early that morning airborne troops led off Operation NEPTUNE, the code name for the assaults themselves. The British 6th Airborne Division landed on the left, or east, flank of the invasion area and took the Caen Canal and the Orne River bridges with ease, while the

American 82nd Airborne Division, under Major General Matthew Ridgway, landed near Sainte-Mere-Eglise at the base of the Cotentin Peninsula, and the 101st Airborne, under Major General Maxwell Taylor, landed nearby to anchor the right flank of the Normandy landing areas. After naval and air bombardment of the beaches and the areas behind them, 176,000 soldiers began landing from 4,000 landing craft at 0630 in the morning. Fortunately for the Allies, the Germans were unable to react quickly because Hitler's chief of operations, General Alfred Jodl, had countermanded Rundstedt's orders to move two armored divisions to Normandy

at the very moment the landings were beginning. On Utah Beach, on the far right flank, the 23,000 men of the US 7th Army Corps, under General J Lawton ('Lightning Joe') Collins, had a fairly easy time of it, thanks to effective pre-dawn bombardment and confusion spread in the German ranks by the airborne landings behind the beachheads. Only 197 casualties were suffered the first day, and a substantial beachhead on the Cotentin Peninsula was achieved when the infantry succeeded in joining up with their airborne comrades.

Omaha beach, to the east, was another story. There the 5th Army Corps, under

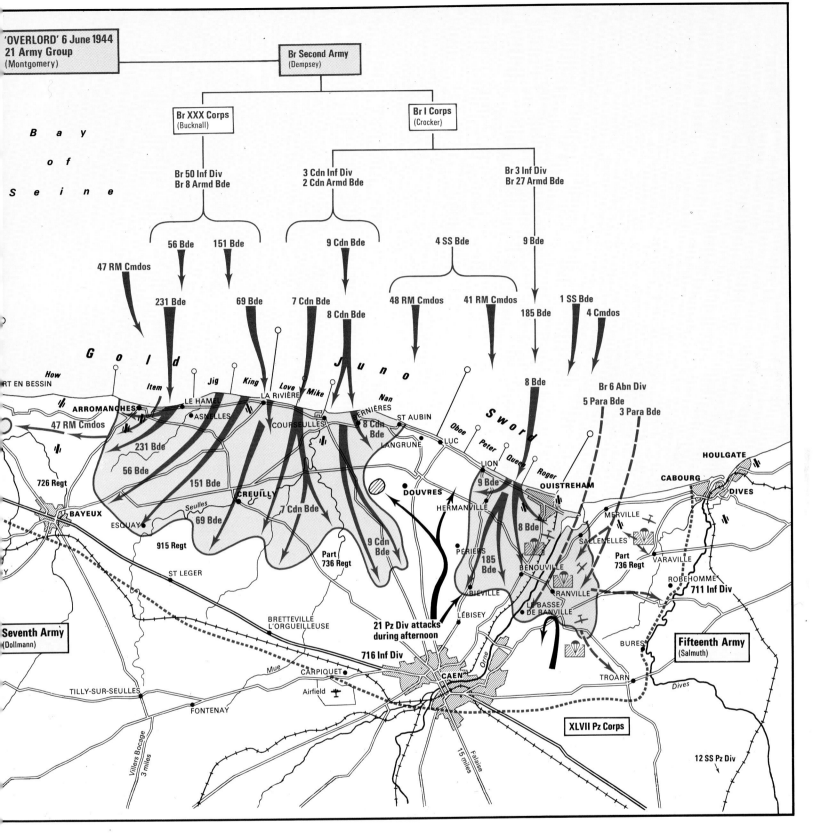

'OVERLORD' 6 June 1944
21 Army Group
(Montgomery)

Br Second Army
(Dempsey)

Br XXX Corps
(Bucknall)

Br I Corps
(Crocker)

Br 50 Inf Div
Br 8 Armd Bde

3 Cdn Inf Div
2 Cdn Armd Bde

Br 3 Inf Div
Br 27 Armd Bde

56 Bde   151 Bde   9 Cdn Bde   4 SS Bde   9 Bde

47 RM Cmdos

231 Bde   69 Bde   7 Cdn Bde   48 RM Cmdos   41 RM Cmdos   1 SS Bde   4 Cmdos
8 Cdn Bde   185 Bde

8 Bde   Br 6 Abn Div
5 Para Bde
3 Para Bde

Bay of Seine

Gold   Juno   Sword

How
RT EN BESSIN
Item   Jig   King   Love   Mike   Nan
ARROMANCHES   LE HAMEL   LA RIVIÈRE   BERNIÈRES   ST AUBIN   Oboe   Peter   Queen   Roger
47 RM Cmdos   ASNELLES   COURSEULLES   8 Cdn Bde   LUC   LION   OUISTREHAM   HOULGATE
726 Regt   231 Bde   LANGRUNE   9 Bde   CABOURG
56 Bde   DOUVRES   HERMANVILLE   8 Bde   DIVES
BAYEUX   151 Bde   CREUILLY   7 Cdn Bde   PÉRIERS   MERVILLE   SALLENELLES   VARAVILLE
ESQUAY   Seulles   69 Bde   185 Bde   BÉNOUVILLE   RANVILLE   ROBEHOMME   711 Inf Div
915 Regt   9 Cdn Bde   BIÉVILLE   LE BASSE DE RANVILLE   BURES
ST LEGER   Part 736 Regt   LÉBISEY
BRETTEVILLE L'ORGUEILLEUSE   21 Pz Div attacks during afternoon   Fifteenth Army (Salmuth)
Seventh Army (Dollmann)   716 Inf Div   TROARN   Dives
Mue   CARPIQUET   CAEN   Orne   BURES
TILLY-SUR-SEULLES   Airfield   XLVII Pz Corps
FONTENAY   Villers Bocage 3 miles   15 miles   Falaise   12 SS Pz Div

Major General Leonard T Gerow, ran into a firestorm of artillery and machine gun fire. With the initial waves pinned down on the 300-yard pebbled beach and unable to move out because of enemy fire, succeeding waves of men and equipment began to pile up. By 0900 Bradley was ready to call off the invasion on Omaha beach, but SHAEF never received his message, and the battle went on. Gradually the soldiers fought their way through the obstacles with their light weapons and established a defensible beachhead, but the cost was 3000 casualties that first day. Had the American commanders not refused to use the specialized armored

equipment available to them, the casualty count would undoubtedly have been lower. But by the same token, had the Navy's destroyers not come in to bottom-scraping depths to cover the soldiers on the beach, the count would have been far higher, and perhaps the beachhead would have been lost.

To the left and east of the American Utah and Omaha Beaches the British Second Army, under General Miles Dempsey, landed on Gold, Juno, and Sword Beaches. Their landings were not difficult, but they subsequently had to beat off countless German armored counterattacks in order to maintain their positions and seize the city of

Caen, the intended pivot-point for the great Allied swing west into the heart of France. Although delayed by fierce German resistance, the British, like the Americans, were greatly aided in the first days of fighting by the fact that Hitler steadfastly refused to believe that this was the 'real' landing and would not unleash his reserves against the Normandy beachheads.

In the days and weeks that followed the landings in Normandy, the Allies slowly but surely improved their positions until it was clear they could not be pushed back into the sea. While the Russians continued to drive ever closer to Germany from the east, Hitler

Top: German propaganda claimed West Wall defenses were impregnable, but few were as formidable as this.

now found his Western enemies firmly in France and equally determined to invade the Fatherland. Yet despite the Allies' successes in OVERLORD, and despite personal testimony from von Rundstedt and Rommel that the situation in Normandy was hopeless and that the Germans should fall back to better defensive positions, Der Führer ordered that there be no retreat.

By 29 June the US 7th Army Corps had taken the port of Cherbourg, at the top of the Cotentin Peninsula, and the British were encircling Caen, the key to holding the Normandy beaches. By 18 July the American 7th and 8th Corps had fought their way through the almost impenetrable hedgerow country, the *bocage*, and had reached St-Lô. In August the American First Army had moved into Brittany, while the new Third Army, organized under General Patton, swung around to the left and headed east.

Hitler now attempted a counterattack toward Avranches, but this succeeded only in destroying 10,000 German soldiers and causing another 50,000 to be wounded in the 'Falaise Gap,' where the British First and Second Armies, on the north, and Patton's Third Army, on the south, converged to trap the German forces. By 20 August Patton was

Top: D-Day troops in a landing craft.
Below: Special intakes helped this M4 Sherman tank to get through the tidal waters, but it finally foundered in the soft sand of a Normandy beach.

on the Seine at Fontainebleau, and on 25 August Paris was liberated, the honor of first entering the city being given to the Free French forces who had fought alongside the Allies. By the end of July, over a million Allied soldiers were on French soil, backed up by 150,000 vehicles and some million tons of supplies. The cry was now 'On to Berlin.'

In the meantime, Operation ANVIL, an amphibious landing on the southern French coast between Cannes and Toulon, had taken place. This 15 August 1944 invasion was carried out by the US Seventh Army, under Major General Alexander M Patch. Once the landings had been made successfully, the accompanying French 2nd Corps was allowed to pass through the Seventh Army and lead the advance through Marseilles and up the Rhône to Lyons and Dijon. They linked up with the Third Army in September and then continued to march north and east on the

Third Army's flank toward Germany. All of France was being liberated, and it looked as though the war might be over in 1944, but in fact many months would have to pass and many thousands of people would have to die before Europe would see peace again.

Phase IV: The Final Drive on Germany

No sooner had the Allies broken out of the Normandy beachheads and begun to sweep east across France, with the British on the left and the Americans on the right, than a dispute broke out among the commanders as to how next to proceed against the German enemy. Montgomery and Bradley preferred operating on a narrow front on the left, while the right merely maintained pressure on the German defenders. Circling left around through Belgium and Holland toward the vital Ruhr Basin north of Cologne, they would aim to beat the Russians into Berlin. Patton and other American generals preferred to advance on a broader front, Montgomery's 21st

Army Group seizing the Channel ports on the left flank, while the American armies advanced in a series of moves against the Saar, the Ruhr, and the Rhineland.

Eisenhower opted for the second strategy. On the left the British moved into Belgium, seizing Brussels and Antwerp, with its giant port facilities. At the same time, the US First and Third Armies pushed vigorously ahead on the center and right, the Third Army crossing the Meuse at Verdun and entering the area of the great American victories of 1918. But now Montgomery's advance against the Germans in the channel ports and along the 60-mile Scheldt Estuary was beginning to slow down. Without control of the Scheldt the great port of Antwerp was useless because the estuary controlled all shipping into the city. As a result, the American First and Third Armies were soon running short of fuel, and their advances too slowed to a walk, despite the unlimited opportunities for victory which lay before them.

In order to speed up the bloody, slow-moving offensive in Belgium and Holland,

Paratroops, eight miles from Utah Beach at Carentan, pass the bodies of comrades killed by German snipers.

Montgomery devised and had approved by SHAEF Operation MARKET-GARDEN, a combined ground-airborne operation to open a narrow 60-mile front through which the British 30th Corps would rush to turn the north end of the Siegfried Line, or West Wall. The key to the success of the operation was the swift capture of the bridges at Veghel, Zon, Grave, Nijmegen, and Arnhem in the Netherlands by British and American airborne troops, so as to allow the 30th to pass through swiftly. This was to be one of the most ill-fated operations of the entire war.

On 17 September 1944 the American 101st Airborne Division jumped behind the German lines and captured the Veghel and Zon bridges, and the next day the 30th Corps, coming up from the south, linked up with them. On 17 September, too, the American 82nd Airborne dropped to take the Grave bridge, and two days later the 30th Corps had made its way to this location, as well. By 20 September the now-combined British-American forces had also taken the Nijmegen bridge. So far, the operation seemed to be going well, but farther to the north, at Arnhem, disaster was building.

The British 1st Airborne Division had landed to take it on 17 September, but the Germans had quickly rushed reinforcements into the area. In short order the British airborne forces had been cut off, with the 30th Corps unable to cut through to rescue them. On 25 September a remnant of the besieged 1st Airborne, about 2200 men, managed to withdraw across the Neder Rhine to British lines, but they left many comrades behind within the swiftly-closing German encirclement. The next day the British pocket was wiped out: the 1st Airborne had lost 7000 men killed, wounded or captured in the vicinity of Arnhem. And in the meantime General von Rundstedt had brought 86,000 men of the XV Army into the vicinity of the Scheldt Estuary, where they contributed to the prolonged and

Right: The campaign in France would show the colorful Patton to be one of the war's greatest commanders.
Below: The Normandy breakout.

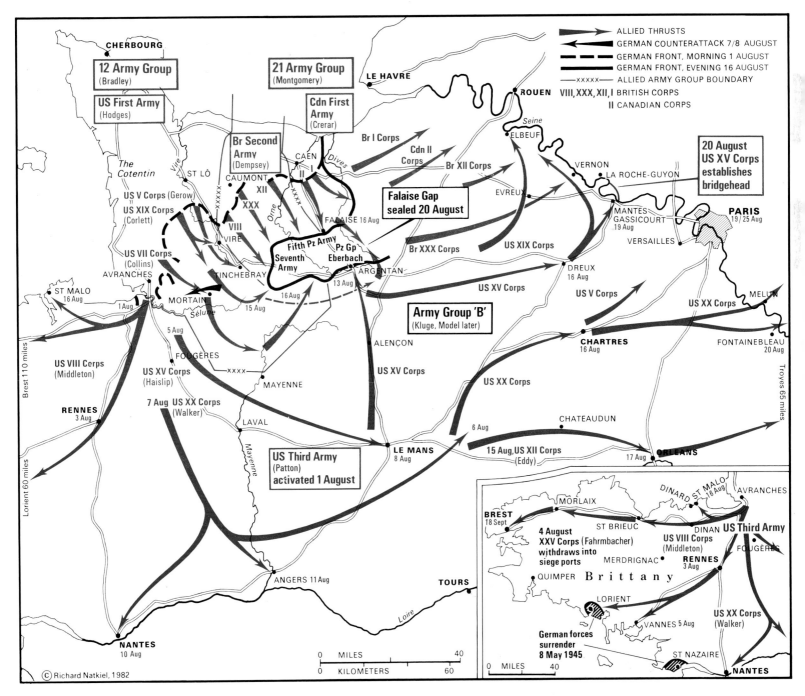

Paris was liberated on 25 August 1944. The honor of first entering the city was given the Free French. Four days later there was a great victory march down the Champs Elysées. Shown here, troops of the 28th Infantry Division.

stubborn defense of that vital area and continued to deny the Allies the use of Antwerp. In the aftermath of the fighting, MARKET-GARDEN was stoutly defended by the British and Montgomery as a proper move, but controversy over the operation continued for decades thereafter.

Although Antwerp was still useless to the Allies, while the Arnhem operation was underway the Canadian First Army continued clearing the Channel ports. During September they drove the Germans out of Dieppe, Le Havre, Boulogne, and Calais, the latter city of great importance as the launching site for the V-1 rockets now being fired on Britain. But not until 8 November was the Scheldt Estuary taken, primarily by Canadian troops, and not until 26 November was it cleared of mines and made usable. These delays held up the American armies to the south and east, forcing them to rely on the 'Red Ball Express' of trucks to bring them

gasoline and other supplies all the way from Cherbourg, 350 miles away. And now the Allies found that winter was moving in. The end of the war would not come in 1944: They would have to wait out the winter and resume the offensive in the spring.

But Hitler had other plans. He was contriving a giant counteroffensive intended to break through the densely forested and semi-mountainous Ardennes region in Belgium and Luxembourg and drive all the way to Antwerp 100 miles to the west, thus splitting the advancing Allied armies. He would then destroy the British and American armies piecemeal before turning to face the Russians advancing from the east. Hitler's generals were opposed to this daring operation because they were convinced they did not have the numbers and supplies to mount such a massive counteroffensive. But Hitler insisted, and the Germans began to scrape together men and equipment from all over

the Reich to carry out the unexpected and daring Ardennes offensive.

By the time the German offensive jumped off, on 16 December 1944, to begin what has come to be called the 'Battle of the Bulge,' 25 divisions, including 10 armored divisions, had been secretly assembled behind their lines. The VI SS Panzer Army, under General Josef Dietrich, and the V Panzer Army, under Lieutenant-General Hasso von Manteuffel, were to spearhead the attack directly through the American lines, while VII Army and XV Army protected their flanks. A Panzer brigade of 20,000 men, led by Lieutenant-Colonel Otto Skorzeny and dressed as Americans, was to commit sabotage and spread confusion behind the American lines. Over 250,000 men, 1900 artillery pieces, and 970 tanks and armored assault guns were to take part in the offensive, and some 1500 planes were promised in order to assure local air superiority. Hitler intended to run

Above: In September the Allies attacked key Dutch bridges with paratroops. All of these attacks succeeded except that on the farthest bridge, Arnhem, which proved a bloody British defeat.
Right: A German Panther tank.

the show himself, the nominal commander, Field-Marshal von Rundstedt, having been placed in that position only for his prestige and morale-building power among the German troops.

While the Germans were building up for their Ardennes offensive, the Americans had been suffering badly in their attempt to take the Hurtgen Forest. They had sustained 24,000 casualties in this offensive (that lasted from 2 November to 13 December), and they lost 9000 more men to disease or battle fatigue. The 8th Corps of the First Army, against whom the German attack was to be directed, was thinly stretched and plagued with faulty intelligence as to what the Germans were up to. (An intelligence officer who told the First Army commander, Lieutenant General Courtney H Hodges, 'It's the Ardennes,' was sent off to Paris for a rest.) In miserable winter weather, marked by low clouds, fog, and heavy snowfalls that grounded Allied airpower over the Ardennes, on 16 December the Germans launched the most famous counterattack of the war.

Only 83,000 Americans stood as defenders when the 250,000 Germans attacked on a 60-mile front, with the communications centers and road junctions of Saint-Vith and Bastogne as their first objectives. The initial attacks carried all before them, despite desperate efforts by the American troops to halt the onslaught. In some areas of the front the Germans had a 6-to-1 advantage. Wave after wave of Germans drove out of the Ardennes, some of them following Hitler's orders for a 'wave of terror and fright' in which 'no human inhibitions should be shown.' This resulted in the slaughter of 140 American prisoners by SS Panzer troops in what came to be known as the 'Malmedy Massacre.' Behind the Allied lines all was confusion as the Germans poured through, with Eisenhower desperately trying to transfer troops into the Ardennes as soon as he and his advisors finally realized that a major German offensive was underway.

Men of an SS unit ready to open fire with their machine gun.

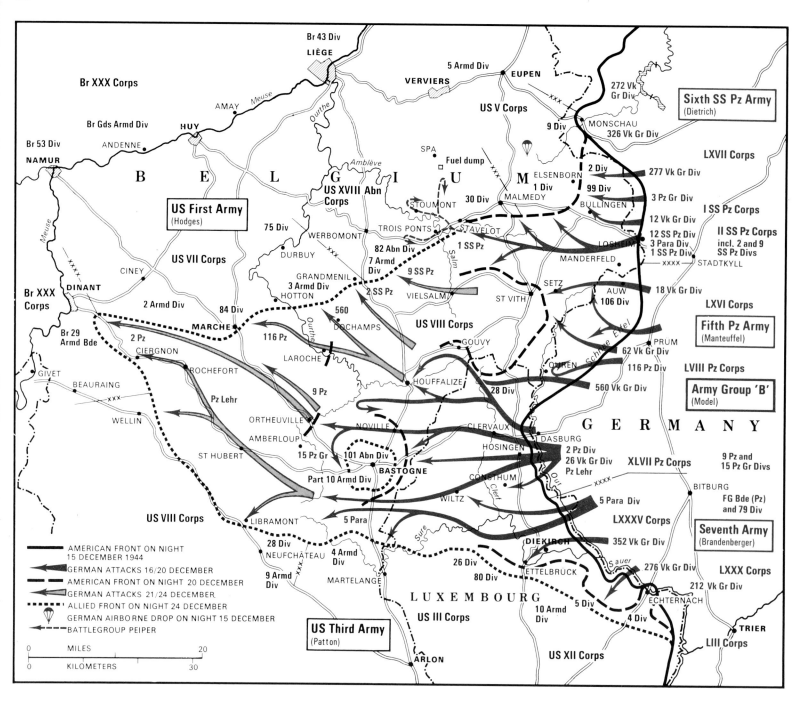

Map of the Battle of the Bulge.

Above: Map of the Battle of the Bulge.
Right: A US 105mm howitzer in action during the German advance.

Saint-Vith was the key to the northern Ardennes. Every available unit was sent to its defense, including the 7th Armored Division. Within three days of the opening of the offensive, Eisenhower also ordered the 82nd Airborne, now in reserve and recovering from MARKET-GARDEN, into the Saint-Vith area. Once they arrived, they and the 7th Armored Division held out near the tiny town against continued German attacks until 23 December, thereby throwing the entire German attack off schedule.

Thirty miles southwest of Saint-Vith, at Bastogne, another drama was being played out. On 18 December 3000 men of the 101st Airborne Division, the 'Screaming Eagles,' began moving toward the area to relieve its defenders. In command was Brigadier General Anthony C McAuliffe. By 20 December the entire 11,000-man 101st, along with some men of the 10th Armored Division, was in place and ready to take on the German attacks. For two days they held out against all odds, cheered by the knowledge that 'Georgie' Patton was sending the 4th Armor-

ed Division to their rescue from the south. When the Germans sent a surrender ultimatum to McAuliffe, his written reply simply said 'Nuts!' To be sure Germans understood, the American officer delivering the reply said, 'If you don't understand what "Nuts" means, in plain English it is the same as "Go to hell,"' adding, 'And I will tell you something else – if you continue to attack we will kill every goddam German that tries to break into this city!'

The siege of Bastogne was not lifted until 26 December, when Patton's armored units fought their way into the city. The 4th Armored Division lost 1000 men in carrying out the rescue, and they found 2000 more Americans dead in and around Bastogne. But at Bastogne and Saint-Vith the Americans had fatally disrupted the German timetable. By Christmas Day the Panzer armies had been stopped, with dry fuel tanks, 30 miles short of Antwerp, and, as the skies cleared, the Allies soon had complete control of the air. On 30 December the First Army began to counterattack from the North, while the Third Army

moved in from the south. By 16 January the giant pincers had met at Houffalize, north of Bastogne. On 28 January 1944 the Battle of the Bulge was declared officially over. The Germans had suffered over 100,000 casualties, to the Americans' 81,000. Hitler's grand counteroffensive had failed, and the last great reserve of German men and equipment was gone.

In February and March 1945 the Allies began to cross the Rhine into Germany. The 21st Army Group, under Montgomery, moved from the north into the vital Ruhr. To the south the US 12th and 6th Army Groups continued to press toward Cologne. When units of the US First Army discovered the bridge at Remagen over the Rhine intact on 7 March and crossed over and held it, Eisenhower shifted the attack south to support this opening. Patton's Third Army crossed at Nierstein on 22 March, and by early April the

General Anthony McAuliffe, famous at Bastogne for one word: 'Nuts!'

east bank of the Rhine had been cleared of German troops.

In line with American promises to Stalin, Roosevelt and Eisenhower had decided they would not conduct a race for Berlin with the Russians and that the Allies would stop at the Elbe (a decision that dismayed and angered the less naive British). Nevertheless the drive

into Germany continued during April and early May, and all along the western terrain the Allied armies were soon breaking through the weakened German resistance. On 25 April American and Russian troops met at Torgau, on the Elbe east of Leipzig. On 30 April Hitler committed suicide as the Russians fought their way into Berlin, and on 4 May Montgomery accepted unconditional surrender from the representatives of Admiral Karl Dönitz, Hitler's successor, at Luneberg Heath. The Allied war against Germany ended on 8 May 1945, and by 11 May all Germans had lain down their arms.

Between D-Day and 8 May 1945, 5.4 million Allied troops had been poured into Western Europe, supported by 970,000 vehicles and 18.2 million tons of supplies. In this last year of the European war, in which the US Army had over 3 million men in the theater, the Americans had suffered 568,000 casualties, including 135,000 dead. America's allies suffered 179,000 casualties, including 60,000 dead. German losses were probably equal to or greater than the total Allied losses. No one on the Allied side doubted that the sacrifices had been well worth while.

The Army Air Force over Europe

Whatever doubts remained from the military debates of the 1930s about the importance of air power were largely erased during the first year of the war. The German Luftwaffe had played a stellar role in the Blitzkriegs

against Poland, the Low Countries and France; and in the Battle of Britain the fate of England, and possibly the outcome of the war, had been decided by the RAF. As a consequence, there was little sentiment in the US to stint the air services, and General Henry ('Hap') Arnold, chief of the Army Air Forces (as the Air Corps was re-christened in June 1941), now received unqualified support for airpower both from the Army and the Congress. By the time of America's entry into the war in December 1941 the nation had an Air Force of 354,000 men and 2800 planes. At peak strength, in early 1945, it would have 2.4 million men and nearly 800,000 planes.

Shortly after Pearl Harbor the Eighth Air Force was formed, and Brigadier General Ira Eaker was sent to England to set up its headquarters. Eaker was a strategic bombing enthusiast who had stood beside Billy Mitchell during his court martial. Since then his belief had not flagged, which placed him in close agreement with Air Chief Marshal Arthur Harris of the Royal Air Force Bomber Command.

Not until August 1942 did Eighth Air Force and Eaker (who had now replaced General Carl ('Tooey') Spaatz as Eighth Air Force commander) have enough men and four-engined Boeing B-17 Flying Fortresses in

Right: The drive into Germany.
Below: Snow-clad Shermans lined up for counterattack near St Vith, one of the key US positions in the battle.

DENMARK
BALTIC SEA
NORTH SEA
FLENSBURG
RÜGEN
Kiel Canal
KIEL
ROSTOCK
STETTIN
7 May
LÜBECK
WISMAR
HAMBURG
SCHWERIN
3 May
NEUSTRELITZ
WILHELMSHAVEN
BREMERHAVEN
STARGARD
EMDEN
18 Apr
BREMEN
DANNENBERG
DÖMITZ
GRONINGEN
26 Apr
OLDENBURG
Lüneberg
ULZEN
WITTENBERG
Belsen
Heath
TANGERMÜNDE
BERLIN
AMSTERDAM
KUSTRIN
Army Group 'H'
(Blaskowitz)
OSNABRÜCK
4 Apr
HANNOVER
US Ninth Army
POTSDAM
FRANKFURT
NETHERLANDS
MINDEN
10 Apr
BRUNSWICK
Twenty-fifth Army
ARNHEM
HAMELN
MAGDEBURG
Twelfth Army
MÜNSTER
GERMANY
BARBY
ROSSLAU
Cdn First Army
First Para Army
Eleventh Army
(Crerar)
WESEL
PADERBORN
Harz Mts
BLANKENBURG
DESSAU
Br Second Army
HAMM
Brocken Pk
24 Apr
COTTBUS
(Dempsey)
DORTMUND
LIPPSTADT
GÖTTINGEN
US First Army
HALLE
US Ninth Army
BOCHUM
(Simpson)
Ruhr
KASSEL
NORDHAUSEN
21 Army Group
DUISBURG
WUPPERTAL
Sauerland
4
MERSEBERG
LEIPZIG
(Montgomery)
DÜSSELDORF
Apr
Buchenwald
WEISSENFELS
GÖRLITZ
Fifteenth Army
Army Group 'B'
ERFURT
ZEITZ
COLDITZ
COLOGNE
(Model)
GOTHA
WEIMAR
DRESDEN
Fifth Pz Army
JENA
Thüringian Forest
US Third Army
CHEMNITZ
LIEGE
BONN
Sieg
MARBURG
OHRDRUF
USTÍ
REMAGEN
US First Army
GIESSEN
FULDA 2 Apr
Seventh Army
BELGIUM
KOBLENZ
Lahn
(Hodges)
BAD ORB
HOF
Erzgebirge
Rhine
Seventh Army
KARLOVY VARY
PRAGUE
12 Army Group
WIESBADEN
FRANKFURT
HAMMELBURG
(Bradley)
HANAU
SCHWEINFURT
BAYREUTH
CZECHOSLOVAKIA
LUX
MAINZ
US Third Army
Main
ASCHAFFEN-
WÜRZBURG
BAMBERG
PILSEN
LUXEMBOURG
TRIER
OPPENHEIM
(Patton)
BURG
Odenwald
KITZINGEN 5 Apr
THIONVILLE
WORMS
US Seventh Army
4 Apr
Bohemian
NÜREMBERG
CESKE
(Patch)
MANNHEIM
FÜRTH
20
18 Apr
BUDEJOVICE
SAARBRÜCKEN
Neckar
Army Group 'G'
Apr
7 May
6 Army Group
First Army
(Hausser)
ANSBACH
Forest
(Devers)
KARLSRUHE
HEILBRONN
18 Apr
Vltava
4 Apr
PFORZHEIM
Löwenstein
REGENSBURG 26 Apr
Fr First Army
Hills
US Seventh
LINZ
(de Lattre de Tassigny)
8 Apr
STUTTGART
Franconian
Army
Danube
CESKE
NANCY
ESSLINGEN
KIRCHHEIM
INGOLSTADT
Isar
LANDAU
STRASBOURG
DONAUWÖRTH
LANDSHUT
PASSAU
TÜBINGEN
Jura
30 Apr
FRANCE
Highlands
DILLINGEN
First Army
Nineteenth
ULM 23 Apr
AUGSBURG
Swabian
Inp
Army
Schwarzwald
Dachau
BRAUNAU
COLMAR
EHINGEN
US Third Army
SIGMARINGEN
LANDSBERG
MUNICH
LINZ
FREIBURG
30 Apr
5 May
MEMMINGEN
ROSENHEIM
SALZBURG
Fr First Army
US Seventh Army
4 May
Lake
OBERAMMERGAU
BERCHTESGADEN
Constance
4 May
BASLE
FÜSSEN
GARMISCH-
Enns
Oberjoch
PARTENKIRCHEN
KUFSTEIN
Pass
Fern
KITZBÜHEL
BREGENZ
Pass
IMST
SWITZERLAND
TAMSWEG
Aarlberg
INNSBRUCK
A U S T R I A
Pass
LANDECK
Tyrol
A L P S
Brenner
4 May
Pass
Resia
Pass
KLAGENFURT
BOLZANO
I T A L Y
YUGOSLAVIA
US Fifth Army

OCCUPIED BY ALLIED FORCES, 28 MARCH 1945
BRITISH ATTACKS
US ATTACKS
FRENCH ATTACKS
GERMAN POCKETS
OCCUPIED BY RUSSIAN FORCES, 16 APRIL
CONCENTRATION CAMPS
0   MILES   120
0   KILOMETERS   200

Right: The victors: (L to R) Omar Bradley, Dwight Eisenhower, George Patton.
Below: Almost as vital as the ground war was the battle raging in the sky. Here, B-17s of the 381st Bomb Group.

England to make their first bombing raid, on Rouen in France. A dozen more followed, as the Americans learned the art of high-level daylight bombing. In the meantime, four-engined Consolidated B-24 Liberators had joined the B-17s. Liberators were slightly faster than the 'Forts' and had a greater bomb capacity, but the B-17 could operate at greater altitudes and could defend themselves better. Together these two bomber types would form the backbone of the American air offensive against Germany in the years that followed.

By late 1942 the Eighth had nearly 300 bombers in England, and its air crews were gaining in proficiency daily as they raided more and more targets in France. But Eaker had yet to realize his dream of launching his daylight precision bomber fleets against Germany itself. Indeed, he was beginning to encounter a growing sentiment in both England and America against this ever being done. The problem had to do with the lack of long-range fighters. Neither the Americans nor the British yet had fighters able to escort bombers beyond the borders of Germany, and it was widely held that the losses Ger-

B-24s had better range than B-17s, but their weaker defenses made them less favored for raids deep into Germany.

man day fighters could inflict on unescorted bomber formations would prove not merely unacceptable but probably appalling. It was for this reason that the British had long ago abandoned daylight strategic bombing entirely, confining their long-range heavy bomber operations to the hours of darkness. They strongly urged the Americans to do the same, but Eaker and other precision bombing enthusiasts scorned the inaccuracy of night bombing and insisted that their Forts could take care of themselves in air combat. In the end, Roosevelt and Churchill, at the Casablanca Conference (January 1943), agreed to give the Eaker faction a chance to prove their contentions about the viability of unescorted daylight bombing. To what extent they succeeded in doing so is still moot, but in the process of trying they undeniably visited fearsome destruction on Germany.

The Eighth Air Force's daylight bombing campaign against Germany began in earnest in June 1943. Kiel, Warnemünde, Hannover, Oschersleben, Kassel, and various points in the strategic Ruhr Valley were among the targets struck during the next 60 days. Perhaps the most famous raid of this period was the attack on Hamburg, conducted in con-

junction with the RAF in late July. In that battered city superheated air from burning buildings was drawn into a gigantic convection current that produced tornadic winds of 150 mph and temperatures of 1800° Fahrenheit. Approximately half the city and 50,000 people were destroyed in this attack.

So far, bomber losses had been significant but far from intolerable. This was to change in August, as the Luftwaffe fighter defenses began to organize to meet the new challenge. The climactic day was 17 August 1943 (the same day the invasion of Italy began). The Eighth Air Force had been assigned two targets deep in Germany. The first was Regensberg, site of a major Messerschmitt aircraft manufacturing complex. Although the introduction of drop tanks had begun to extend the ranges of Allied fighters significantly, Regensburg was still well beyond their radius, and the 146 B-17s had to fly unescorted over Germany most of the way to the target. Luftwaffe Messerschmitt Bf 109s and 110s, Focke-Wulf Fw 190s, and Junkers Ju 88 nightfighters kept the Forts under continuous attacks. Seventeen Forts were lost, and casualties to aircrews on surviving planes were heavy. But this was only the warm-up.

The second raid that day, on the Schweinfurt ball-bearing factories, also deep in Germany, was to have been launched 10 minutes after the Regensburg bombers flew

off, but weather delayed the bombers' take-offs for more than three hours, thus negating any advantage to be had from simultaneous attack. Some 300 German fighters were waiting for the 230 Flying Fortresses as they crossed the German border. They hectored the Forts unmercifully all the way to Schweinfurt and back, shooting down 36. Although the Americans did considerable damage to both Regensburg and Schweinfurt, 53 of the 376 B-17s sent out on these two missions were shot down, and 47 others never flew again. So great was the damage to the bombers on this single day that the Americans did not return to German skies for another two months. When they did, on 14 October, in the form of another giant raid on Schweinfurt by 291 Flying Fortresses, the results were much the same. Some 60 American bombers were lost, to only 38 German fighters. Further raiding deep into Germany in 1943 was suspended until the range of fighters could be sufficiently extended to escort bombers all the way to their targets.

The Eighth Air Force was by no means the only US Army air force operating in the European Theater. In the summer of 1942, while the Eighth was assembling in England, the nucleus of a US Army Middle East Air Force was being established in North Africa. Composed at first of a handful of B-17, B-24, B-25 (a twin-engine medium bomber built by

North American) and P-40 units, it grew rapidly. After the battle of El Alamein it was redesignated the Ninth Air Force, and by August of 1943 it had become so large that it had to be subdivided, some of its units being given to the newly created Twelfth Air Force, while the remainder of the Ninth was transferred to England to supplement the Eighth Air Force's growing daylight bombing offensive across the Channel. Since, unlike the Eighth, the Ninth had, in addition to its heavy bombers, a large medium bomber component, it was able to mount nearly continuous low-level short-range attacks against targets in France and the Low Countries, even at times when, either for reasons of policy or bad weather, the heavies were

grounded. And after D-Day, when the mediums could operate from bases on the continent, they, too, were able to join in the aerial assault on Germany. By the end of the war the Ninth was a very large and powerful organization, indeed, containing no fewer than 11 Bomb Groups and 18 Fighter Groups (three more than the Eighth).

While the Eighth and Ninth assailed Hitler's Reich from the west, the Twelfth kept up the attack from the south, now, increasingly from bases in Italy. By the beginning of 1944 it, also, had grown so large that it had to be subdivided, the heavy bomber units and their fighter escort groups being transferred to a new command, the Fifteenth Air Force, while the Twelfth continued to operate an

impressive collection of medium, attack and fighter units.

With respect to daylight raids by unescorted heavy bombers flying deep into enemy territory, the experience of the Mediterranean air forces was much the same as that of the air forces flying out of England. Perhaps the most memorable example was the great raid mounted against Rumania's Ploesti oil refineries in August 1943 (the same grim month as the Regensburg and Schweinfurt raids). Of the 165 unescorted B-24s that finally made it to the target 43 were downed by

A bomber's-eye-view of the Eighth Air Force's most notoriously dangerous and expensive target, Schweinfurt.

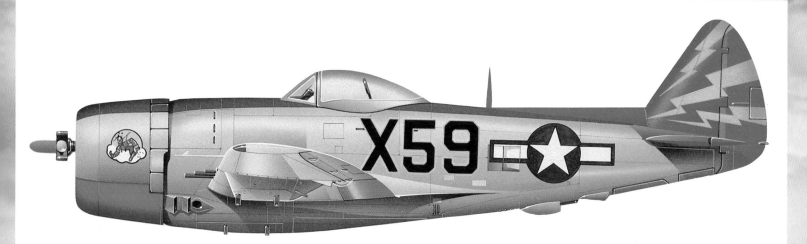

The P-47 Thunderbolt fighter (*above*) lacked the range to escort bombers deep into Germany. But any Luftwaffe hope of halting the raids ended when the long-range P-51 Mustang appeared.

enemy flak and fighters and eight more were so badly shot up they had to crash land in Turkey; and of the 114 that managed to straggle back to their bases more than half had sustained serious damage.

By the end of August it was plain that, despite the contentions of enthusiasts, the future of daylight strategic bombing would, after all, depend on the provision of suitable fighter escort. Of the American fighters available in 1943, the big Lockheed P-38 Lightning had

the necessary range but could not maneuver with Lufwaffe fighters on equal terms, while the more formidable Republic P-47 Thunder bolt decidedly did *not* have the range. Yet there was hope in the offing, in the form of North American's spectacular new P-51 Mustang, an American-designed airframe powered by Britain's famed Rolls-Royce Merlin engine, that promised not only unparalleled speed and maneuverability but a range that put virtually the whole of Germany

Above: Messerschmitt Bf 110 fighters, one of many air-defense types used.
Left: By 1945 Mustang-escorted B-24s could raid Berlin almost at will.

within its combat radius. Mustangs began to appear in the ETO in early 1944, and within six months they had radically changed the character of the European air war. Allied bomber losses dropped sharply, while Luftwaffe fighter losses soared to such levels that German industry was hard put to make them good. What could not be made good, of course, was the relentless loss of trained German fighter pilots. The Luftwaffe was, in effect, hemorrhaging to death, while the whole of Germany lay increasingly exposed to the fury of the Allied air offensive.

Although British and American air strategists protested, Allied air power in 1944 was largely turned to supporting OVERLORD. The Eighth and Ninth Air Forces, along with their British air colleagues, flew over 200,000 sorties to cripple the main transportation lines in France and northwest Europe. They virtually shut down rail traffic in France, although always bombing at a 2-to-1 ratio on the Pas-de-Calais area over the Normandy

area to preserve the landing site deception. They also flew against the German rocket-launching sites in northwest Europe, and on D-Day 8000 bombers and fighters flew over 14,000 sorties in support of the amphibious landings, having already played their deceptive role in Operation FORTITUDE farther north. In the days that followed, the Allies had complete air superiority over the Normandy beaches, a major factor in the success of the invasion.

Major daylight strategic bombing of Germany resumed with a vengeance in 1945. The declining Luftwaffe tried desperately to limit the destruction. One hope for turning the tide of air battle was the development of the Messerschmitt Me 262, the world's first jet fighter, but Hitler delayed development of this remarkable plane until late 1944, insisting it should be used as an offensive bomber, since it had the ability to carry a bomb. Once in the skies, the Me 262s proved to be very effective against their propeller-driven adversaries, but there were never enough of them even to begin to threaten Allied air supremacy.

Aircraft of the RAF and all four of America's European air forces now ranged virtually at

will over Germany. In February Allied strategic bombers dropped nearly 125,000 tons of bombs on German cities, while medium and attack bombers added approximately another 30,000 tons. By March the Eighth Air Force alone was capable of sending 1500 heavy bombers over Germany in a single day, and the RAF of dropping nearly 5000 tons of bombs on a single target. The gruesome Anglo-American attack on Dresden, made in mid-February, is perhaps the best remembered of these late-war raids. In it, 1600 acres of the old city were leveled and about 70,000 persons lost their lives.

On 16 April 1945 the air offensive against Germany ended. There was by then hardly anything left to destroy. Exactly how great a contribution aerial bombardment made to Germany's eventual collapse is still a matter of debate, but none denies that that contribution was significant. The 73,000 American airmen – as well as the like number of RAF fliers – who were killed during the European bombing offensive certainly did not give their lives in vain. Yet it was to be in the Pacific, rather than in Europe, that the truly decisive role of air power would at last be demonstrated.

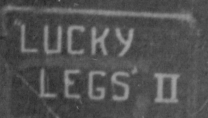

WORLD WAR IN THE PACIFIC: 1941-1945

In September 1941 the military rulers of Japan made a fateful decision. Unless the United States reversed its policy of resisting Japanese expansion in the Far East, American outposts in the Pacific would have to be attacked and destroyed, for they stood as barriers to the fulfillment of the Japanese dream of dominating the western Pacific. Not satisfied with her conquests of Manchuria, Korea, Formosa, and the Ryukyu Islands prior to 1921, in the next ten years Japan had seized large portions of northern China and important Chinese southern seaports and had then moved into French Indochina, with the acquiescence of the Vichy government in France.

Now it was time to complete the Japanese empire in the Pacific by seizing the American-owned Philippine Islands and Guam, the Dutch East Indies, Borneo, New Guinea, Burma, Thailand and Malaya, plus Wake Island in the central Pacific and the Gilbert

The first six months of the Pacific War saw Japan everywhere triumphant over her Western foes.

and Solomon Islands in the southwest Pacific. With these conquests completed, Japan would rule the Pacific for decades to come. As her leaders and people saw it, this was her destiny.

Seizing Far Eastern territories from the British and Dutch did not seem too dangerous an undertaking, since these nations were tied up with their war against Hitler. The problem was the United States. American ownership of the Philippines, Guam, and Wake meant that the Americans had territories and military installations within the area coveted by Japan. As long as the Americans stood astride and on the flank of the Japanese routes of conquest, Japanese holdings, both real and anticipated, would be endangered. If, therefore, the United States would not acquiesce in Japan's Far Eastern plans (and it would not: American hostility to Japanese expansionism became clearer and clearer after 1939), Japan would have both to seize American territories in the western Pacific and neutralize her military bases in the central Pacific.

Such brave defenses as that of Wake Is. (*right*) salved American pride but were no substitute for victory.

Of course this would mean war, but, it was hoped, within six months the Japanese army and navy would have realized all of Japan's objectives in the Pacific. The Americans and their severely weakened European allies would be left on the periphery of Japan's empire, with no alternative but to accept her conquests. America could launch a counter-offensive only from the Hawaiian Islands or from her own West Coast, and it would have to extend all the way across the vast reaches of the Pacific. This would be a nearly impossible task, especially in the absence of significant help from the British, French, or Dutch. America would thus have to accept the inevitable and learn to live with Japan's conquests.

These strategic calculations gave birth to a Japanese plan to attack Pearl Harbor, the Philippines, and Guam early in December 1941, and simultaneously to mount offensives against the British, Dutch and Australian territories west and south. The western and central Pacific would be firmly in Japanese hands by mid-summer 1942. The plan was audacious to the point of being breathtaking, and it almost succeeded.

At 0755 on the clear Sunday morning of 7 December 1941 the Japanese launched a superbly executed surprise attack on the giant American naval base at Pearl Harbor. Within two hours most of the US Pacific Fleet's battleships were either sunk or severely damaged, 18 warships overall. In addition, 177 Army and Navy planes were destroyed, 159 damaged, and over 2,000 sailors and Marines were dead or dying. Intelligence information that a Japanese attack was imminent, information that in retrospect would appear to be crystal clear, had produced no advance warning. Radar blips picked up by the Army Aircraft Warning Service's five mobile radar units on the northern tip of Oahu (blips that indicated great numbers of planes coming from the north) were first misunderstood and then ignored. The Americans were totally unprepared.

At the Army's Schofield Barracks, Hickam Field and Wheeler Field, as elsewhere on Oahu, the enemy struck without warning. Army Air Force bombers and fighters at the airfields had been lined up wingtip to wingtip as protection against sabotage. They made perfect targets for the Japanese airmen, who wiped them out in the first waves. Almost no American aircraft were able to rise to meet the enemy. A flight of B-17s arriving from the mainland, stripped of armor and ammunition for the long over-water haul, became a prime target as the Flying Fortresses flew into the area to land at Hickam Field. One was destroyed as it crash landed, another landed on a golf course, and the others set down anywhere they could on any

The Japanese attack on Pearl Harbor (*right and top right*) so crippled the US Pacific Fleet that no retaliatory action was possible.

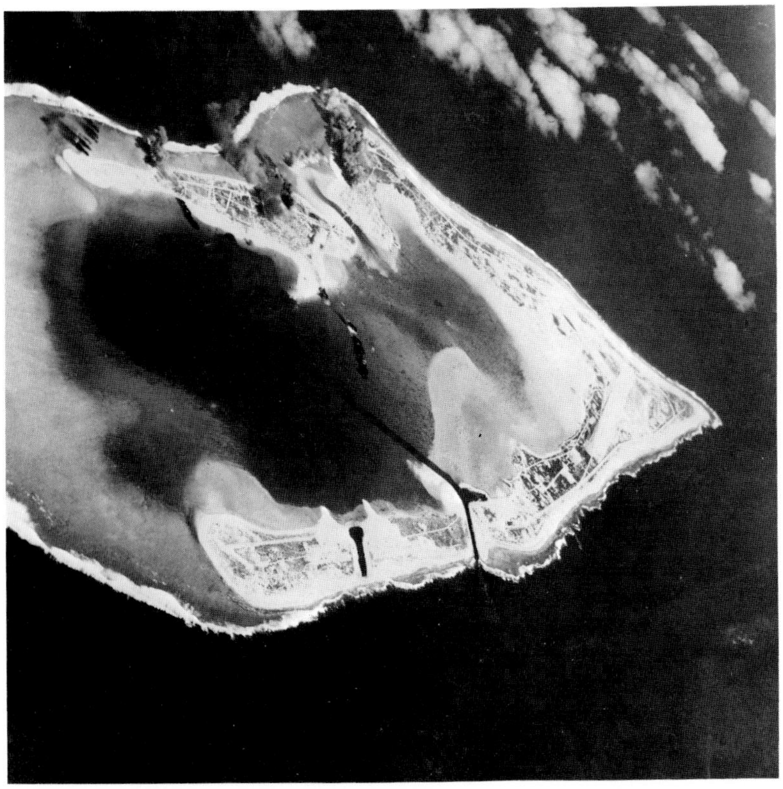

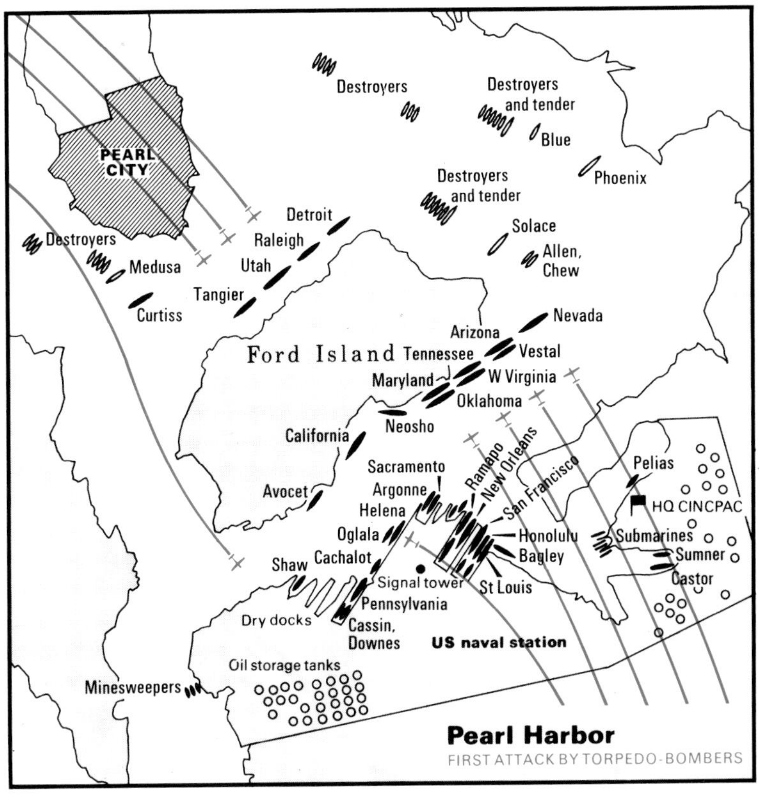
PEARL CITY
Destroyers
Destroyers and tender
Blue
Phoenix
Destroyers and tender
Solace
Allen, Chew
Detroit
Raleigh
Utah
Tangier
Destroyers
Medusa
Curtiss
Arizona
Nevada
Ford Island
Tennessee
Vestal
Maryland
W Virginia
Oklahoma
Neosho
California
Sacramento
Argonne
Helena
Avocet
Ramapo
New Orleans
San Francisco
Pelias
HQ CINCPAC
Oglala
Cachalot
Shaw
Honolulu
Bagley
Submarines
Sumner
Castor
Signal tower
St Louis
Pennsylvania
Dry docks
Cassin, Downes
US naval station
Oil storage tanks
Minesweepers
Pearl Harbor
FIRST ATTACK BY TORPEDO-BOMBERS

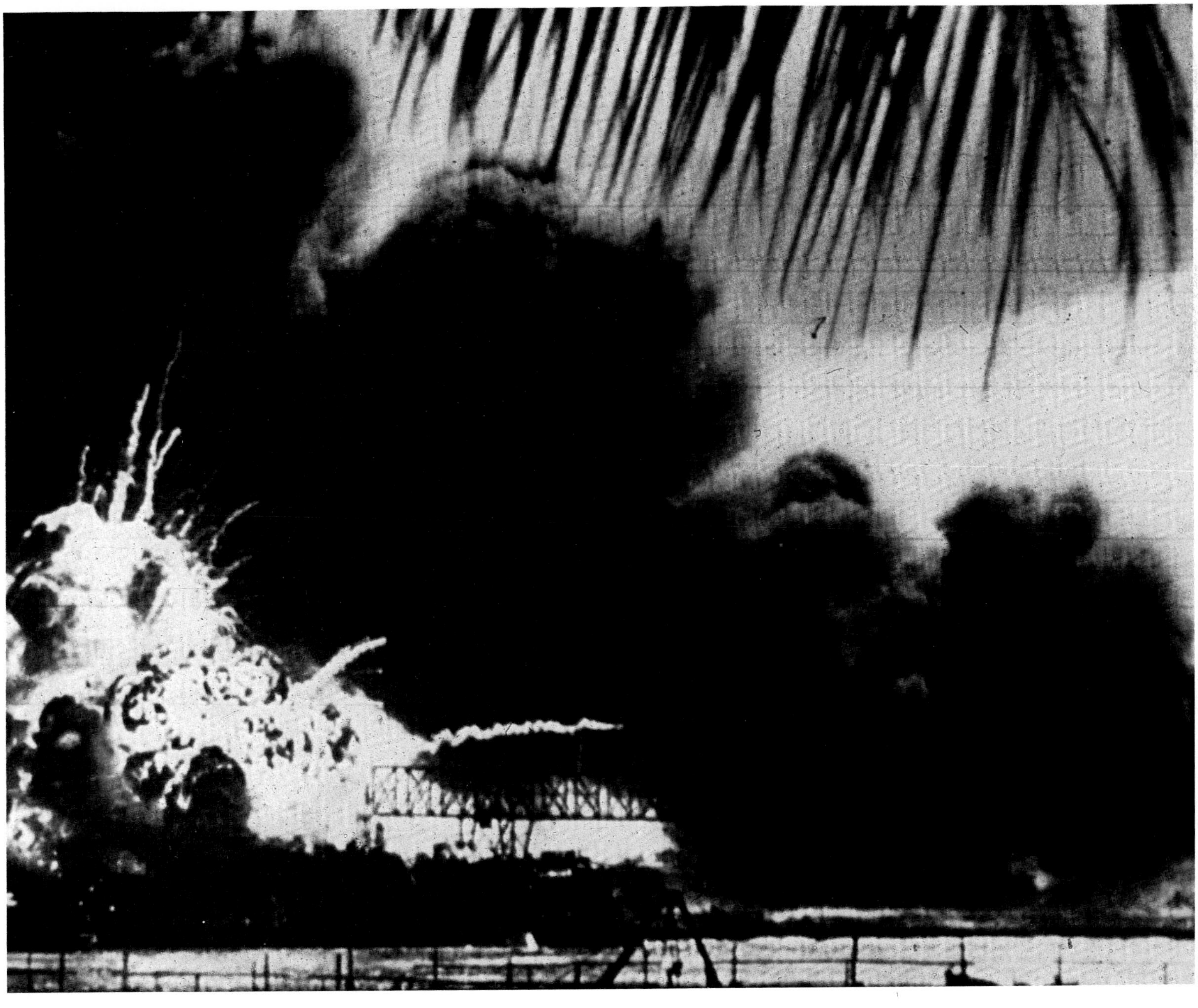

small airstrips available in the Hawaiian Islands.

Like his naval counterpart, Admiral Husband E Kimmel, Lieutenant General Walter C Short, the Army commander in Hawaii, was soon relieved of command and held accountable for the devastation. He had not consulted with Kimmel and had failed to put his men on full war alert prior to the raid. Whatever Short's real guilt in the controversial matter as to why the military was not ready for the attack, the grim fact remained that the Army, like the Navy, was in no position either to protect the Hawaiian Islands against further attack or invasion or to begin the process of fighting back against the forces of Nippon.

Defeat: Guam, Wake, the Philippines

On that same December day, at 1220 in the afternoon, 108 Japanese bombers and 84 fighters swept in over Clark Field northwest of Manila, the capital of the Philippines, on the island of Luzon. Below they found 18 B-17s, over 50 P-40 fighter planes and 30 other aircraft all neatly lined up in rows. Not one defensive aircraft was in the air to oppose them, despite the fact that the news of Pearl Harbor had by now been flashed throughout the Pacific command. In short order, and with their only challenge coming from feeble antiaircraft fire, the Japanese planes swoop-

ed down to destroy General Douglas MacArthur's air force parked on the ground. Only 17 B-17s sent south to a base on Mindanao, the southernmost main island in the Philippines, were saved from destruction. As at Pearl Harbor, the Americans in the Philippines had been caught unprepared. Plans had been underway for a B-17 attack on the Japanese air forces on Formosa, but they had been delayed by a lack of reconnaissance photographs. Now, the thousands of Army personnel in the Philippines, along with their naval and Filipino comrades, were left without air cover as the Japanese prepared to launch their invasion of the archipelago.

Almost at the same time, the 400-plus naval and Marine garrison on Guam in the Marianas, some 1,500 miles east of Manila, was attacked by over 5,000 Japanese troops. Within two days the island fell.

Wake Island, a small atoll 2,300 miles west of Hawaii, then being converted to a naval aircraft station, was scheduled for attack on 8 December. On the island were 450 Marines, 1200 civilians from the construction crews working on the islands, and a handful of Army Signal Corps and naval personnel. They were hit first in the forenoon by Japanese aircraft from Kwajalein, in the Marshall Islands, 600 miles away. Three days later a Japanese invasion squadron of 13 vessels arrived off Wake. Although the Marine defenders, with valuable aid from the Navy and Army personnel, held off two invasion at-

tempts with their accurate gunnery, sinking one ship and damaging five others, they could not stop the inevitable. Air raids continued on the besieged garrison, and finally, on 23 December, a major Japanese invasion was launched. The island fell that day, and 1555 Americans were taken prisoner.

The main Japanese target, though, was the Philippines. Here General Douglas MacArthur, former Army Chief of Staff, Field Marshal of the Philippine army, and now commander of the American-Philippine army forces, had only about 25,000 regulars on hand. These consisted of the Philippine Division of the US Army, 12,000 Filipino Scouts (members of the US Army), a division of Philippine Army regulars, and a few Marines. With these few men he would have to hold off a major Japanese invasion force.

Lieutenant General Masaharu Homma led the 43,000 men of his Japanese 14th Army ashore on Lingayen Gulf, north of Manila, on 22 December. Homma's forces soon had the Northern Luzon Force, under Major General Jonathan ('Skinny') Wainwright, in retreat. Meanwhile, a second force landed at Lamon Bay, 70 miles southeast of the capital. The American and Filipino forces could not stop the Japanese moves toward Manila, despite their bravest efforts, so MacArthur ordered all his forces back, some taking up positions on the Bataan Peninsula at the northern end of Manila Bay, while others moved onto the fortress island of Corregidor – 'The Rock' – in

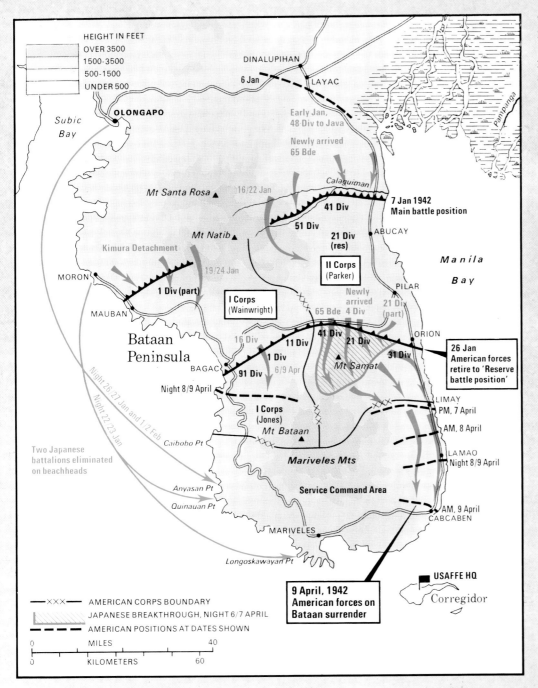

The fall of Bataan.

the middle of the entrance to the bay. This meant abandoning the city of Manila, but MacArthur felt he had no choice if the garrison was to hold out long enough for aid to arrive. By 2 January Manila had fallen.

Although faced with shortages of food, ammunition and medicine, 15,000 American troops and their 65,000 Filipino allies dug in on Bataan to await the Japanese juggernaut. Army headquarters was deep inside the 1400-foot reinforced Malinta Tunnel on Corregidor, and from there the defense of Bataan and Corregidor would be directed. Beginning on 11 January, the Japanese again and again mounted artillery and infantry attacks against the American and Filipino positions on Bataan, first at the northern end of the peninsula and then, when this line had to be abandoned, across the center. Slowly the American-Filipino forces were pushed back, but they took a grim toll of Japanese as they went. By mid-February Homma had lost over 7000 dead and wounded, and he had still not taken Luzon. He called a two-month halt and asked Tokyo for reinforcements.

During the lull the American and Filipino soldiers tried to strengthen themselves for the offensive that was sure to come, but MacArthur's army was slowly falling victim to

Left: The fall of Bataan.
Below: The Japanese 14th Army coming on shore at Lingayen Gulf. In less than a fortnight they would be in possession of Manila.

disease, as supplies of medicine, especially precious quinine, ran out. And morale, too, was sinking, particularly after a radio broadcast from President Roosevelt in late February revealed that reinforcements were not coming. Then MacArthur himself was ordered out of the Philippines by Roosevelt: He was to go to Australia to assume command of forces that would launch a grand counter-offensive against Japan. MacArthur reluctantly followed orders. On 11 March he turned over command on Luzon to General Wainwright and, with his family, left by PT boat for Mindanao, to the south, and thence by Flying Fortress to Darwin, Australia. Before leaving his beloved Philippines, MacArthur promised Wainwright he would return, a vow the flamboyant general reiterated upon arriving in Australia: 'I came through, and I shall return.' This public promise would cast a long shadow over subsequent Pacific strategy.

Back in the Philippines the suffering and dying went on. The revitalized forces of General Homma renewed their offensive on Bataan on 3 April, and six days later Major General Edward King, who had replaced Wainwright as Bataan commander when Wainwright replaced MacArthur on Corregidor, surrendered what was left of the American-Filipino forces in his command, 76,000 men. For another month the 13,000 defenders on Corregidor and its three surrounding fortified islands were subjected to

Left: The surrender of Corregidor.
Below: One of Col. James Doolittle's 16 B-25s taking off from USS *Hornet* for the famous first raid on Tokyo. The raid did little damage, but its effect on enemy morale was considerable.

constant artillery barrages. Then, on 5 May, Japanese troops and tanks rolled ashore. Two days later Wainwright was forced to surrender not only Corregidor and its defenders but the entire Philippine archipelago to General Homma. The Philippines had fallen after five months, but not before the Army troops there, along with their Navy, Marine and Filipino comrades, had written a glorious chapter in defensive warfare, and not before several thousand troops slipped away to fight the Japanese as guerrillas until MacArthur fulfilled his promise to return.

For those soldiers forced to surrender in the Philippines, the suffering was only beginning. The 13,000 men on Corregidor were left without food for a week and were then driven through Manila like animals before being shipped by train to a harshly-run POW camp at Cabanatuan, north of Manila. Here, within two months, 2000 American prisoners died of hunger and disease. The 76,000 American and Filipino prisoners from Bataan underwent a worse fate, the infamous Bataan Death March to Camp O'Donnell, 65 miles away. Most were forced to walk and to endure the cruelty of the Japanese guards who, in their contempt for any soldier who would surrender, frequently stabbed and shot those who straggled. At least 7000 Americans and Filipinos died on the Death March.

By the end of the war, of the 25,600 Americans captured in the Philippines, on Wake Island, and elsewhere in the Pacific (22,000 of these in the Philippines), 10,650 died in captivity, a grim figure of over 41 percent. The saga of the Corregidor and Bataan prisoners was but a foretaste of the cruelty and fanaticism of the Pacific war that was about to unfold.

The Solomons Campaign

The Americans were able to strike back at Japan on 18 April 1942, in an astonishing raid by 16 land-based Army B-25 bombers led by Lieutenant Colonel James H Doolittle. They flew 700 miles from the carrier *Hornet* to bomb Tokyo and four other major Japanese cities. The raid served to buttress American morale early in the war, but it caused little damage. The Navy also scored some minor victories in the Pacific, but none great enough to offset the grim fact that most of the miniscule American Asiatic Fleet, including the cruiser USS *Houston*, had either been destroyed in the Battle of the Java Sea on 27-28 February or in other isolated actions that occurred as Japanese forces swept inexorably down through the southwestern Pacific. The meager British and Dutch forces working with the Asiatic Fleet were also decimated.

The Japanese armies moved on. Malaya, Singapore, the Dutch East Indies, Rangoon, Hong Kong, more of China, the remainder of the Philippines, and New Britain all fell to the Japanese forces. Only at sea could the Americans score any victories: first in the Battle of the Coral Sea on 4-8 May 1942, when an American task force was able to turn back a Japanese invasion force steaming for Port Moresby on New Guinea, and then, a month later, in the mid-Pacific, when two American carrier task forces (with only three carriers between them) sank four Japanese carriers in the Battle of Midway. Although no one realized it at the time, the Battle of Midway represented the turning point of the Pacific war. Japanese expansion had been stopped,

178

and the Japanese navy had been seriously weakened. From this point on, the Americans and their Allies would be gradually shifting to the offensive in the Pacific, and American superiority in numbers and in warmaking capabilities would begin to make itself felt.

Yamamoto had had his six months. Now it was the Allies' turn. As the Japanese were, at first slowly, and then with increasing speed, pushed back from their farthest perimeter of conquest to their home island base, the US Army would be called upon to play a major role in this bloody war of reconquest.

The first step back came in the Solomon Island chain, deep in the south Pacific northeast of Australia. The Japanese had begun to menace both Australia and New Zealand by seizing New Britain Island and the port of Rabaul from the Australians, capturing the towns of Lae and Salamaua, on the northeast shore of New Guinea, and bombing Port Moresby, on the southeast coast of New Guinea. In March 1942 the Japanese had seized the Solomon islands of Guadalcanal and Tulagi, intending to use them as airbases to interdict Allied traffic to Australia and to endanger the other island chains along the shipping routes from America. The Japanese had to be ousted from Guadalcanal and Tulagi, and thus was born the first American offensive operation of the Pacific War, hastily mounted and, initially, small in scale.

The assignment was given to the 1st Marine Division, and on 7 August 1942 the Leathernecks began their assaults on Guadalcanal and on Tulagi, 20 miles to the north, across Sealark Channel. The Japanese reacted violently, rushing reinforcements to the area and trying by every means to dislodge the marines from the islands, especially Guadalcanal, with its vital airstrip, Hender-

Right: The South Pacific offensives
Below: Wounded US soldiers returning from the front in New Guinea, 1942.

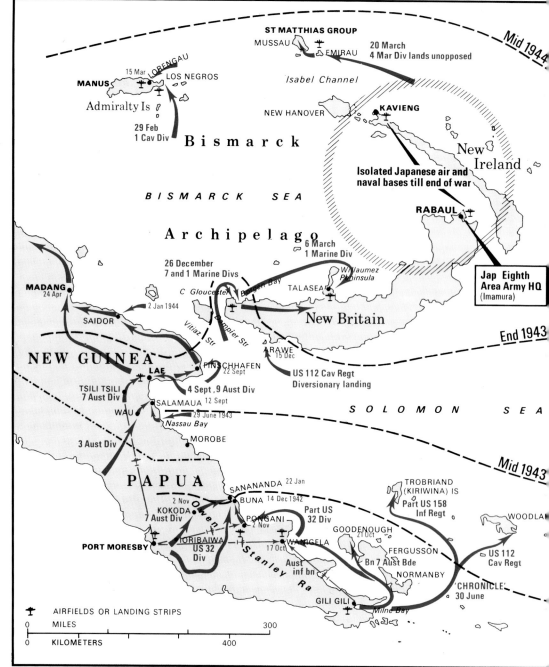

son Field. No fewer than six major naval battles were fought as the Japanese tried to cut off the Marines from reinforcement by sea, while at the same time bringing in more troops and supplies of their own.

In early December the 1st Marine Division was withdrawn from the island, its place being taken by the 2nd Marine Division and the Army's Americal and 25th Divisions, Major General Alexander M Patch commanding. Patch immediately sent his troops against rugged Mount Austen, a 1500-foot peak, still in Japanese hands, that overlooked Henderson Field, six miles away. There the soldiers ran into savage opposition, a bitter indoctrination into the fighting quality of the Japanese soldier. Patch finally decided to bypass the mountain and go after the main Japanese force that was escaping to the west, but the 13,000 Japanese (all that were left of 36,000 crack troops) managed to get away when their navy moved in to evacuate them. Guadalcanal and nearby Tulagi were now freed of Japanese, and the Americans had a solid hold on the southern Solomons. The

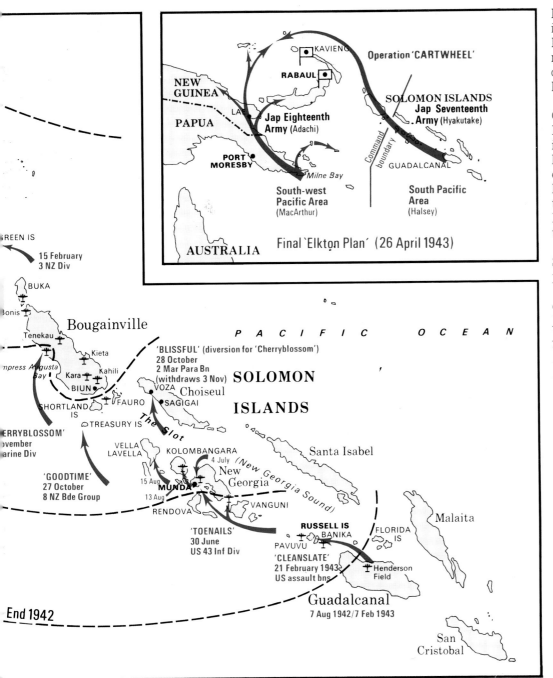

Final `Elkton Plan' (26 April 1943)

Operation 'CARTWHEEL'

KAVIENG

RABAUL

NEW GUINEA

PAPUA

Jap Eighteenth Army (Adachi)

LAE

PORT MORESBY

Milne Bay

SOLOMON ISLANDS
Jap Seventeenth Army (Hyakutake)

Command boundary

GUADALCANAL

South-west Pacific Area (MacArthur)

South Pacific Area (Halsey)

AUSTRALIA

GREEN IS
15 February
3 NZ Div

BUKA

Bonis

Bougainville

Tenekau

Kieta

Empress Augusta Bay

Kara

Kahili

BIUN

SHORTLAND IS

FAURO

TREASURY IS

'CHERRYBLOSSOM'
1 November
3 Marine Div

'GOODTIME'
27 October
8 NZ Bde Group

'BLISSFUL' (diversion for 'Cherryblossom')
28 October
2 Mar Para Bn
(withdraws 3 Nov)

VOZA

SAGIGAI

Choiseul

The Slot

VELLA LAVELLA

KOLOMBANGARA

New Georgia

4 July

15 Aug

MUNDA

13 Aug

RENDOVA

VANGUNI

'TOENAILS'
30 June
US 43 Inf Div

RUSSELL IS

BANIKA

PAVUVU

'CLEANSLATE'
21 February 1943
US assault bns

SOLOMON ISLANDS

Santa Isabel

New Georgia Sound

Malaita

FLORIDA IS

Henderson Field

Guadalcanal
7 Aug 1942/7 Feb 1943

San Cristobal

End 1942

PACIFIC OCEAN

Port Moresby once before by water, but the invasion fleet had been turned back in the Battle of the Coral Sea in early May. Now, two months later, they had begun a second operation to seize the vital Allied base by land instead.

The only route for the 100-mile trek from Gona to Port Moresby was a perilous trail, the Kokoda Track, over the mountains. In places it was so narrow one could traverse it only by holding onto branches to avoid falling hundreds of feet down into the jungle gorges below. Yet the Japanese were as determined to make this daunting trek and take Port Moresby as the Australians were to prevent them from doing so.

Through late July, all of August, and into September 1942 the Japanese resolutely pushed against the Australian defenders. By 17 September they had reached Ioribaiwa, only 30 miles from Port Moresby. But here the Japanese overland drive was stopped. The Japanese troops were utterly exhausted, and their supply lines were providing only a trickle of the food and material they needed, thanks in large measure to incessant attacks conducted by MacArthur's Fifth Air Force, under Major General George C Kenney.

The Japanese, meanwhile, had also suffered defeat in their attempt to seize Milne Bay, on the southeast tip of Papua, in early September. Here 1300 American troops had stood side by side with their 7700 Allied comrades to stop a Japanese amphibious attack and force the survivors back to their ships. The failure at Milne Bay, combined with the constant necessity of moving more troops to Guadalcanal, meant that the Japanese outside Port Moresby could not be reinforced. With no aid possible, and with his troops suffering from disease and starvation, Major General Tomitaro Horii accepted the

By mid-1943 the Solomons advance had gone from Guadalcanal to New Georgia. Here, the 43rd Infantry hits Rendova.

routes to Australia were safe, and the US Army had entered the Pacific war in force, the beginning of a commitment that would last for three more years and would involve the Army in dozens of major operations throughout the Pacific fighting area.

New Guinea and the Solomons Ladder

While the Japanese were being expelled from the lower Solomons, Australia, aided by ground and air units of the US Army, was fighting desperately to halt the spread of Japanese power in New Guinea. In July 1942 Japanese troops had begun landing on the northern coast of Papua, the easternmost part of New Guinea, near the small mission station at Gona. Their objective was to cross the Owen Stanley mountain range, rising in places to 13,000 feet, and to take the town of Port Moresby on the southern shore. With Port Moresby in hand, they could attack Australia, only 300 miles away across the Torres Strait. The Japanese had tried to take

Long before the island had been fully secured, Seabees were building vital landing strips on Bougainville.

high command's decision to retreat. He began to lead his weary and despondent men back across Papua to the northern shore, pursued all the way by the 7th Australian Division.

Once back on the northern shore, the Japanese turned to meet their pursuers in the Buna-Gona area. The US Army dispatched units of the 32nd Infantry Division, transported by the Fifth Air Force, to small fields in the Buna area. While the 7th Australians advanced on nearby Gona, the Americans began their attacks on the well-emplaced Japanese at Buna on 19 November 1942. When they failed to break through, General MacArthur, on 30 November, named newly-promoted Lieutenant General Robert L Eichelberger to command the American troops at Buna. His final words to Eichelberger reflected his determination: 'I want you to take Buna, or do not come back alive.'

General Eichelberger whipped the disheartened American troops into shape and launched a devastating attack on 5 December. This, coupled with spectacular Australian victories at Gona, had the Japanese in retreat by Christmas, and by 22 January the Japanese had been driven out of Papua. The cost had been high: 3000 men had been killed and 5400 wounded.

The Buna-Gona victories coincided with the defeat of another Japanese drive, this time from Lae and Salamaua, in Northeast

New Guinea, toward Port Moresby (a defeat in which the Fifth Air Force played a major role by bringing in reinforcements to the Australians at the mountaintop airstrip at Wau to stop the Japanese drive). Together, the Allied forces had managed one of the most significant triumphs of the Pacific war. But at the end of the bloody fighting, MacArthur pledged 'No more Bunas.' He kept his word.

After the successes of Guadalcanal and Papua, jubilant American strategists began to think in terms of mounting major offensive campaigns. MacArthur wanted to drive up New Guinea, through the Philippines, and on to the Japanese home islands. The Navy wanted to storm across the central Pacific, conquering islands and building airbases and anchorages as they went, until Japan was within bomber and carrier-based aircraft range. The outcome of this high-level strategic argument was that the Joint Chiefs of Staff decided on a compromise, a giant two-pronged movement toward Japan. MacArthur would advance toward the Philippines along the island chains in the southwest Pacific, while the Navy, assisted by the Army and Marines, would fight its way across the Pacific from the east.

The two giant pincers would converge on the Philippines, although a decision was deferred on whether to liberate the Philippines or bypass them. In any event, both the Army and the Navy now had clear mandates for action, and by the spring of 1943 they were on the move. For the Army the first part of the job meant clearing New Guinea and moving

'up the Solomons ladder' toward the great Japanese base at Rabaul on New Britain, a task that would require the cooperation of both the Navy and the Marines. It would take longer than anyone then realized.

The plan was that MacArthur's forces would clear the Huon Peninsula, including the Japanese base at Lae, in Northeast New Guinea, and then move across the Vitiaz and Dampier Straits to land on the western end of New Britain Island. Rabaul was on the eastern end of the island. Meanwhile, Halsey's forces would move up through the Solomons, with Rabaul also as their target. On 30 June 1943 elements of the 41st Infantry Division landed 60 miles below Lae at Nassau Bay. They soon joined with Australian troops (which had crossed the mountains) and moved toward Lae. On that same day 5000 troops of Lieutenant General Walter Krueger's Sixth Army took the undefended islands of Kiriwina and Woodlark in the Trobriand Islands east of New Guinea, and both were soon equipped with airstrips.

On New Guinea the American and Australian troops advanced toward Lae during July and August. Then, in September, an amphibious landing was made by the Australians 20 miles east of Lae, while the Army's 503rd Airborne Regiment parachuted in 20 miles west of the city (the Fifth Air Force dropping 1,700 paratroopers in one minute). Although the Japanese were ordered to evacuate the base at Lae, 9000 withdrew into the mountains, and it took the American-Australian force until the end of the year to complete the capture of the Huon Peninsula.

On 15 December 1943 soldiers of the 112th Cavalry Regiment finally crossed the Vitiaz and Dampier Straits and landed at Arawe on New Britain. MacArthur and the Army were now less than 300 miles from Rabaul. On 25 December MacArthur sent the 1st Marine Division, the Guadalcanal veterans, to take Cape Gloucester, on the western tip of New Britain, which they did after three weeks of fighting. MacArthur, with the Straits securely in American hands, now had gained clear naval passage west and north.

In the meantime Halsey's forces were moving up the Solomons toward Rabaul, in the process undergoing some of the roughest fighting of the Pacific campaign. The islands of New Georgia, Kolombangara, and Bougainville were considered the primary steps up the Solomons ladder, but no one realized how costly seizing these steps would be. In Halsey's assault on New Georgia, Marines were landed on the night of 20 June 1943 at Segi Point. Their object was to make their way behind crucial Viru Harbor by D-Day, 30 June, but the jungle delayed them, and they arrived too late. Similarly, the assault troops that landed on the island of Rendova, across from Munda Point on New Georgia, to set up artillery cover also found

the jungle and mud too much to handle. It took four days for them to set up their 155mm guns and commence firing on their objective, the Japanese airfield on Munda. By that time, the troops of the 43rd Infantry Division had already landed on New Georgia itself, but they too soon became bogged down by the jungle morass and met fierce Japanese resistance. An American all-out attack on Munda, launched on 9 July, failed completely. Thoroughly frustrated, Halsey removed the commander of the Munda operation and sent in the 37th and 25th Divisions to help out, but not until 5 August were the determined Japanese defenders blasted from their well-prepared jungle entrenchments and the airfield taken. Some 10,000 Japanese had held off 40,000 Americans for five weeks.

Fearful that an attack on Kolombangara, with its 10,000 defenders, would result in another such blood bath, Halsey decided to bypass the island and take nearby Vella Lavella instead. The American landing on Vella Lavella on 15 August 1943 met with almost no opposition, Kolombangara was neutralized and the Americans had learned, almost by accident, the tactic of leapfrogging.

Bougainville, only 250 miles from Rabaul

by air, still remained, and it could not be bypassed. It had six airfields and was defended by 40,000 well-seasoned veterans of the China wars. Yet Halsey was able to throw the Japanese somewhat off balance at first. He sent the 2nd Marine Parachute Battalion to take the island of Choiseul, southeast of Bougainville, on the night of 27 October, for a while convincing the Japanese that it was the site of the major landing. He also fooled the enemy completely by making his main landings at Cape Torokina, on the western coast of the 125-mile-long island, rather than at Buin, on the southern part of the island, where the Japanese had major installations. But on Bougainville, as on the other islands, Japanese resistance was furious. The 3rd Marine Division and the Army's 37th Division were quickly subjected to the kind of bloody combat their fellow soldiers had experienced before them on New Georgia. Although the Americans were able to establish a perimeter at Cape Torokina, the Japanese counterattacked to drive them back into the water, and the battle raged for 17 days be-

An artist's impression of the landing on Bougainville, the start of one of the bitterest of the Solomons' battles.

fore the Japanese were driven off. Protracted fighting followed. In fact, Bougainville was not fully secured until April 1944, by which time the Japanese had lost 7000 dead, the Americans 1000.

But long before the fighting ended, the Americans had built three airfields on Bougainville, and from them the airmen could both strike at Rabaul and support MacArthur's move across the Vitiaz and Dampier Straits to New Britain on 15 December 1943. Then, with Rabaul at last within easy striking distance of land-based and carrier-based planes, the decision was made simply to bypass it. It had been effectively neutralized as a naval, air, and land staging area, and MacArthur was free to resume his advance on the Philippines.

Across the Pacific

The first objectives in the Navy's central Pacific offensive were the Gilbert Islands, over 1500 miles southwest of Hawaii and 500 miles southeast of the Marshall Islands. The two main targets in the Gilberts were Makin Atoll, to the north, and Tarawa Atoll, 100 miles to the south. The taking of Makin was assigned to the Army; the Marines were to seize Tarawa.

There were only 300 soldiers and 400 laborers on Makin. Assaulting them would be the 165th Regimental Combat Team of the 27th Infantry Division, a contingent of 6500 men. But the expected one-day fight beginning on 20 November 1943 (as the battle for Bougainville was raging in the Solomons), took four days, as radio equipment failed and men and artillery were misused by the undertrained troops. The overall landing commander, Marine Major General Holland M ('Howlin' Mad') Smith, was contemptuous of the slow action of the 27th Division (which had a 20-to-1 advantage in numbers over the enemy) and said so. But Smith soon found that he had greater problems on his hands when the Marines attacked tiny Betio, in the Tarawa Atoll to the South.

The attack on Betio, the first Marine amphibious assault in the central Pacific, turned into a bloodbath. It took three days of furious fighting to dig out the Japanese from an island of less than half a square mile in area. The defenders had been virtually untouched by pre-invasion naval and air bombardment, and now they held to their defensive blockhouses, pillboxes, and caves to their deaths, taking a grisly toll of Marines in the process. By the time the fighting was over 4700 Japanese troops and laborers had died in their places. Over 1000 Marines were dead, and some 2200 had been wounded. But at least some valuable lessons were learned at Tarawa, such as the need for more reliable radio equipment and secure communications command vessels, for high-trajectory

The Gilberts were the first target of the Central Pacific offensive. Army troops had some trouble taking Makin (*above*), but nothing like the bloodbath that faced the Marines on Tarawa (*right*).

artillery rounds that gave greater penetration of emplacements, and for amtracs (armored amphibian tractors with propellers and caterpillar tracks) to replace the flimsy Higgins assault boats that often could not cross coral reefs. Such lessons would serve both the Marines and the Army well as they drove across the central Pacific. Amphibious warfare would, in their hands, reach unimagined levels of tactical sophistication.

On 1 February 1944 Kwajalein Atoll came under US attack. At the northern end of the atoll the 4th Marine Division assaulted and secured the islands of Roi and Namur, giving them control of the Japanese airbase there. Meanwhile, the Army's 7th Division took Kwajalein Island. Neither assault met much resistance, and few Americans died.

With barely a pause, Admiral Nimitz ordered Rear Admiral Marc A Mitscher's fast carrier task force's planes to attack the major naval base at Truk, 1100 miles west. They responded with a pounding of Truk that netted over 40 ships sunk and 200 planes destroyed on the ground. This left Nimitz's forces free to take Eniwetok Island, in the western Marshalls, 380 miles beyond Kwajalein, without harassment. The job of taking Eniwetok and nearby Engebi and Parry Islands was given to the 106th Infantry

Left: Landing craft evolved steadily throughout the war. Here, LVTA-1s, small amphibian tanks with 37mm guns.
Below: The invasion of Saipan.

of the 27th Division and to the Marines of the 22nd Regiment. It took just one day of combat to seize these islands. Soon all of the Marshall Islands were either taken or bypassed, and the central Pacific drive rolled on toward the Marianas Islands, the final steppingstones to the Philippines.

The Marianas Islands lie 1500 miles east of Manila Bay. Once their main islands of Saipan, Tinian, and Guam were taken, the Americans could cut Japanese supply lines to the south, isolate Truk to the southeast, and build airfields from which to bomb the Japanese home islands with the new long-range Boeing B-29 Superfortresses. The Navy's Fifth Fleet, that had assembled for the attack on the Marianas, included over 600 ships. The Marines of the 2nd, 3rd, and 4th Divisions and the Army's 27th Division totaled over 127,000 men.

Nimitz scheduled the first attack for Saipan, in the middle of the island group. Invading to engage the 32,000 Japanese soldiers and naval troops on the island would be the 2nd and 4th Marine Division. On 15 June 1944 the Marines launched their attacks on Saipan and were able to establish a beachhead, despite furious Japanese opposition and counterattacks. To try to save the defenders, the Japanese First Mobile Fleet and Southern Fleet sailed out of bases in the southwest Pacific to take on the American Fifth Fleet in a decisive battle to save the Marianas. The Japanese fleets contained much of what was left of the once-great Imperial Fleet. The result of this major Japanese naval sortie was the two-day Battle of the Philippine Sea, 19-20 June, in which Mitscher's Task Force 58 decimated the First Mobile Fleet and destroyed its air power in what the Americans called 'The Great Marianas Turkey Shoot.'

In the meantime the advance up the island of Saipan from the southern landing points was bogging down. 'Howlin' Mad' Smith put the blame on the Army's 27th Division, in the center of the northward-thrusting American line, the same unit he had previously castigated for its slowness on Makin. This time 'Howlin' Mad' demanded and got the relief of the 27th Division's commander, Major General Ralph Smith. The 27th thereafter began to advance, but on the morning of 7 July had to face the most furious *banzai* attack of the war. Some 3000 Japanese, drunk with *sake* and faithful to their commander's wish that they follow him in death, charged the American lines at Tanapag Harbor. The death-seeking Japanese were stopped only by furious hand-to-hand fighting and 105mm howitzers fired into their ranks at point-blank range. When Saipan was finally declared secure on 9 July 1944, over 16,000 Americans had been killed or wounded. The Japanese dead numbered 29,000.

On 24 July nearby Tinian was invaded by 15,000 Marines. It fell within a week. In the meantime Guam, to the south, had been invaded by elements of the 3rd Marine Division, the 1st Provisional Marine Brigade and the Army's 77th Division. It took two weeks of hard fighting and the death of 3500 Japanese troops before the island fell.

With the Marianas now in American hands, the Philippines seemed the next logical target. But Nimitz insisted, over Halsey's protests, that the Palau Islands in the western Carolines be taken to protect his southern flank. The result was disastrous for the 1st Marine Division, given the task of invading the island of Peleliu, the largest island in the chain, on 15 September 1944.

The Japanese were absolutely determined to hold Peleliu, and the 6500 seasoned soldiers on the island were instructed that they were to fight from prepared positions to the last man, taking as many Marines with them as they could. They carried out their orders to the letter, and after six days of bitter fighting still controlled much of the island, despite the heroic efforts of the Marines to drive them from their positions. At this point the Army's 321st Regimental Combat Team of the 81st Infantry Division was sent in. More savage fighting followed, but the Japanese could not be dislodged, even though by the end of October only 700 Japanese remained alive. By then the Marines had suffered so many casualties they could fight no more. The 81st Division took over, and the gallant 1st Marine Division was pulled out.

Slowly and carefully the 81st reduced the remaining Japanese positions, and within a month the battle had been won. But the battle for Peleliu cost the Americans over 1200 Marines and about 275 soldiers dead and over 6000 of both services wounded. Whatever the justification for the decision to invade Peleliu, unlike the similar blood bath of Tarawa ten months before, this time few Americans at home took note of the carnage. All eyes were now riveted on the action in the Philippines. True to his promise, MacArthur had returned. The road that he had traveled had been strewn with difficulties. He had negotiated it with genius.

Victory in New Guinea

While the great right arm of the American Pacific strategy was moving across the central Pacific, MacArthur, in the southwest Pacific, had taken Papua New Guinea, including much of the Huon Peninsula west of Buna-Gona, and was in the process of neutralizing Rabaul by his landings on the western end of New Britain Island. But the remainder of New Guinea remained a Japanese stronghold, and it had to be taken. MacArthur had to get at least to Hollandia, halfway up the coast, before he would have a jump-off point for the island of Mindanao in the southern Philippines. Accordingly, as the Australian troops moved west on an inland route through New Guinea, MacArthur and the US Army moved along the north coast in a simultaneous paralleling movement.

He first sent the 126th Regimental Combat Team of the 32nd Division to assault the town of Saidor in order to trap a major Japanese troop concentration between his troops and the Australians. This failed, and many of the enemy got away to Madang, up the coast, but MacArthur, in a surprise move in February 1944, sent his army to take the Admiralty

Japan. They were also to take Okinawa and other islands in the Ryukyu Island chain, less than 400 miles from the Japanese homeland. The altered two-prong strategy, if successful, would ring Japan with air and sea power preparatory to an invasion of the home islands in 1945.

The Philippines

Four American Army divisions, under Lieutenant General Walter Krueger, commander of the Sixth Army, hit the beaches on Leyte, in the central Philippines, on 20 October 1944. Air cover was provided by General Kenney's Fifth Air Force and by naval task forces under Admiral Halsey. The Japanese reacted quickly to the invasion, fearing that the entire archipelago would be lost if Leyte fell to the Americans. Ground and air units were hurried to Leyte, while the Japanese mustered their last naval units to destroy the invasion fleet off the invasion beaches. In the ensuing Battle of Leyte Gulf

A wounded Marine on Peleliu, site of a bloody battle in which nearly 1200 Marines and 275 Army soldiers died.

Islands, to the north. This gave him air bases from which to launch the Fifth Air Force against the Japanese stronghold at Madang. After Madang had been duly bombed, MacArthur launched his land attack. Led by the 1st Cavalry Division (Armored), the attack succeeded, despite fierce Japanese resistance. The Japanese commander moved his forces west to prepare himself for MacArthur's next move up the coast. He assumed the new targets would be Hansa Bay and Wewak.

But MacArthur had other plans: he would bypass these intermediate points and strike directly at Hollandia, 500 miles up the coast. With invaluable aid from General Kenney's Fifth Air Force, which neutralized Japanese air power in the target area, and with the Navy's Task Force 58 standing by, Hollandia was invaded on 22 April 1944 and taken with little trouble. The 1st Division, the 24th Division, and the 163rd Regimental Combat Team made up the force that landed in three locations in the Hollandia area.

Although 55,000 Japanese of the Eighteenth Army were still between himself, at Hollandia, and the pursuing Australians, MacArthur did not hesitate to move west from Hollandia towards the Vogelkop Peninsula, at the far west end of New Guinea. Along the way he was obliged to fight many battles, and resistance was often savage, as on the island of Biak in Geelvink Bay, just east of the Vogelkop Peninsula, where 11,000 Japanese troops fought ferociously until late July. Meanwhile, MacArthur had convinced President Roosevelt that the left flank of the American advance in the Pacific – his flank – should now move on to Mindanao, then to Leyte, in the central Philippines, and finally to Luzon, in the north of the archipelago. MacArthur thus prevailed over the Navy's

preference for bypassing the Philippines and striking for Formosa instead.

But first something still had to be done about the Japanese Eighteenth Army and other scattered units which remained in New Guinea. The Eighteenth Army had launched an attack on the 32nd Division, the 124th Regimental Combat Team, the 31st Division, and the 112th Cavalry Regimental Combat Team at Aitape. The intention was to dilute American strength and halt the Army's outward thrust toward the Philippines. The assault started on 10 July and ended only on 9 August. In that one month, 10,000 Japanese were lost, against an American toll of 400 dead and 25,000 wounded. Completely decimated and exhausted by their futile efforts, the remainder of the Japanese force fled back toward Wewak and then into the New Guinea mountains. At the end of the war what remained of this Japanese army finally surrendered to the Australians.

With New Guinea under effective control as of late July 1944, MacArthur turned north toward Mindanao. In early September, as MacArthur's forces were preparing to attack Morotai, in the Moluccas, so as to protect the left flank of his route north to Mindanao, the general received a message from Admiral Halsey, whose Third Fleet was already carrying out air attacks on the Philippines. The central part of the archipelago was wide open, said Halsey, and he had urged the Joint Chiefs to change the Pacific strategy to bypass Mindanao and strike directly at Leyte. Nimitz and the Joint Chiefs, then meeting with Roosevelt and Churchill, agreed. MacArthur was given the green light to invade Leyte.

The decision to liberate the Philippines also entailed an important shift in the central Pacific strategy. Nimitz' forces, having advanced over 4500 miles from Hawaii to the Palaus in ten months of fighting, were now to veer north to strike the Bonin Islands and seize Iwo Jima as a fighter base to protect the bombers flying out of the Marianas against

(23-25 October) the Japanese decoyed Halsey's main force far off to the north of the Philippines, while sending two sizeable squadrons through straits in the central and southern parts of the islands to converge at Leyte Gulf and destroy the invading Americans. But for the gallantry of the sailors on the relatively few fighting ships left behind at Leyte Gulf, the beachhead on Leyte might well have been lost and the Army units isolated. In fact, the Japanese Navy accomplished nothing at Leyte Gulf but its own destruction.

On Leyte itself the reinforced Japanese continued to hold out and slowed the American drive to a crawl until December, when the 77th Division made a surprise landing on Leyte's west coast. This effectively broke the

MacArthur's strategy was almost as dependent on amphibious operations as was Halsey's.
Right: MacArthur inspects the beach after his landing in Dutch Borneo.
Below: US troops pouring out of an LST to invade Middleburg Is.

stalemated war, although some Japanese units held out for several more months. In the meantime MacArthur and the Army were moving onto the main island of Luzon. After seizing a supporting airfield in December, four divisions landed on Lingayen Gulf, north of Manila, on 9 January 1945. MacArthur's forces on Luzon quickly built to more than five divisions in a matter of days. He then began his move down the Central Plains toward Manila. Many of the intervening Japanese forces fled to the mountains, but 20,000 Japanese naval and army service troops decided to fight it out in Manila. This resulted in a month-long campaign that left the city virtually destroyed and 100,000 civilians dead, many executed by the Japanese.

Meanwhile, the 503rd Parachute Infantry struck to retake Corregidor, the 38th Division landed near Subic Bay to secure the Bataan Peninsula, and the 11th Airborne hit southern Luzon. As the Japanese moved into the

Left: Generals MacArthur and Horace Fuller viewing damage done by naval gunfire to a Japanese supply dump at Hollandia, New Guinea. MacArthur used naval support brilliantly
Below: The invasion of Leyte.

An LST with landing pontoons lashed to her side heading for Okinawa, the costliest island battle of the war.

mountains, MacArthur continued to pour in reinforcements. Eventually 11 divisions, three regimental combat teams, and thousands of Filipino guerrillas were used against the Japanese in this, the largest land war in the Pacific theater. Japanese resistance in most areas of Luzon had ended by June 1945, after General Eichelberger's new Eighth Army had taken over from General Krueger's exhausted Sixth Army. At war's end, some 50,000 Japanese were still holding out in Luzon's mountains.

With the American Army in full control of the Philippines, and the Navy in full control of the surrounding seas, the fate of Japan was effectively sealed. Yet a good deal of blood remained to be spilled before the war in the Pacific finally came to an end.

Iwo Jima and Okinawa

Iwo Jima, in the Bonin Islands, 660 miles southeast of Tokyo, was the key to supplying fighter protection to the B-29s attacking the Japanese home islands. The task of taking the island was assigned to the 70,000 Marines of the 4th and 5th Divisions. They launched their attacks on 19 February 1945, reinforced by the 3rd Marine Division, and ran into fanatical Japanese resistance. A month of hard fighting was required before the tiny eight-square-mile island was secured. About 6800 Americans were killed on Iwo Jima. Almost all of the 22,000 Japanese defenders died in the savage fighting.

A landing by the 77th Division was made on the Kerama Islands, off Okinawa, on 26 March. The main amphibious assaults on crucial Okinawa were made on Easter Sunday, 1 April 1945. The Army's 7th and 96th Divisions and the Marines' 2nd and 6th Divisions made the initial landings. Overall command was in the hands of the Tenth Army commander, Lieutenant General Simon B Buckner. To the surprise of the American forces, the defending 130,000-man Japanese Thirty-second Army made no effort to impede their landings. Instead, the Japanese pulled back into entrenched positions in the hills, where they fought the Army and Marine units almost to a standstill, especially on the southern part of the island. Meanwhile, Japanese aircraft subjected the Navy to *kamikaze* attacks that resulted in the sinking of 25 ships and the damaging of more than 150. Ashore, the Japanese held out along the Shuri Line and on the Oroku Peninsula, until finally withdrawing for a last stand on the Kiyamu Peninsula, on the southern tip of the island. The soldiers and Marines pursued them over the craggy surfaces of southern Okinawa, blasting and burning the Japanese out of their caves and entrenched positions, until the enemy finally surrendered on 22 June. In 83 days the Japanese had lost at least 110,000 men killed; the Army and Marines, over 7600 killed and 31,807 wounded. *Kamikaze* and other air attacks had accounted for an additional 4300 naval personnel dead and another 7000 wounded.

The combatants on both sides now knew what the next steps would be: stepped up aerial bombing, followed by an invasion of the home islands. For this, bloodily-won Okinawa would be the staging area.

The Pacific Air War

American air power in the Pacific was roughly handled by the Japanese in the opening days of the war. Of the 231 USAAF aircraft

Nearly 6800 Marines died on Iwo Jima to give B-29s a forward base.

based on Oahu on 7 December 1941, 97 were destroyed and 88 were heavily damaged. On the same day the Navy lost 80 aircraft, 50 percent of its total in Hawaii. The situation was even worse in the Philippines: Major General Lewis H Brereton's 249-plane Far Eastern Air Force lost 67 percent of its aircraft in the first hours of the Japanese attack on 8 December, and by Christmas FEAF had virtually ceased to exist.

Almost as dismaying as the devastation itself was what America was learning about the calibre of the Japanese Army and Navy air arms. Far from being composed of the second-rate pilots and third-rate planes attributed to them by most western 'experts' before the war, they proved to be equipped with large numbers of formidably modern aircraft flown by battle-tested veterans. The single Japanese warplane that best symbolized this unpleasant reality was the Imperial Navy's Mitsubishi A6M Zero, which was not only revealed to be the most advanced carrier-based fighter in the world, but seemed likely to prove technically superior to most of the USAAF's land-based fighters, as well. And there were several other Japanese types which were, in their own combat categories, almost as impressive as the Zero. Thus America and her allies entered the Pacific air war in a state of such quantitative and qualitative inferiority that none could predict when the tables might be turned.

By the beginning of 1942 the Army had only two significant concentrations of air power left in the Pacific: the Hawaiian Air Force, still trying to recover from the damage it had sustained during the Pearl Harbor attack, and a motley collection of bomber and fighter squadrons that was being hastily

Right: The Luzon campaign.
Below: US cruisers shell Bataan and Corregidor.

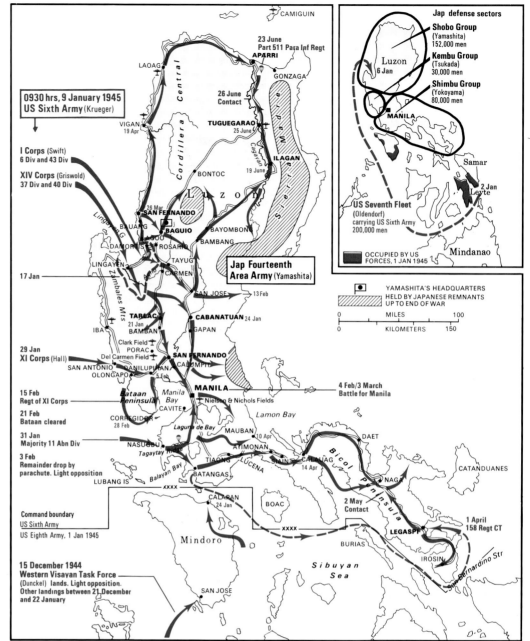

assembled in Australia to help meet the looming threat of Japanese invasion. On 2 February the Hawaiian group was redesignated the Seventh Air Force. In time it would become the principal Army air component of the right half (*ie.* the Central Pacific wing) of America's vast two-pronged offensive against Japan. Similarly, the Australian group, which would be christened the Fifth Air Force in September, would become MacArthur's principal air weapon in the left-hand wing of the great offensive.

It was General Kenney's Fifth that was to see the most combat. When it was activated in the autumn of 1942 it had only 75 operational fighters and 80 bombers, and these were already engaged in a precarious struggle for supremacy in the New Guinea skies with what was then perhaps Japanese military aviation's most elite formation, the daunting Lae Air Wing. Despite heavy casualties the Fifth survived this trial by fire and was able subsequently to give valuable support to US and Australian troops in their successful Buna-Gona campaign. By the end of the year the Fifth had established a major airbase on New Guinea (at Dobodura) and its

The Bell P-400 was no match for the brilliant Mitsubishi A6M Zero (*below*).

B-17s and B-24s were making regular raids on the big Japanese base at Rabaul, a bombing campaign that would continue with mounting intensity for the next 12 months until Rabaul ceased to be a significant factor in the prosecution of the war. Simultaneously, throughout 1943 and 1944 the Fifth gave often crucial close support to MacArthur's ground forces as they leap-frogged their way to victory along New Guinea's north coast.

In aerial combat the Fifth also made steady progress in overcoming the qualitative deficiencies that had plagued it at the outset. Pilots and aircrews, now highly proficient veterans, devised new tactics to offset the technical limitations of their equipment. To be sure, some hopelessly outclassed machines, such as the Bell P-39s and the Douglas A-24s, had to be withdrawn, but the marginal inferiorities of other types were gradually dissipated through incremental technical improvements and ever more refined tactical employment. The case of the Lockheed P-38 is perhaps the most striking example of what improved tactics could accomplish. This ponderous twin-engine fighter was plainly no match for the agile Japanese fighters in dogfights, but it could at least operate at significantly higher altitudes. This single advantage permitted the P-38 pilots to perfect a spectacularly successful 'bounce' tactic, in which the American fighters would come down on their enemies in thunderous power dives, make single firing passes, and then, using the great speed accumulated in the dives, zoom back up to the safety of altitudes where the Japanese could not follow. In time the Fifth would receive fighters much superior both to the P-38 and the Zero, but the fact remains that the Fifth's two highest-scoring aces – indeed, the highest-scoring aces in American history – Major Richard Bong and Major Thomas McGuire, made most of their kills in P-38s.

Quantity eventually came to favor the Fifth (as it did all US air forces) as much as quality. By early 1944 it comprised 803 fighters, 780 medium and heavy bombers, and 328 transports, a ten-fold increase over its inventory eighteen months earlier. By the end of 1944 this massive force was ashore on Leyte, and six months later it was joining the Seventh and other Pacific air forces on Okinawa and Ie Shima in the Bonin Islands in preparation for the final assault on Japan.

The route by which the Seventh Air Force had come to the Bonins was somewhat more circuitous. Obliged to follow the island-hopping course of the central Pacific arm of America's two-pronged grand strategy in the Pacific, the Seventh was constantly on the move and sometimes widely dispersed. The roster of its various bases – among others, Midway, Espiritu Santo, Guadalcanal, Makin, Kwajalein, Iwo Jima, and Okinawa – reads like a capsule history of the Central Pacific campaign itself. Since the Seventh was smaller than the Fifth, and less continuously engaged with the enemy, its contribution to victory is not so easily expressed in raw statistics. Yet in strategic terms, that contribution was considerable.

There were other US Army air forces active in the Pacific, as well. The Tenth and Fourteenth Air Forces, operating in the China-Burma-India theater, may not have played major parts in America's grand offensive strategy but made important contributions to the crucial campaigns being fought by her British and Chinese allies on the Pacific's Asian perimeter. The Thirteenth Air Force wrote some glorious chapters in the history of the bitter air war over the Solomons before joining forces with the Fifth in the battle for the Philippines. Finally, there was the new XXI Bomber Command, already in place in the Marianas even before the Fifth and Seventh finally converged in the Bonins in the late spring of 1945. To the XXIst would

go both the honor of ending World War II and the onus of ushering in the awesome new age of the atom.

The End of the Pacific War

During the summer of 1945 the 1000 Boeing B-29 Superfortresses of XXI Bomber Command (which was made part of the Twentieth Air Force in July) conducted almost daily raids on the cities of Japan from the Marianas, Okinawa, and Iwo Jima, aided by carrier-based planes from the American and British Pacific Fleets. Simultaneously American planes, surface ships, and submarines shut down any outside help for the beleaguered Japanese in the home islands. Already plans were being made for the invasion of Japan itself. Now that the war had ended in Europe, all of the Allied might could and would be applied for this most massive invasion in world history. Casualties on the Allied side were estimated to reach 1.5 million, and on the Japanese side, up to 10 million military and civilian, ten percent of the population. All expectations were that the Japanese would display even more fanaticism in protecting their home islands than they had shown in defending their Pacific possessions, for their 'Ketsu-Go' ('Decisive Battle') home defense plan was designed to cause such high Allied casualties as to induce the Americans to give up the fight and go home.

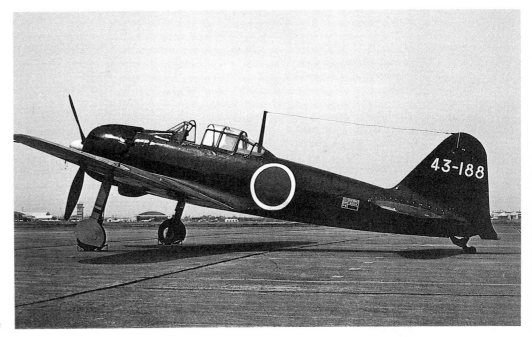

Left: The greatest US Pacific aces flew Lockheed P-38s, yet the plane's European record was only mediocre.
Below: US air power alone neutralized Japan's giant naval base at Rabaul.

how many more weapons of this type America had at its disposal, asked for peace. Japan formally accepted the Allied terms on 14 August 1945.

With the signing of the surrender terms on board the US battleship *Missouri* in Tokyo Bay on 2 September the Pacific war came to an end. As in the European phase of the war, the US Army, cooperating with its American sister services and those of the Allied nations, had brought a stubborn foe to its knees at a terrible cost in blood. Some 235,000 Army personnel had lost their lives in the war effort in the European and Pacific theaters. But victory had been won, and now it was time to look to a world without war.

Over 193,000 men of the Sixth Army, including seven Army and three Marine divisions, were set to strike the southernmost Japanese home island of Kyushu on 1 November 1945 in Operation OLYMPIC. Some 457,000 men would follow. They would be backed by the Fifth Fleet, with 3033 vessels (even more than at Normandy) and 2000 carrier-based planes. Some 6000 land-based planes would also participate in the operation. On 1 March 1946 the US Eighth and First Armies, with 14 divisions, would land on the main island of Honshu in the Yokohama-Tokyo area as part of Operation CORONET. It was estimated that Japanese resisistance would end only after many months of shocking bloodshed.

All plans for invasion were cut short when, on 6 August 1945, a Twentieth Air Force B-29 dropped an atomic bomb on the city of Hiroshima. Despite the weapon's unprecedented destructive power, the Japanese government refused to surrender. Two days later the Russians declared war on Japan and invaded Manchuria. On 9 August a second B-29 dropped an atomic bomb on the city of Nagasaki. Although the Japanese still had over two million men (including seven regular divisions and seven reserve divisions) under arms and willing to defend their homeland, plus 10,500 operational aircraft (5000 to be used in *kamikaze* attacks), the devastation wrought by the atomic bombs was so great that the Japanese government, not knowing

Top: From first to last the workhorse USAAF fighter in the Pacific was the Curtiss P-40. Here, a P-40 M Warhawk.
Right: Nagasaki, 9 August 1945.

Top: Kobe, 1946. Even before Hiroshima,
conventional bombing had lain waste many
Japanese cities.
Below: History's most famous bomber.

Korea, 1950: Four M26 tanks firing on a Communist
observation post.

COLD WAR AND GLOBAL COMMITMENT: 1945-1985

Peace had returned in 1945 with the defeat of Germany and Japan, but the world had changed significantly. Most of Europe's major powers had been brought close to prostration by the bloodletting of the war. Elsewhere in the world, people who had been living under European political and economic domination for decades or centuries were eager to take advantage of their masters' exhausted condition to demand more freedom, if not outright independence. Moreover, the destruction of the short-lived German and Japanese empires had left power vacuums in western Europe and in the Far East that must, in the nature of things, somehow be filled.

In America, a vague fear, waiting only to be confirmed, began to arise that the Russian Communists, now victoriously standing astride eastern and central Europe, would surely seize the moment to ensnare millions of people in their expanding power network. True, the United Nations, with its emphasis on peaceful solutions to future quarrels between nations, had been created in San Francisco, but few Americans were willing to put their complete trust in an organization that looked so suspiciously like the old League of Nations. Furthermore, the United Nations included as a signatory peace-keeper the Soviet Union, a nation that had given ample evidence in word and deed that its commitment to peace might be less than total.

Perhaps it would all work out, but the United States would have to keep its guard up and learn to live with the fact that America had inherited the mantle of protector of freedom in the postwar world. Few realized how high the price would be for playing that role.

Demobilization and Readjustment

Whatever the state of the world, it was widely expected that the GIs of World War II would quickly be returned to their homes and families, now that the fighting had stopped. The Army devised a method of releasing individual troops on the basis of their length of service, time in combat, overseas deployments, and number of dependents. But the scheme was hardly in place before increasing public pressure forced the high command to release men even faster, so that by the end of 1945 half of its eight million men under arms had been separated. When the Army tried to slow down the return of troops from overseas early in 1946 in order to meet its worldwide commitments, the attempt was met by protests and demonstrations in all the former theaters of war. Quick release procedures were resumed, and another 25 percent were discharged by mid-1946.

Because President Harry Truman's budgets mandated a postwar Army strength of only one million men (instead of the four million the Army had planned on during the war), the Army cut the remainder of its draftees. By mid-1947 the Army counted only 680,000 ground troops and 300,000 airmen. It was all-volunteer and pared down for peacetime duty. The Navy and Marine Corps

suffered corresponding reductions in manpower, and little money was available for acquisition and maintenance of equipment in any of the services.

While the strength of the military was being curtailed, action was taken to bring unity to the nation's armed forces in both planning and operating. Under the provisions of the National Security Act of 1947, the Air Force was created as a co-equal service with the Army and the Navy. (The Navy retained control over the Marine Corps, despite the objections of the Army, which wanted responsibility for all ground troops.) The Act also created the National Security Council to co-ordinate and integrate national security policies. NSC members were the Secretary of State, the Secretary of Defense (a new position with cabinet rank), the secretaries of the three military branches, and other agency heads appointed by the President.

Harry S Truman, whose presidency saw the end of World War II and the dawn of the Cold War and the Atomic Age.

A second body created by the Act was the National Military Establishment. It was headed by the Secretary of Defense and included the secretaries of the services. Under the Secretary of Defense were the Joint Chiefs of Staff, represented by the military chiefs of the Army, Navy, and Air Force. The Joint Chiefs were charged with giving advice to the Secretary of Defense, the National Security Council and the President, not with running the services. Under the first Secretary of Defense, James V Forrestal, each branch was accorded its area of responsibility: the Army for land warfare; the Navy for sea and sea-based operations, plus the Marine Corps; and the Air Force for strategic air warfare, tactical air support for the Army, and air transportation. Area commands were

established throughout the world, wherein a single commander appointed by the Joint Chiefs of Staff would exercise coordinating control within that geographical region.

The National Security Act was amended in 1949 because it had left the Secretary of Defense with too little power to enforce co-operation in the federated military service system now established. The office was also weak because the three civilian secretaries of the services had direct access to the President, thus bypassing the Secretary of Defense. The amendments of 1949 strengthened the office of Secretary of Defense by converting the National Military Establish-

Even as Americans enjoyed such post-war pleasures as dancing to Rock 'n Roll (*below*) they were haunted by the looming spectre of the atom bomb (*left*).

The 1948 Soviet blockade of Berlin and the US airlift was one of the first of many Cold War confrontations.

Briton Klaus Fuchs was among several Soviet spies who helped to break the American monopoly of atomic secrets.

ment into the Department of Defense, with the Secretary of Defense holding full cabinet rank and the service secretaries clearly placed below him. The Army, Navy, and Air Force retained their autonomy, but were also plainly and directly under the Secretary of Defense. The Joint Chiefs of Staff (now with another member, in the person of a chairman without a vote) still held a somewhat amorphous position. The JCS was charged with co-ordinating military strategy and planning but had no responsibility for their being carried out. That responsibility lay with the Secretary of Defense, the three service secretaries, and the various chiefs of staff.

As part of this unification process, three interservice schools for senior officers were created to assure joint service planning and execution: the Armed Forces Staff College for planning, the Industrial College of the Armed Forces for mobilization of resources, and the National War College for execution of military plans. In these same years other important changes were also made. A new Uniform Code of Military Justice was enacted in 1950, and President Truman ordered all services to become racially integrated. All-black units ceased to exist in the Navy and in the Air Force in June 1950, and in the Army by 1954.

While unification and reorganization were proceeding apace in the five years after World War II, the size of the services (with the exception of the new Air Force, which seemed to promise more defense for less money with its atomic bombers ready to fly anywhere in the world) continued to decline, particularly after the advent of cost-conscious Secretary of Defense Louis A Johnson, who succeeded James Forrestal in 1949.

President Truman had, in 1945, called for UMT (universal military training) for one year for all young men in order to assure an adequate and trained military force, but the idea had died after years of acrimonious debate in Congress. The Army was, accordingly, forced to depend on the National Guard and the reserves to supplement its regulars, but restricted budgets held down the Guard to only 325,000 members in undertrained and underequipped units, and the reserves to only 186,000 men. And, under the budget-cutting axe, the Army found that by 1950 its regulars only amounted to 591,000 men and women, despite the continuing need for it to provide occupation forces in Germany, Japan, and Korea. The Navy and Marine Corps were similarly undermanned and underequipped, and even the Air Force, despite its favored status, faced serious deficiencies in planes and materiel. All of this erosion was still taking place, when the escalating Cold War finally spilled over into actual combat in Korea. Again peacetime neglect produced near-disastrous results.

Cold War, Containment, and Korea

Disputes over occupation forces and policies did not arise in Japan because of President Truman's insistence that Japan come under American occupation alone after the war, but situations in Germany and Korea foreshadowed inter-Allied tensions that eventually led to open hostility. The American, French, and British zones of occupation in western Germany and in the capital of Berlin, far inside the Soviet occupation zone in eastern Germany, experienced swift disarmament and restoration of German rule under Allied tutelage. In eastern Germany, however, the Soviet Union steadfastly erected barriers to reunification of the entire country by its insistence upon Soviet domi-

nation of the eastern section of the nation, which it ruled as a client state. After Russia's failure to oust the Western powers from Berlin by a blockade of the city in 1948-49 – a blockade broken by an Allied airlift of food and supplies for the people of Berlin – there emerged two separate and distinct German states, the German Federal Republic, made up of the Western zones of occupation, and the German Democratic Republic, a Soviet-dominated Communist regime in the east.

Lack of Soviet co-operation also prevented reunification of the peninsula of Korea after its Japanese conquerors had been removed in 1945. The Russians moved onto the peninsula north of the 38th parallel as a temporary zone of occupation, while American soldiers from Okinawa moved in south of that line. Despite wartime agreements that Korea would be reunited and free, meetings in late 1945 revealed that the Soviets saw the 38th parallel as more than just a temporary boundary between occupation zones. In fact they would not agree to a reunited Korea unless the initial interim government was Communist-dominated. As a result, the 38th parallel developed into a *de facto* boundary between a Communist-dominated North Korean government and a pro-Western South Korean government.

These disputes in Germany and Korea over occupation policies gave clear warning that the Soviets viewed occupation as a means of aggrandizement and control. They helped to initiate a broadening postwar confrontation between Soviet and Western blocs that hardened into a semi-permanent Cold War.

Western fears of Soviet aggressive intentions in the aftermath of the war seemed con-

Above: The US suffered what was then seen as a Cold War defeat when Mao Tse-tung's Communist Party came to power in mainland China.

Sensational spy trials such as that of the Rosebergs (*left*) fostered the anti-Communist demagoguery of men like Joseph McCarthy (*top left*).

firmed by Soviet policy in eastern Europe. Here, one state after another was drawn behind what Winston Churchill called the 'Iron curtain' in a celebrated speech at Fulton, Missouri, in 1946. And it soon became clear that Russia and her 'satellites,' as the dominated central and eastern European countries came to be called, were playing a leading part in attempting to bring Greece into the Soviet orbit via a civil war. Russia was also supporting Mao Tse-tung in his attempts to overthrow the pro-Western government of Chiang Kai-shek in China. The American response to Communist aggrandizement was a policy of 'containment,' i.e., helping friendly governments resist encroachments on their sovereignty by the Soviet Union or other Communist states.

Containment assumed an economic stance in 1947 when Congress, at the urging of President Truman, put up $400 million in aid to Greece and Turkey to assist these two countries in their fight against Communist incursions. This trail-blazing step soon became known as the 'Truman Doctrine' and, since it was couched in terms of helping free people throughout the world resist outside forces, placed the United States squarely in opposition to Soviet and Communist expansionism. The next year the principle was specifically extended to Europe, when the United States adopted the Marshall Plan, whereby $16 billion was funneled to Europe to help the Western democracies get back on their feet economically to resist Com-

The formidable T-34/85 tank was one of the modern weapons the Soviets had supplied to their North Korean ally.

munist encroachments. Congress finally became convinced of the necessity of such aid when the Soviet Union staged a coup and overthrew the government of Czechoslovakia, putting a Communist government in its place in April 1948.

The year 1948 also saw a permanent division of Korea when the Soviet Union refused to allow free elections in the country to establish a unitary government, even though the elections would be supervised by the United Nations. Accordingly, the UN held an election in South Korea later that year and established the Republic of Korea in the south. The Soviet Union, in turn, established a Com-

munist government in the north, the Democratic People's Republic, and the temporary occupation boundary of 1945 became a permanent political boundary. Both Russia and the United States withdrew their occupation troops in 1949.

Containment also took on a military form in these years when, in 1947, the United States and 21 American republics signed the Inter-American Treaty of Reciprocal Assistance (the Rio Pact) to resist collectively any armed attack on any of the signatory powers. And the next year saw the US enter into a military alliance with five Western European democracies in the Brussels Treaty, the forerunner to the North Atlantic Treaty Alliance, signed in 1949. Under the provisions of NATO (the North Atlantic Treaty Organization), the United States, Canada, and ten European

democracies pledged their mutual help in case of attack, the expected aggressor being the Soviet Union or one of its satellites. By 1949, too, the United States was sending Army advisory groups to friendly nations under the Mutual Defense Assistance Program. And containment took on a new urgency in this pivotal year when the Soviet Union exploded its own atomic bomb and when Chiang Kai-shek was driven off the mainland of China onto the island of Taiwan (Formosa) by the forces of Mao Tse-tung, who quickly signed a treaty of mutual assistance with the Soviets.

While the Western powers had continued to disarm, the Soviet Union, along with the Communist Chinese and the leaders of Russia's puppet states in the East and West, had maintained and extended their military strength. By 1950 Russia had an army of over two and a half million men, to America's 640,000, and 9000 warplanes, to America's 3300. The Cold War atmosphere was now very tense. The question was whether confrontation would somehow spill over into actual warfare. That question was answered on 25 June 1950 when thousands of soldiers of the North Korean army swept across the length of the 38th parallel in a well-planned invasion of South Korea.

The North Korean government had been waging clandestine warfare against the Republic of Korea government of Syngman Rhee with little success for two years before the invasion. Perhaps misreading American willingness to defend South Korea, the inva-

sion in force of 25 June, aided by Soviet-built T-34 tanks and perhaps encouraged by Soviet advisors, swept all before it in the days that followed. The ROK (Republic of Korea) army, basically a constabulary force and not well trained or equipped, numbered only 95,000 men; the North Korean army had at least 135,000 regulars plus as many as 100,000 trained reserves. Within three days the South Korean capital of Seoul, 35 miles below the 38th parallel on the western shore of the peninsula, had been entered by the main North Korean force, while parallel attacks were taking place down the center and eastern shore of the country.

The United Nations Security Council had condemned the invasion and had authorized force to meet it. (The Soviet Union was absent and unable to cast a veto on UN reaction to the invasion because it had walked out of the Security Council six months earlier over the UN's unwillingness to replace Nationalist China's delegation with one from Communist China.) By this time President Truman had already ordered General Douglas MacArthur in Tokyo to use all available American forces to stop the North Korean drive, including the use of ground, air, and naval forces. Concurrently Truman had ordered the Seventh Fleet to stand off Taiwan to prevent both the Chinese Communists from attacking the Nationalists on Taiwan and the Nationalists from attacking the Communists on the mainland, since either move would have widened the conflict. Truman was also putting the wheels in motion to back up MacArthur's stand with more soldiers and supplies. As the feisty Truman saw it, if South Korea fell, the policy of containment would be rendered worthless. It was a time of testing for America and the Western democracies.

In Japan MacArthur had available to him one armored division and three infantry divisions in his Eighth Army command, but all were undermanned and underequipped. He also had little tactical air support, since the Air Force units in Japan were primarily defensive and only equipped with short-range interceptors. But with North Korean units marching down the Korean peninsula, and

Right: The Korean War.
Left: A 57mm recoilless rifle in action against a Communist position in Korea.
Below: Some US 'Cold Warriors' of the Korean War period. L to R: Philip Jessup, Dean Acheson, John F Dulles and Charles Bohlen.

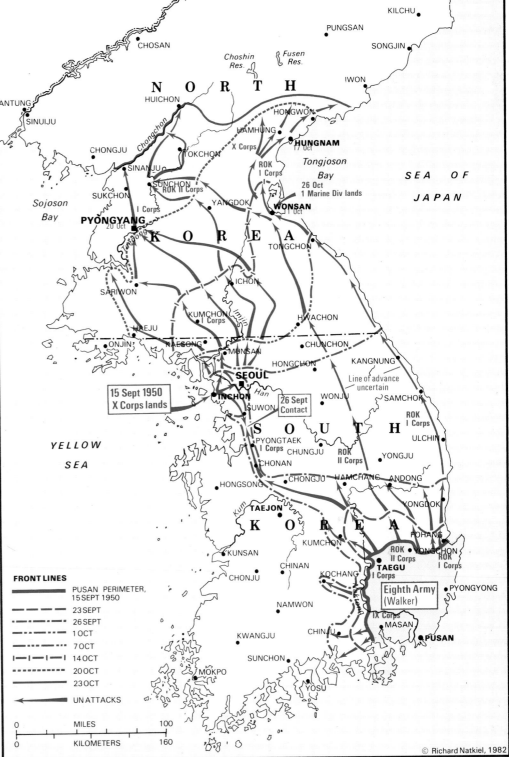

with the ROK forces only able to delay them slightly, something had to be done. MacArthur began to feed in elements of the Eighth Army piecemeal. Lieutenant General Walton H Walker was named Eighth Army commander in charge of both American and South Korean forces, but he could only slow, not stop, the North Korean drives. American armored and infantry units facing the enemy were constantly forced to withdraw to avoid capture in double envelopments by the numerically superior enemy forces.

By early August the Americans had suf-

fered 6000 casualties (and the South Koreans 70,000), and General Walker's forces had been almost pushed out of South Korea. They held only a small area in the south behind the 'Pusan perimeter,' a line around the vital resupply port of Pusan. This 140-mile-long curved perimeter of American and ROK troops, however, proved strong enough to hold off the enemy and allow MacArthur time to feed in more troops and supplies. As additional Army troops, plus Marines, British infantry, and armor, assembled behind the line, Navy and Air Force planes mastered the techniques of close air support for the defenders below. Although it was not clear at the time, the tide was beginning to turn against the North Koreans. Now MacArthur was about to make the finest strategic coup of his long and distinguished career.

Even while ROK and American units were being forced back toward Pusan, MacArthur was planning his offensive. The farther the North Korean forces advanced to the south, the more vulnerable they were to envelopment, and in this MacArthur saw his opportunity. He quickly assembled X Corps, commanded by his chief of staff, Major General Edward M Almond, out of the 7th Infantry Division, the 1st Marine Division, and almost 9,000 ROK soldiers. Its purpose: to stage an amphibious landing at Inchon, the Yellow Sea port on the west coast of Korea only 25 miles from the capital of Seoul, far behind the enemy lines. Since most major highways and rail lines converged at Seoul, seizing the city would cut off the North Korean invaders to the south and force them to retreat through the mountains of eastern Korea. Ideally, most of them would be trapped and destroyed.

MacArthur's plan for the invasion at Inchon was as dangerous as it was audacious. Inchon had to be captured quickly, but the port could be approached only through mile-wide mud flats on which ships could easily be stranded, especially since the tides at the port rose and fell an incredible 30 feet. Furthermore, the harbor was guarded by defenses on the island of Wolmi-Do at its mouth, and, once ashore, the assaulting forces would have to clamber over a high seawall into the built-up urban area. Resupply could come in only at high tide every 12 hours: At falling, low, or early rising tidal periods the port was useless for reinforcement. And X Corps would be the last of MacArthur's reserves.

Most of MacArthur's Army and Navy colleagues were adamantly opposed to the operation, some estimating its chances of success at 500-to-1, but MacArthur was given the go-ahead, and the landings took place as planned on 15 September 1950. They were

Right: After Inchon the Allies were able to make use of new offensive possibilities. Here, paratroops of the 187th Airborne make a drop in Korea in April 1951.

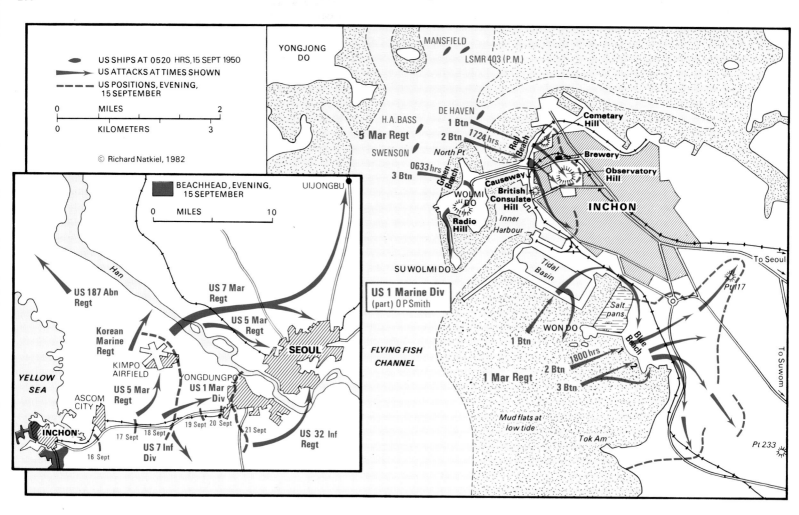

US SHIPS AT 0520 HRS, 15 SEPT 1950
US ATTACKS AT TIMES SHOWN
US POSITIONS, EVENING, 15 SEPTEMBER

MILES 0 — 2
KILOMETERS 0 — 3

© Richard Natkiel, 1982

BEACHHEAD, EVENING, 15 SEPTEMBER

MILES 0 — 10

successful beyond anyone's imagining. The 1st Marine Division and the 7th Infantry Division troops met only light resistance, quickly established a beachhead for re-supply, and began to sweep inland toward strategic Kimpo Airfield and Seoul, despite heavy fighting. Within two weeks, by 29 September, MacArthur was able to turn over the capital once again to President Rhee. In the meantime, General Walker's Eighth Army broke out of the Pusan perimeter and swept north. Some 30,000 North Koreans managed to escape back across the 38th parallel, but another 135,000 were killed or captured in MacArthur's superbly executed trap.

South Korea had been effectively cleared of the invading North Korean forces, but what now should be the next step? President Truman wanted to limit the war to the defense of South Korea, fearing that a move into the north might bring North Korea's supporters, China and Russia, into the war. On the other hand, the enemy troops who had escaped, combined with their reserves in the north, could still mount a considerable threat to the existence of the South Korean government. Furthermore, reunification of all of Korea *was* a long-standing American and United Nations goal. Faced with a difficult choice, the President told MacArthur, on 27 September, that he could enter North Korea but was to use only ROK forces as he neared the Chinese or Soviet borders on the north. Within two weeks the United Nations had given its *de facto* approval to the move to the north by calling for a restoration of peace and security throughout the entire country.

By late October American and ROK forces had moved deep into North Korea and in places were only 50 miles from the Chinese border. At a conference between Truman and MacArthur held on Wake Island on 15 October the general assured the president that Communist Chinese warnings that they might intervene only constituted sabre-rattling bluffs. Yet ground commanders of US and ROK units were already finding Chinese soldiers among the increasingly-stubborn defenders they faced as they approached the Yalu River, the northern border of the country.

By early November it was clear that thousands of Chinese 'volunteers' were fighting alongside the North Koreans, although still not in sufficient strength to check seriously the United Nations Command's armies push-

Top: The Inchon landing.
Below: House-to-house fighting near Seoul after the Chinese offensive.

ing north. But by late November the scale of the Chinese intervention had increased dramatically. Now some 300,000 Chinese troops had crossed into North Korea. It was, MacArthur said, an 'entirely new war.' He ordered his troops back from the Yalu to prevent their being overwhelmed or captured by the swarming Chinese. Once again the Allies were in retreat.

The American and ROK withdrawal from North Korea was carried out in good order, despite the severe Korean winter, but Chinese pressure was intense. The X Corps was withdrawn from Hungnam by sea to Pusan in a dramatic evacuation, and the United Nations force soon found itself back in the vicinity of the 38th parallel, having lost all of its territorial gains in the north. On 24 December General Walker was killed in a traffic accident, and Lieutenant General Matthew B Ridgway, the paratrooper commander of World War II fame, was hurriedly flown in to take his place as the head of Eighth Army. Although Ridgway found his UN lines to be thin and weak, he took all possible steps to protect the 38th parallel and Seoul. But Chinese attacks on New Year's Eve 1950 forced him to pull back even farther, and on 4 January 1951 the Chinese swept into the capital.

Despite this setback Ridgway managed to take advantage of weak Chinese logistical support and to end their incursions, stopping them roughly along the old 38th parallel line. With Ridgway holding that line the President and the Joint Chiefs decided to accept a stalemated war rather than become engaged in a major conflict with China or Russia. But MacArthur demurred. He was fully prepared to escalate the war in order to

By the end of 1951 the Korean front had stabilized a little north of the 38th parallel. The static war that followed consisted largely of small raids and artillery duels (below).

win, and his suggested options included blockading China, launching air attacks on China's war industries, using Chinese Nationalist troops in Korea, and allowing Chinese Nationalist troops to attack the Chinese mainland.

The President and the military chiefs rejected MacArthur's proposals. Since Ridgway had stabilized the front and there was diminishing danger of the UN forces being driven off the peninsula, the decision was made to stay and defend South Korea, but widening the war was out of the question. Even under these strategic limitations Ridgway was able to make some gains by cautious offensive moves north of the 38th parallel after recapturing Seoul in March 1951.

President Truman considered sending out feelers for a negotiated settlement at this point, but MacArthur maintained his bellicose public stance. He even sent an offer for peace talks to the enemy commanders, its tone being that of a victor addressing the vanquished. MacArthur's arrogant assumption of a nearly independent diplomatic-political role highly displeased the peppery president, but Truman held his fire. But then, despite presidential orders that all comments on national policy be cleared beforehand by his office, MacArthur informed the Republican party leader in the House of Representatives that he favored the use of Nationalist Chinese forces and that he was at odds with official policy for a limited war in Korea. (There could be, he said, 'no substitute for victory.') President Truman, on 11 April 1951, relieved the general from command and appointed General Ridgway in his place.

The 'firing' of General MacArthur seemed to crystallize national sentiment over the Korean War. The nation was already bitterly divided over a limited war in which there seemed no chance of gaining a clear-cut

victory. To millions of Americans MacArthur was the symbolic martyr to a misguided policy of no-win warfare. The old general returned to the United States as a hero, to be feted with the largest parade ever staged down Fifth Avenue in New York City and to be invited to address Congress. It was great show, a heaven-sent issue for the opposition Republicans, and a catharsis for a nation involved in a military situation fraught with controversy and frustration. Eventually, after memories of MacArthur's return and dramatic speech before Congress had dimmed (at the conclusion of the speech he had announced that, like an old soldier, he would 'just fade away'), and after the Korean hostilities had ended, most Americans concluded that, in the long run, Truman had done the right thing in releasing the hero-general from his duties.

But while the Truman-MacArthur controversy flared at home, the Army, the Marines, and the ROK forces were still fighting on in Korea. Chinese and North Korean troops continued to attack the UN positions, and Lieutenant General James A Van Fleet, the new Eighth Army commander, and his soldiers beat off these attacks and then advanced north of the 38th parallel to the 'Kansas-Wyoming line,' terrain suitable for tenacious defense. There the fighting stopped in June 1951, and the peace talks began.

Delays by the Communists precluded setting an armistice date throughout the summer, and hostilities flared now and again into the fall. The North Korean and Chinese forces finally agreed on an armistice on 27 November (to begin in 30 days along whatever battle line existed at that time), but further negotiations for fixing the armistice date broke down. Through the winter of 1951-52 the negotiations dragged on, the major issue of contention being the United Nations proposal that prisoners of war who did not wish to be sent home would be set

Eisenhower 'goes to Korea,' January 1953. In his presidential campaign he had promised to end the increasingly unpopular no-win war.

free, as provided for in the Geneva Convention of 1949. The Communists vigorously objected to this proposal. Negotiations continued through the summer of 1952; finally, in October 1952, the talks went into recess.

The negotiations were only resumed after the election of Dwight D Eisenhower as president in November 1952. In his run for the presidency Eisenhower had promised to 'go to Korea' and do something about the stalemated war, and in January 1953, before his inauguration, he flew to Korea to confer with General Mark Clark, now the Far East commander. Clark was ready to resume the war, but Eisenhower was not. He wanted an armistice and was willing to use threats to get it. After taking his oath of office, he informed the Communists in China, the Soviet Union, and North Korea via diplomatic channels that if an armistice were not forthcoming the United States would 'move decisively without inhibition in our use of weapons' and without necessarily confining its actions to Korea. In March 1953 continued American persistence finally led to an agreement for renewal of the talks, although battles flared through July. An

armistice agreement was finally signed on 27 July 1953, and fighting ended that day.

In the 37 months since the original North Korean invasion, 142,000 American men had been killed, wounded, or captured, about 75 percent being Army personnel. The North Koreans and Chinese had lost about one and a half million men, the vast majority Chinese. In all, about two million American fighting men were committed to the war. When the line of demarcation was drawn in 1953 (slightly south of the 38th parallel on the western side of Korea and slightly north of the parallel across the center and eastern end of the peninsula) it signaled that the United States had, at the least, contained an aggressor and defended a friend.

Yet precisely what the legacy of the controversial Korean War would be was unclear when the fighting finally ended in 1953. What was very evident, however, was that the world was becoming an increasingly dangerous place, that America had fallen heir to active leadership among the Western democracies, and that the American military would play a major role in world affairs in the decades to come. It now seemed probable that limited wars fought under a nuclear umbrella might become permanent features of the post-war world.

New Technologies, New Postures, New Problems

The years 1953 to 1963 represented a decade of fundamental realignment both within the Army and within the American military establishment. Korea was fought largely on a World War II basis, although within the new American political-military strategy of containment. But rapid changes in the 1950s and 1960s in armaments, technologies, and mission concepts forced the American military to adapt to new modes of warfare occasioned by the presence of atomic weapons of overwhelming destructive power. These called for a basic alteration of the traditional American concept of victory in war. The gradually escalating conflict in Vietnam would demonstrate to what extent freedom of military action had become hostage to political calculation, though, to be fair, it should be added that politics may not have been solely responsible for the lack of a clearcut US victory in Vietnam.

There was no question, even after the Korean War, that the United States would continue to resist Communist and Soviet expansionism as a matter of duty. The only question was how. Surely nuclear weapons would play the largest part in America's

forces, which were cut back to meet the administration's goal of reducing military spending from its Korean War levels. The Army, for example, was forced to cut six divisions during the 1950s. Crucial to the Eisenhower defense policy of nuclear superiority, as enunciated by Secretary of State John Foster Dulles, was greater emphasis on intelligence gathering to assess Soviet capabilities and intentions. This was gained partially through high-flying reconnaissance planes, such as the U-2, which could fly at 70,000 feet and take crystal-clear photographs of Russian military installations. Radio intelligence, spies and, by 1960, a functioning satellite reconnaissance program were also used.

For land power in case of war, the Eisenhower administration, ever mindful of trying to get 'more bang for the buck,' looked to reduced regular forces and the greater utilization of reserves and the National Guard. These forces were enlarged through laws of 1952 and 1956 that allowed men to spend part of their active duty time with reserve units or the Guard. This raised the number of reservists and Guardsmen in active training to one million, but did nothing to answer the Army's need for greater firepower and mobility on the battlefield.

The Army, therefore, used its limited funds to modernize its armored divisions and to procure armored personnel carriers for its infantry. Perhaps most important, the Army quickly moved to adopt the helicopter for carrying troops and for vertical envelopment techniques in battle. 'Helos' had been used in Korea for reconnaissance and medical evacuation missions, but newer, larger, and more dependable helicopters opened vistas of troop movement and tactics never seen before. The Army also formed 'sky cavalry' units for close fire support, using helicopter gunships. The Army believed, with the Marines, that the helicopter represented the wave of the future in infantry tactics. Thus the

plans for deterrence. Such weapons could be delivered by the Air Force's newer long-range bombers operating from Strategic Air Command (SAC) bases at home, in Europe, and on the periphery of the Soviet empire. Intercontinental ballistic missiles (ICBMs) and the Navy's submarines armed with ballistic missiles could also be used as delivery systems. The Air Force had functional ICBM systems by 1960 with the solid-fuel, concrete-silo-survivable 'Minuteman' on the ways, and the Navy carried 1500-mile-range 'Polaris' missiles in its nuclear-powered submarines.

As a secondary echelon of nuclear deterrence it was also necessary to deploy in Western Europe and in the Far East shorter-range IRBMs (intermediate range ballistic missiles), Air Force planes with tactical nuclear bombs, and carrier-based aircraft. These steps, of course, required the co-operation of America's allies in Europe through NATO, and in the Far East in the form of the Southeast Asia Treaty Organization (SEATO), formed in 1954. Other regional alliances were also formed during these years, so that the United States was bound by commitments to aid its allies against Communist aggression throughout the world.

Emphasis on nuclear deterrence meant de-emphasis on the build-up of conventional

New challenges to US security arose at the end of the 50s. *Top:* the trail of a Soviet space rocket. *Below:* Fidel Castro, Cuba's new ruler, soon became a Soviet client.

Eisenhower years, despite the administration's tilt toward nuclear weaponry and a strategy of massive retaliation, produced significant steps toward modernization and crystallization of the Army's role in the nation's defense posture.

When John F Kennedy came into the White House in 1961 he brought with him a concept of military strategy at variance with that of Eisenhower. Kennedy and his advisors believed that the strategy of massive retaliation not only brought with it the deadly danger of overreaction, but also left the nation unready for lower level, localized conflicts that could best be contained by conventional, non-atomic means. He called his new strategy 'flexible response.' The concept included not only matching or super-

seding the Russians in atomic capabilities through increased warheads, better missiles and more accurate targeting, but also having multi-use conventional forces at the ready at all times. This combination, of course, would cost more, but the young president believed that increased defense spending, combined with domestic tax cuts, would bring the economy out of the doldrums, making 'flexible response' good domestic policy too.

Conscious, however, of the potential waste inherent in defense spending, Kennedy (no doubt influenced by the movement toward more efficiency promised for the business world by systems analysis and budgeting) brought with him to Washington a new breed of managers for the Department of Defense, each fully convinced that greater national defense at restricted costs could be gained by cost analysis and its application. This approach to defense would bring more centralization and systemization to the

American military, as well as an unprecedented amount of civilian decision-making.

Kennedy's point man for the 'new look' in military matters was his Secretary of Defense, Robert S McNamara, former head of Ford Motor Company. McNamara brought with him to Defense an entire upper-tier team of management-systems-engineering experts, soon dubbed 'defense intellectuals' by their admirers and 'whiz kids' by their critics. As Kennedy's first-line advisor on military matters, McNamara instituted a number of reforms, such as budget requests based on strategic functions. Having budget requests that were 'function based' gave McNamara's analysts a quantifiable end by which to measure cost effectiveness and, presumably, military worth. But the result was that weapons systems were often chosen for their lower cost relative to a given end, rather than for their optimum combat effectiveness. For example, the Air Force and the Navy found themselves ordered to produce a model for a fighter plane (the TFX) that would serve both services, even though both argued that, given their different missions, each needed an airplane specifically suited to their respective combat roles. Though the military chiefs resisted McNamara's planning-programming-budgeting system (PPBS) and argued against its efficiency in combat situations, and even though McNamara's 'revolution' caused vast disarray in the military services, it remained in place during the Kennedy years and was carried over into the presidency of Lyndon B Johnson, who succeeded Kennedy after the popular leader's assassination in 1963.

What would eventually prove to be of greatest consequence for the military and the nation was that under both Kennedy and Johnson the principles of systems analysis tended also to be applied to many aspects of foreign policy and to military decisions in Vietnam. This approach had far-reaching implications for the effective conduct of war, where non-quantifiables play an equal or greater role than quantifiables. McNamara's quantifiable analyses also led the nation into a labyrinth of 'assured destruction' requirements for atomic warheads and delivery systems, all based on a number of hypotheses regarding Russian capabilities and intentions. In the end, 'assured destruction' wound up looking much like the old 'massive retaliation' quantified.

'Flexible response' also sent unclear signals to America's allies. France, for example, became fearful that the United States might not use its full arsenal to defend Western Europe, and under Charles de Gaulle France not only pulled its troops out of their integrated status in NATO and forced NATO to move its headquarters out of the country, but also set France on the road to developing its own nuclear arsenal.

Yet whatever its shortcomings, 'flexible response' led to some measurable improvements in America's conventional non-nuclear forces. For the Army this meant development of infantry and armored divisions with greater mobility and firepower. The Army

Three months after his inauguration in 1961 John Kennedy had to face the humiliating Bay of Pigs failure.

also joined the Air Force in 'Strike Command,' whereby two Army airborne divisions were wedded operationally to the Tactical Air Command (TAC) and the Military Airlift Command (MAC) for greater tactical striking power. The 'air cavalry' tactic of using armed helicopters in conjunction with ground forces was also developed and refined. And since the administration had been shocked by the unreadiness of Army Reserve and National Guard units called up at the time of the crisis over the building of the Berlin Wall in 1961 (the Air Force and Navy reserves made a much better showing), Kennedy and McNamara concentrated on trying to improve the reserves and the Guard, paring their numbers somewhat but emphasizing increased training and readiness for those who remained.

Fortunately for the nation there was no conventional Soviet challenge to the nation's new defense posture. The abortive Bay of Pigs invasion of Cuba by Cuban refugees to topple Fidel Castro in April 1961 proved

Left: Kennedy's Secretary of Defense, Robert McNamara, advocated flexible response and function-based budgets.
Below: The worst crisis of the Cold War erupted when the USSR attempted to send MRBMs to Cuba. Here, missile crates on the Soviet ship *Kasimov*.

25 OCTOBER 1962

MRBM LAUNCH SITE 1
SAN CRISTOBAL, CUBA
22-40N 83-18W

OXIDIZER TRAILERS

FUEL TRAILERS

MISSILE TRANSPORTER & PRIME MOVER

MISSILE SHELTER TENTS

FIRING TABLE

MISSILE TRANSPORTERS

Top: A US reconnaissance photograph of a Cuban missile site, October 1962.
Left: North Vietnamese leader Ho Chi Minh. The Kennedy years saw a sharp rise in US involvement in Vietnam.

nothing about the military because it was almost entirely a CIA-conducted operation. The nation's military leaders were not privy to the planning and execution of the invasion except in the most peripheral sense.

Despite the painful failure of the Bay of Pigs operation, Kennedy remained convinced that counterinsurgency was a valid and valuable military-diplomatic tool. This led to his personal interest in the development of the Army's Special Forces, an elite and high-ly-trained force to be used for sabotage, counterintelligence, and counter-guerrilla action. Thus the 'Green Berets' found a champion in Kennedy, and by late 1961 they were at work in South Vietnam.

If America was spared any very serious conventional military challenges during the Kennedy years, the nation nevertheless had to face what was probably its most alarming nuclear confrontation. This was the Cuban missile crisis of October-November 1962. It

began when military intelligence revealed that allegedly defensive missile sites being installed in Castro's Cuba by the Soviets were in fact being readied for offensive medium-range nuclear missiles. Calling to full alert the Strategic Air Command's bombers with nuclear payloads, putting the Army's NATO forces with tactical nuclear weapons on guard to protect Western Europe, and imposing a naval blockade on Cuba with the Navy's carrier battlegroups and submarines, Kennedy was able to force the Russians to withdraw the missiles from Cuba in return for a promise not to invade the island and to remove American missiles from Turkey. This successful use of America's en-tire spectrum of responses in complement-ary fashion, combined with effective threats of escalation, was taken by many as proof that 'flexible response' was meeting America's national defense needs. Yet in retrospect it is difficult to say just how serious the Soviet threat ever actually was. If it were a dan-gerous but essentially frivolous probe, the success of the American response would fall short of proving the absolute validity of the nation's overall defensive strategy.

Crucial to the Army and to the nation were

steps taken during the Kennedy years that would drag the United States deeper and deeper into a quagmire in Southeast Asia. From this the nation would extricate itself only in 1975, after the fighting there had removed one president from office, fractured the national consensus on both foreign policy and national defense goals, left the US with an unacceptable casualty list from a conflict in which America was clearly defeated and humbled, and caused a shuddering among the nation's allies as they came to doubt America's willpower and ability to defend itself and them.

The Vietnam War

American involvement in Vietnam began in 1950 with modest aid being offered to the French, who were trying to regain control over their former colony of French Indochina in the face of Vietnamese determination that this would not be allowed to happen. Only a few Americans were involved at first. These included Army officers and enlisted men in the Military Assistance Advisory Group sent to dispense military and financial aid. Opposed to the French and their puppet

emperor, Bao Dai, were Communist forces called the Viet Minh. Their leader was the venerable Communist and Vietnamese leader Ho Chi Minh. Under Ho, the Viet Minh claimed jurisdiction over the entire country in the name 'the Democratic Republic of Vietnam.' The French, with weak support at home, were finally driven to the conference table in 1954, after they suffered a humiliating defeat at the fortress of Dien Bien Phu.

The conference held at Geneva to settle the conflict was attended by all the major nations, plus delegates from the Democratic Republic of Vietnam and the State of Vietnam (the Bao Dai government). The resulting Geneva Accords ended the fighting, set up a temporary demilitarized zone at the 17th parallel, with the Viet Minh administering Vietnam to the north and the French to the south, and provided civilians with the right to choose whether to live in the south or the north. Free elections were to be held in two years to determine the permanent government of the reunited country. Both Vietnamese governments objected to any permanent division of the country, and the South Vietnamese government, in particular, objected to the elections, since it believed

'Non-combatant' US advisors teaching grenade drill to South Vietnamese soldiers in the late 50s. By 1965 US forces would be openly at war and fighting the enemy face-to-face.

that truly free elections would never be allowed in Ho Chi Minh's north. The United States declined to push them on this matter.

Thus Vietnam was divided into two countries. Some 100,000 South Vietnamese moved north (Ho Chi Minh calling on Viet Minh agents to stay in the south in their guerrilla base areas), and 800,000 North Vietnamese moved south. To strengthen the South Vietnamese government, about 400 Americans remained in the south to train the South Vietnamese army of 200,000 men and to provide economic aid to the government, now led by Ngo Dinh Diem. Initially, the American intention was simply to help South Vietnam to maintain its independence in the face of Communist aggression from the north. No one imagined that this was a commitment that would last until 1975 and eventually draw the United States into armed conflict on a massive scale.

The government of Ngo Dinh Diem proclaimed itself a republic and initiated steps to

214

Above: The 'Ho Chi Minh Trail' in Laos, the enemy's main supply route.
Right: General William C Westmoreland commanded US forces in Vietnam 1964-8.
Far right: The Vietnam War.

gain control over the countryside by suppressing dissidents, resettling refugees, and making modest land reforms. When the time for the scheduled national elections came up in 1956, President Diem insisted that free elections could not be held in the north and refused to participate. The United States backed him, and it appeared that the Communists would have to acquiesce in the inevitability of a divided Vietnam.

But Ho Chi Minh, having consolidated his power in the north by stern repression, now gave the green light to the Viet Minh in the south to rise once again and to attack the Diem government. Soon the South Vietnamese government was being seriously harassed by Ho's Viet Cong (Vietnamese Communist) insurgency campaigns within, and by his movement of regular North Vietnamese troops into the South. Local authority over South Vietnam was challenged by VC assassinations, sabotage, terror, and small-scale military attacks, all carried out under a thinly-disguised Communist organization labeled the 'National Front for the Liberation of South Vietnam' (NLF). Under this pressure the United States sent more advisors to Vietnam to aid the South Vietnamese military in its counterinsurgency efforts. Until 1960 the US advisors operated only in rear-echelon organizational training units; thereafter they began gradually to be drawn into the field to help stiffen the South Vietnamese army against its enemies in the countryside.

By 1960 the Viet Cong was enjoying marked success by terrorizing Vietnamese civilians into aiding and protecting them, and the government of President Diem was hard pressed to resist the growing danger from the north. Ho Chi Minh, on the other hand, allowed no dissent at home and enjoyed the support of both China and the Soviet Union in carrying out his campaign to bring down the Diem government and reunite Indochina under his banner.

Reacting to these unfavorable developments, President Kennedy decided to increase American support to Diem. By 1962, 11,000 men, the great majority of them from the Army, were serving as part of the Military Assistance Command, Vietnam (MACV), then under General Paul D Harkins. These troops, many of them Green Berets, now began to work directly with South Vietnamese regular and irregular forces in the field. But the military situation still failed to improve. Since the Communists had control of large sections of Laos, they were able to dominate the frontier along the long common border between that country and Vietnam and thus establish and maintain a supply route in 'neutral' territory. Their 'Ho Chi Minh Trail' ran all along the western border of South Vietnam. With it they could re-supply their regular or insurgent forces at will without outside interference. On the other side, the 60,000 South Vietnamese troops trying to control infiltration into South Vietnam in the highlands and along the frontier were hard pressed to do so effectively.

Seeking to aid the South Vietnamese in destroying VC enclaves in the south, the US in 1962 began to ferry their troops to the enemy by means of helicopters such as the CH-21 Shawnee and the UH-1 Huey. Armed helos were also added to the vertical envelopment forces. By early 1963 the United States was clearly in the war, and some progress was being made against the North Vietnamese, but the government of President Diem was at the same time becoming more and more unpopular. In view of this, and hoping to restore political stability in South Vietnam, President Kennedy gave his tacit blessing to a plot to overthrow Diem.

In the resulting coup both Diem and his brother Nhu were murdered by the conspirators (a development Kennedy insisted he never intended), but the result was not the political stability anticipated. Instead, there followed a year and a half during which numerous South Vietnamese generals jockeyed for control and influence, creating a splendid opportunity for the Viet Cong to

reassert itself and extend its influence.

As the North Vietnamese continued to pour regular army units and insurgents into the south, the South Vietnamese government, even with 23,000 American advisors, seemed unable to stop their gradual extension of control over the countryside. President Lyndon B Johnson, Kennedy's successor, was unsure how to react. He did not want to escalate the war, since it would endanger his domestic programs, but he did not want to be saddled with losing it. In the event, he took advantage of an August 1964 attack by North Vietnamese patrol boats on American destroyers carrying out electronic surveillance missions in the Gulf of Tonkin to gain

from Congress almost *carte blanche* authorization to repel attacks on US forces and to curb aggression in Southeast Asia. But even with the Tonkin Gulf Resolution he still seemed unsure of what to do and was not inclined – as was his Secretary of Defense, Robert McNamara – to listen to the military's suggestions. By the spring of 1965 he was forced by events to make his decision.

Under pressure of major North Vietnamese and Viet Cong victories in the central highlands of Vietnam, Johnson, in February 1965, ordered both that American Army and Marine combat troops should go into direct action against the enemy and that military targets in North Vietnam should be

The helicopter was a crucial weapon in Vietnam. Here, troops on a 'search and destroy' mission land from UH-IDs.

bombed. Within three months Air France B-52s were also hitting enemy enclaves in South Vietnam. Yet pressure by the North Vietnamese continued to threaten the existence of the South Vietnamese government, and still more US ground troops had to be committed to the fight. By the end of 1965, 180,000 American troops were in Vietnam, and more were on the way.

For a time it appeared that perhaps the situation might be saved. A government had emerged, under Army General Nguyen Van Thieu and Air Force Marshal Nguyen Cao Ky, that promised some stability and a willingness to allow a return to civilian rule once the war was over. And new tactics were being developed. In order to thwart the Viet Cong and North Vietnamese Army in the south, General William C Westmoreland, commander of US forces since the year before, ordered 'search and destroy' operations to hold off any further incursions and destroy enemy enclaves.

But despite notable victories over the enemy, such as the Army's successful seizure and holding of the Ia Drang Valley in the central highlands in the late summer of 1965 (which proved the feasibility of massed helicopter transport of infantry troops), the combined US and South Vietnamese forces could not destroy the invading and infiltrating enemy forces. They could not break the enemy's will and compel him to call a halt to the war, especially when his supply ports in North Vietnam and Cambodia and his Ho Chi Minh Trail were still politically off limits for destruction by superior American air power.

Thus the war dragged on, and by February 1968 American military personnel in Vietnam totaled over 490,000 men. South Vietnamese regulars and militia totaled another 640,000. By this time as many as 180,000 North Vietnamese had been killed and another 70,000 had been captured, but the 240,000 Communist combatants still in the field could not be subdued. Now both time and American impatience with a long, indecisive war were Ho Chi Minh's greatest allies. As he had said in 1945, 'If we have to fight, we will fight. You will kill ten of our men and we will kill one of yours, and in the end it will be you who will tire of it.'

The American soldier, although backed by excellent medical care (less than 1 per cent of battle casualties died in the war) and equipped with new armored personnel carriers, the new automatic M16 rifle, new anti-tank rockets, superbly effective Claymore anti-personnel mines, helicopter gunships, and other technological improvements, was caught in a war in which the enemy was always elusive, ready to take casualties, and willing to fight on. Worse, the American soldier was hamstrung by the government's

Left: Both weather and terrain made Vietnam a difficult theater. Here, a mortar fires in monsoon-sodden jungle.

inability to clarify the strategic goal of the fighting and dying; the inability of the American public, influenced by media coverage that by and large was not sympathetic to the cause, to comprehend the nature of the war; and the willingness of the military high command to accept policy decisions that brought the fighting men no closer to final victory.

Some clear American successes had been scored in 1966 and 1967 when sizable units moved out of their base camps against enemy strongholds, and the pacification programs carried out by the civilian-military units under CORDS (Civil Operations and Revolutionary Development Support) seemed to be effective in rooting out Viet Cong influence in the villages of South Vietnam, but still the war went on. Indeed, although taking casualties as high as 10-to-1 over American forces in the field, North Vietnmaese troops, reflecting Ho Chi Minh's prophetic warning, showed every sign of continuing, and by 1967 they were preparing for a major offensive to begin with the lunar new year (*Tet*) in early 1968.

The Tet Offensive that began on 30 January 1968 was built around a series of massive attacks on South Vietnamese cities. Its object was both to bring about a general uprising against the government and to encourage anti-war sentiment in the United States. It failed in the former but succeeded in the latter. In their pre-dawn attacks in the provinces and in the Saigon and Mekong Delta areas, the 84,000 North Vietnamese and Viet Cong attackers struck the capital, 36

provincial capitals, and dozens of other cities and hamlets. Particularly hard hit were the cities of Saigon and Hue. Fighting was heavy in all locations, but, to the dismay of the North Vietnamese, the US and South Vietnamese soldiers, Marines, and Rangers, aided by massive close air support, inflicted heavy losses on the enemy. Especially noteworthy were the vigorous defenses put up around the Green Beret camp at Dak To, around the Marine base camp at Khe Sanh, and in Hue and Saigon. By the time the month-long offensive had died out, the Communists had suffered 32,000 troops killed and 6000 captured, against only 4000 killed on the American and South Vietnamese side.

The Tet Offensive had been an overwhelming Communist defeat, and soon the American and South Vietnamese pacification program in the countryside was reinstated with greater vigor than before, but the picture of initial military losses presented to the American public by the media, coming on top of general American disenchantment with the war, spurred vigorous demands at home for a complete pull-out from Vietnam. Thus an American and South Vietnamese military victory was interpreted as a great defeat at a crucial time in the continuing public debate over Vietnam. It became, in fact, a strategic psychological victory scored by the Communists. Understandably, many US servicemen saw this as a form of betrayal.

An M113 APC pulls an M48 tank out of the mud. Although Vietnamese terrain was unsuitable for armor, tanks often proved indispensable in battle.

Top: Bombing of Haiphong, April 1972, as seen from an American B-52.
Above left: Vietnam exposed some weaknesses in US equipment. The postwar Bradley M2 is a more battle-worthy personnel carrier than the old M113.
Below left: Vietnamese aftermath: Boat People.

The Tet Offensive also meant the end of the presidency of Lyndon B Johnson, who announced in March 1968 that he would not be a candidate for re-election, that he was curbing the air offensives against North Vietnam, and that he would welcome talks with the Communists. He was succeeded by Richard M Nixon who promised throughout his campaign against Hubert H Humphrey, the 'peace' candidate for the Democrats, that he had 'secret plans' and would end the war 'with honor.'

President Nixon had no secret plans, but he was determined to remove the American fighting men from the war and pursue peace through diplomacy. Aided by an impending Russo-Chinese split and by popular support for his announcement that he was determined to end the draft in favor of an all-volunteer Army, Nixon moved toward diplomatic solutions and toward a policy of 'Vietnamization,' wherein the South Vietnamese army, with American financial and advisory aid, would henceforth shoulder the burden of the fighting.

Withdrawal of American troops began in the summer of 1969 as the Army, now under General Creighton Abrams, held off the enemy by isolated actions against North Vietnamese base camps. Nixon also allowed the Air Force to begin pounding the Ho Chi Minh Trail and to destroy the 'neutral' Cambodian port of Sihanoukville, in both cases severely damaging the North Vietnamese ability to carry on its war against the south. Finally, Nixon authorized American and South Vietnamese troops to wipe out major North Vietnamese enclaves, across the border in Cambodia called the 'Parrot's Beak' and the 'Fish Hook.'

Even as the Americans were pulling out of Vietnam, anti-war sentiment continued to grow at home. News of the My Lai massacre of 400 villagers in 1968 (wherein the officer in charge had not been court martialed and punished by his superiors) leaked out to damage the Army's reputation, and the 'Pentagon papers,' revealing Defense Department uneasiness over the conduct of the war, were purloined and published. Now the North Vietnamese decided on another Major offensive to achieve final victory. This 'Easter Offensive' of 1972 by the North Vietnamese was bloodily rebuffed by surprisingly effective South Vietnamese troops. It was also foiled by President Nixon's decision to allow the military to mine the major North Vietnamese harbor of Haiphong, a move the generals had been urging for years. The resulting Air Force raids on North Vietnamese targets and Haiphong were spectacularly effective and, of great significance, neither the Soviet Union nor China made more than mild protests.

In the meantime presidential advisor Henry Kissinger continued to explore the diplomatic route to peace. By October 1972 it looked as though his efforts had been successful, but when the North Vietnamese balked and continued their military activity, Nixon loosened the Air Force once again, and Operation LINEBACKER II, in which Air Force and Navy planes flew 1800 sorties and dropped 20,000 tons of bombs on North Vietnam, mostly in the Hanoi and Haiphong areas, was carried out. This led the North Vietnamese to agree to end the fighting. America would withdraw, and all other issues would be settled by the Vietnamese themselves. By December 1972 American forces in Vietnam had declined from a wartime high of 565,000 to only 24,000.

America was finally out of the war. A sum of $1 billion was delivered to President Thieu in military aid, and the fighting, now again waged by the original combatants, went on. Nixon won re-election in 1972 but resigned in the wake of the Watergate scandals in 1974, with Gerald R Ford inheriting the weakened presidency. Congress, responding to anti-war and anti-military sentiment in the aftermath of Vietnam, was keeping a tight clamp on military spending, actually reducing the Pentagon's budget in terms of real purchasing power by 37 percent between 1968 and 1974. Congress also passed the War Powers Act in 1973, requiring Congressional approval of overseas troop deployments for longer than 60 days, a severe curb on the president's power as commander-in-chief and as chief diplomatic official in the government.

The year 1973 also saw the end of the draft and the implementation of the 'all volunteer' armed forces, an experiment that at least doubled the cost for each soldier in uniform. The new enlistees tended, if anything, to be somewhat less educated than the former inductees, yet they would have to handle weapons and equipment of unprecedented sophistication. Added to this were problems of integrating more black and female recruits into the service units, of dealing with the widespread availability and use of drugs by military personnel, and of trying to teach military discipline to young men and women coming out of a permissive society. The result was widespread dissatisfaction and disorientation in the services.

A resounding blow to American prestige came in April 1975 when the US-backed South Vietnamese government fell to a concerted North Vietnamese attack, Congress having refused President Ford's request for $700 million in emergency military monies to aid its South Vietnamese ally. (The use of American forces in combat in Southeast Asia had been flatly prohibited by Congress in 1973.) Americans watched on their television sets as Marine helos dropped into Saigon to evacuate the last Americans from the war-stricken country. Vietnamese refugees fought desperately to escape the city in the face of the terror of a holocaust that would surely follow their 'liberation' by the North Vietnamese. The tribulations of their compatriots, the 'boat people,' would intensify the impression of American failure in the months to come.

Since the conflict began in 1950, some 2.6 million American military personnel had served in South Vietnam. Over 47,000 had died there in battle, another 10,000 had died from accidents and disease, and 154,000 had been wounded. The war had cost the

Men of the 82nd Airborne Division on Grenada, October 1983. US casualties in this invasion: 18 dead, 67 wounded.

American government $410 billion. The South Vietnamese had lost 200,000 killed as soldiers, but over one million South Vietnamese of all sorts had died as war casualties. The North Vietnamese had expended 800,000 lives in gaining their victory. As American Marines lowered the flag and departed from Saigon on the last day of the Vietnam War, an American colonel on diplomatic assignment in Hanoi remarked to a North Vietnamese officer, 'You know you nevered defeated us on the battlefield.' The North Vietnamese officer replied, 'That may be so, but it is irrelevant.'

What was relevant was that by the Vietnam War the anti-Communist alliance system, including NATO, had been seriously weakened. SEATO was dead, with Far Eastern

The Army's new main battle tank, the 45mph M1 Abrams, began to enter service in 1980. It was armed with a 105mm gun.

nations looking elsewhere than to America for their security needs. The domestic consensus in favor of 'containment' and the necessity of aiding America's allies was shattered, as the American politicians and the people they represented vowed 'no more Vietnams.' And the American military forces sank into public disfavor, being unfairly burdened with the 'loss' of Vietnam. Only in the next decade would the Army and its sister services regain a modicum of their former prestige. Whether the damage done to the American consensus about containment or to the Western alliance system can be wholly repaired remains to be seen. But there is reason to be optimistic.

Soldiers at the Ready

When he assumed the presidency in January 1977 President Jimmy Carter brought to the White House and to American diplomacy a desire to move international relations and American policy in more humane directions. Accordingly, he tried manfully to curb the spread of nuclear weapons and, at the same time, to reduce American outlays for defense purposes. Although dollar growth of the defense budget went up slightly under the first two Carter budgets, because of inflation real outlays actually declined. In addition, Carter cancelled the B-1 bomber program, curtailed the Navy's shipbuilding and replacement plans, stretched out procurement of MX missiles and tactical aircraft, and reduced spending in the military for operations and weapons maintenance. Indeed, during the first two years of the Carter administration, the military, including the Army, was virtually placed on hold while the new president tried to translate the international power struggle into some less menacing form of competition.

But the president's hopes were frustrated by events. First came the jolt of withdrawing support for the Shah of Iran only to have him replaced by the radical and violently anti-

American Ayatollah Khomeini in 1979. This was followed by the seizure of American embassy personnel in Tehran and their being held hostage for 444 days by the Muslim fundamentalist leader and his followers. Further frustration was later added to the situation in the form of a bungled inter-service attempt to rescue the 53 hostages from the Iranian capital of Tehran in April 1980. As a result, Carter backed off from withdrawing the one American Army divison from South Korea and placed American troops in the Sinai after the Camp David agreements to assure peace there betwen Israel and Egypt. The final shock came with the Soviet invasion of Afghanistan in December 1979, which led Carter to reassessment of his policies and to recommending an increase in real spending on defense.

Now convinced of the need to augment American military power, Carter also increased military aid to Israel, Egypt, and Saudi Arabia to forestall spread of Soviet influence in the Middle East; authorized a Rapid Deployment Joint Task Force of up to 200,000 troops for world emergencies; and began to stockpile military supplies at the newly-leased American base at Diego Garcia in the Indian Ocean. But severe damage had been done to the military by the inadequate budget appropriations of Carter's first two years in office. Disturbed by Carter's perceived inability to handle America's problems, for all his good intentions, the voters turned to Ronald Reagan, the Republican candidate in 1980, and placed him, with his promises to 'rearm America,' in the White House.

During his years in office Reagan kept that promise. Military budgets placed heavy emphasis on weapons procurement and on substantial pay and benefit increases for personnel penalized by years of heavy inflation. Real growth in defense spending under the first three Reagan budgets stood at eight to 12 per cent, and defense spending moved to over seven per cent of the nation's GNP. The Militrary also moved to implement cruise missile and B-1 bomber programs, with Reagan's support, and both MX ICBMs and Pershing II intermediate-range missiles have been deployed, the former in fixed silos at home and the latter on European soil under NATO auspices. In addition, the president called for an anti-ICBM space-based laser or energy beam defense system called the Strategic Defense initiative, dubbed 'Star Wars' by the media. Nor did the Reagan administration hesitate to project American power abroad. It supported both friendly governments and anti-Communist counterinsurgency operations in Central America. It sent US Marines into Lebanon in 1982 (a move that ended in disaster with the bombing of their headquarters in October 1983); and it sent a multi-service force onto the Caribbean island of Grenada, also in October 1983, to deflect a Cuban Communist takeover of the island, already being converted into a military base of operations, an altogether more successful operation.

Operation URGENT FURY, the invasion of

Above: Men of the 82nd Airborne fire rounds from their preferred artillery weapon – the compact M102 105mm light howitzer – into the Grenadian hills during the 1983 invasion.
Right: Small forces from other Caribbean nations joined the US in the Grenadian operation.

Grenada, may have been more successful than the attempt to free the hostages from Teheran in 1980 or the landing of Marines in Lebanon in 1982, but the multi-service operation revealed serious shortcomings in American military operations. These led to probing criticism from outside the military and much soul searching within. The result was some very positive changes in US military doctrine during Reagan's remaining years in the White House.

The 1983 invasion of the tiny Caribbean island came about after Maurice Bishop and his socialist movement were otherthrown by left-wing extremists in October 1983. American policy makers had already been concerned about Soviet and Cuban presence on the island, and since a large airport complex had recently been constructed there, it was feared that Soviet aircraft might now be permitted to operate from the airfield and endanger shipping in the Caribbean and Central America and perhaps even along the southern coast of the United States. Furthermore, there were on the island about 600 American students and tourists whose safety would have to be assured.

222

Above: Happy American students surround a US soldier on Grenada. Ensuring that the students would not be taken hostage by the enemy was one of the US Military's primary concerns during the invasion, an objective that the US Army was able to accomplish successfully.
Opposite: American troops in Greenville, Grenada, after taking the town on 25 October.

When the Organization of Eastern Caribbean States asked the United States to join in military action to restore democracy and political stability on Grenada, Reagan gave the order for American forces to invade to protect the Americans, neutralize the island, and reestablish political harmony and democracy. In the ensuing operation that began on October 25, Marines (assisted by token forces of six area nations) attacked the northern end of the island while Army Rangers and members of the 82nd Airborne Division attacked on the south—even though the American students at St George's University Medical School and the other

American nationals were in the capital at the center of the island. It took three days before the island was secured, despite relatively light opposition from Grenadan and Cuban defenders.

Secretary of Defense Caspar Weinberger claimed that the job had been 'well done,' but there was criticism from the Senate Armed Services Committee, which pointed to poor coordination between the Army and Navy, noting that there was no single service commander with the authority to make tactical decisions. Poor radio communication between the services had also been a major problem, resulting in ground forces not being able to call in supporting naval gunfire. And incredible logistical foul-ups marred the whole operation.

The long-term importance of Operation URGENT FURY lay not in its restoring stability to Grenada or in its thwarting foreign designs in the Caribbean but in the impetus it gave to changes in America's military forces, especially in the areas of command and co-

ordination. The Packard Commission (officially the President's Blue Ribbon Commission on Defense Management, created in 1985 to assess the organization of the Department of Defense and chaired by former Deputy Secretary of Defense David Packard), and the Senate Armed Services Committee, subsequently recommended that DOD be reorganized and that unified commands be created for vitally needed cooperation between the armed forces.

The same year Senators Barry Goldwater (R) of Arizona and Sam Nunn (D) of Georgia, each the respected party leader on the Senate Armed Services Committee, endorsed a comprehensive staff study drawn up by the Department of Defense regarding it s organization and decision-making processes. Thus early in Ronald Reagan's second term in office a fundamental rethinking of the roles of all the armed services was underway. And it would not be long before the fruits of this rethinking would be put to the a fiery test.

Two US M2 Bradley Fighting Vehicles churn through the Saudi Arabian desert during the tense months prior to the start of the war with Iraq in early 1991.

VICTORIOUS PROFESSIONALS
1985-PRESENT

The year 1985 may well prove to be a watershed in the history of the world, for in that year, though no one yet realized it, the very assumptions on which East-West relations had been based ever since the end of World War II began to change. In essence, US policy toward the Soviet Union had not significantly varied since 1947, when American diplomat George Kennan called for 'containment' of Soviet expansionism by military, diplomatic, and economic means. Kennan predicted that if the West could contain the USSR long enough, the internal weaknesses of the Communist system would eventually force the system to change. Events in 1985 and thereafter seemed to bear out Kennan's theory.

In 1985 Mikhail Gorbachev came to power in the USSR and called for change not only in terms of *glasnost* (openness to public debate) but also of *perestroika* (restructuring of the Soviet system). It soon became clear that Gorbachev also included on his agenda the idea of downgrading hostility toward the West at least in part because the arms race, with its consequent high expenditures, was causing an unacceptable strain on the Soviet economy.

In the months and years that followed, Gor-

A soldier at the Air Assault School at Fort Campbell, KY, is instructed in rappelling.

bachev and his reformers, while holding off challenges from old guard Communist leaders, were confronted both with growing demands for political and economic liberalization within the Soviet Union and with secessionist movements in various parts of of the polyglot empire. By the end of 1989 the Soviet puppet governments of all the USSR's European satellites had either been overthrown or fatally compromised, and the hated Berlin Wall had been torn down. The Warsaw Pact was formally dissolved in 1991, and by the end of 1992 the USSR itself had disintegrated into a commonwealth of independent non-communist states.

Yet the fall of the Soviet Union and the end of the Cold War did not automatically end America's security concerns. The mighty ex-Soviet war machine, including its atomic weaponry, was now divided among the unstable nations that made up the new Trans-Ural Confederation of Independent States. But since neither the future character of the CIS nor that of any of its member governments was predictable, how all this military power might be used was unknown.

The Army's Manpower

Unlike previous eras in its history, by the 1980s the US Army was moving to take full advantage of the military skills not only of its active duty personnel but also of its reserve and National Guard units. The all-volunteer Army, in which civilian pay and benefits would have to match or exceed those of the civilian economy, resulted in higher cost-per-soldier expenditures. At the same time, the cost of its equipment and weaponry – from the single bullet to high-technology helicopters and missiles – was soaring to new heights. Army planners, therefore, opted for a smaller but highly trained regular force, supplemented as necessary by fully trained and integratable reserve and Guard forces.

The backbone of the modern Army would be its active duty personnel, standing at 781,000 in 1985 (but due for cuts in the budget deficit years that followed). These men and women in armor, cavalry, air cavalry, mechanized infantry, light infantry, airborne, Ranger, special forces, aviation, and artillery battalions would form the core of the Army's fighting forces. There was evidence of improvement in the caliber of the regular forces in that over 91 percent of the Army's recruits were now high school graduates, and officers in the field reported that these regulars were among the best they had ever commanded. The Army had come a long way since the recruiting doldrums of the 1960s and 1970s.

Backing up the on-line regulars were 261,000 reservists in combat, combat-support, and general-support units which supplemented the regulars in all battalions except air cavalry, airborne infantry, motorized infantry, and Ranger units. By 1987 there were more reserve than active battalions in cavalry, light infantry, and field artillery and an equal number of special forces reserve units. Another 285,000 men and women served in the Individual Ready Reserve (IRR), being subject to call according to their military occupational specialities. Over 80 percent of the Army's reservists were high school graduates, and the Army was moving to provide them with 'the latest' equipment, so that they could be fully integrated into regular fighting units when called to duty.

As with the reserves, the National Guard soldiers were better trained and better equipped than ever before. Numbering over 452,000 paid members in 1986, the guardsmen were expected to be deployable in 30 to 60 days from call-up. They represented 43 percent of the Army's combat units (including 50 percent of its armored cavalry regiments) and 20 percent of its support units. Like the reservists, they were now furnished with some of the latest weaponry in the Army's arsenal and were better trained than ever before. Guard units, like their reserve counterparts, regularly took part in major exercises both in the United States and abroad, and the Army National Guard was also moving to build its own aviation (helicopter) force of 6600 soldiers by 1991.

Opposite top: Army trainees man a forward area radar during an air defense exercise. Such radars give early warning to batteries of anti-aircraft guns or missiles.
Opposite: US Air Assault troops practice rappelling down from a UH-60 Black Hawk.

New Weapons

The weapons that had been developed to give this new-model Army the firepower and mobility it wanted were formidable indeed. Heading the list of new armored vehicles was the M1A1 Abrams main battle tank. By 1985 the Army had 35 battalions of Abrams tanks and was shooting for 7400 of the behemoths by the early 1990s. First produced in 1982, the M1 Abrams weighed in at 60 tons, but its 1500-horsepower engine could drive it at up to 45 miles per hour. Armed with either a 105mm rifled gun or a 120mm smoothbore gun and two machine guns, the Abrams could move and fight equally well in daylight or dark because it was equipped with a laser range finder, a ballistic computer, and thermal-imaging night sights. Furthermore, the Abrams had a 27 percent lower silhouette than its lighter and less powerful predecessor, the M60 Patton. As the Gulf War would illustrate, the Abrams could outduel any tank in existence, including the Soviet-built T-72.

Supplementing the Abrams main battle tank were M2 and M3 Bradley fighting vehicles designed to carry infantrymen and their weapons into war with speed and safety. The Bradleys, replacements for the earlier M113 APCs (armored personnel carriers), were armed with a machine gun, a 25mm cannon, and twin launchers for TOW (Tube-launched, Optically tracked, Wire-guided) missiles and had a cross-country speed of 41 miles per hour. They also had double armor plating of aluminium and steel and were fully

Above: The mighty US M1A1 Abrams main battle tank would silence its many critics with its splendid performance in the 1991 Gulf War.
Opposite: A US soldier stands guard with his TOW (Tube-launched, Optically-tracked, Wire-guided) anti-tank missile launcher.

the workhorse of the Army's vertical assault combat operations.

These machines were rapidly displacing the Vietnam-era AH-1 Cobra attack helicopter, the UH-1 Iroquois utility and transport helicopter, and the OH-58 Kiowa multi-role helicopter as technology proceeded apace. And by the late 1980s the Army had begun development of the even newer LHX (light helicopter experimental) in two versions, a scout-attack version and a light assault version, intending to procure 4200 of these fast machines for the combat of the future.

The Army's missile inventory of the 1980s was headed by the Patriot tactical air defense missile. First deployed in early 1985, the Patriot was a medium- and high-altitude ground-to-air missile. Mobile and having all-weather capability, it functioned by command guidance from the ground to mid-course; then, as it neared its target, it would inform ground radar of its location relative to the target, and a ground computer system would direct it to the kill. Though not really meant to be an anti-missile weapon, the Patriot missile would attain a better than 80 percent success rate when deployed against Iraqi Scud missiles in the 1990-91 Gulf War.

Also in the Army's missile inventory were the Hawk, a medium-range, surface-to-air missile, the Chaparral, a self-contained, heat-seeking anti-aircraft missile, and the Stinger, a man-portable guided missile weighing only 35 pounds, as well as many types of TOW missiles.

Coming on line in the 1980s to aid ordnance targeting for the Army in combat were

JSTARS (joint surveillance and target attack radar system) for deep target intelligence and JTACMS (joint tactical missile system), used in cooperation with the Air Force in attacking deep targets.

The Army's chief shoulder weapon continued to be the M16A2 rifle. With a 5.56mm caliber (the NATO standard for rifles), the M16 in its improved version had a maximum range of 500 meters, and it was also fitted with a new 3-round burst device. In 1982 the Army adopted the light M249 5.56mm automatic squad rifle as a second weapon for its infantry; it could fire an astounding 700 rounds per minute. The standard hand weapon was the 9mm Beretta, a replacement for the venerable Colt .45.

The Army in the Unified Command Structure

Two catalysts for change in the Army's place in the military structure for the late 1980s were the Packard Commission's report, calling for strengthening of the authority both of unified and specified commanders and of the Joint Chiefs, and the Senate Armed Services Committee's report entitled *Defense Organization: The Need for Change*, issued in 1985. President Reagan endorsed the substance of both reports and

Below: AH-64 Apaches, probably the world's most sophisticated attack helicopters.
Bottom: The UH-60 Black Hawk began replacing the UH-1 Iroquois (the "Huey" of Vietnam fame) as the Army's standard all-purpose helicopter in the early 1980s.

amphibious. Also in the armored category and delivering firepower against the enemy on the battlefield were the 155mm M109 and 203mm M110 self-propelled howitzers, these supplementing the non-armored, towed 155mm M114 howitzers, the 155mm M198 howitzers, and the 105mm M101 and M192 howitzers.

In the air, the new Army of the 1980s featured two 'stars,' the AH-64A Apache attack helicopter and the UH-60 Black Hawk combat assault transport helicopter. The Apache, which entered the Army's air inventory in the early 1980s, had a maximum speed of 192 miles per hour and a range of 380 miles, despite its loaded weight of nine tons. Its two-man crew, equipped with a laser target designator, forward-looking infrared sensors, and pilot night-vision capabilities, carried combat ordnance of 8 Hellfire radar-guided anti-tank missiles, 38 2.75-inch Hydra rockets, and 1200 rounds of ammunition for its 30mm cannon. The Apache would prove itself to be a first-class anti-tank weapon in the Gulf War.

The UH-60 Black Hawk, with a crew of three, could cruise at 150 knots and lift an 11-man infantry squad or a 105mm howitzer and its crew into combat. In the 1980s it became

urged Congress to act on them. As a result, Senator Barry Goldwater and Representative William Nichols of the House Armed Services Committee co-sponsored a bill endorsing most of the recommendations contained in the reports. The Goldwater-Nichols Department of Defense Reorganization Act of 1986 was quickly passed by both houses of Congress and was signed into law by President Reagan in October 1986.

By this landmark legislation not only were the office of the chairman of the Joint Chiefs strengthened and duty in unified staff billets required for general-officer rank in the services, but also unified and specified commands were either strengthened or created to direct all American forces worldwide with greater efficiency. The Goldwater-Nichols Act strengthened the four unified commands and one specified command already in place, and in the years thereafter four more unified commands and another specified command were added.

The US Army was slated to play a major role in seven of these ten commands, and its current field manual, *FM 100-5: Operations*, now assumes joint operations throughout. In fact, a multi-service combat operations doctrine for synchronized deep attack had been a keystone of Army-Navy cooperation since the origination of AirLand Battle doctrine in the early 1980s, a fact reflected in *FM 100-5: Operations*.

So great has been the effect of the multi-service commands system on all US military operations that it is now almost impossible to understand fully how any given service functions without first understanding how it fits into these integrated structures. The unified commands in which the Army plays a significant part are the Pacific Command, the European Command, the Southern (ie Latin American) Command, the Central (ie southwest Asian and northern Indian Ocean) Command, the Space Command, the Special Operations Command, and the Transportation Command. In addition, the Army is the primary component of one of the specified commands, the Forces Command. It is certainly worth taking a closer look at these particular organizations.

The US Pacific Command (USPACOM) was created in 1947 as an outgrowth of the unified command practices which developed in that theater during World War II. Its area of responsibility includes not only the Pacific Ocean but also the Indian Ocean area and the Asian land-mass, approximately 52 percent of the surface of the earth. Its commander in chief and his staff are located on Oahu, Hawaii, and about 380,000 defense personnel are assigned to this theater of operations. Directly under the Commander in Chief Pacific Command are subordinate Army, Navy, Marine, and Air Force commanders, all also located on Oahu, with the Army's subordinate unit, US Army Western Command, headquartered at Fort Shafter. Two subordinate unified Army commands report directly to the Commander in Chief Pacific Command: these are US Forces Korea and US Forces Japan.

Traditionally, Pacific Command's primary strategic mission was to cope with whatever regional military challenges the USSR or North Korea might present. The collapse of the Soviet Union greatly reduced one part of the threat but did not completely dispel it, since a formidable array of ex-Soviet land, sea, air and nuclear power still remained in place in the Far East. Although this potent force was nominally under the control of the new CIS, neither the future character of the CIS nor even its survival was certain, and how its military forces might be used was therefore unguessable.

On the Korean peninsula the North Korean government has over 800,000 troops in its Korean People's Army. It is, by some estimates, the fifth largest army in the world, with 70 infantry divisions or separate brigades and 80,000 special operations forces. Some 65 percent of its ground forces are south of Pyongyang and thus constitute a potential threat to the South Korean capital of Seoul. South Korea has only about 650,000 troops, and its armed forces are outnumbered by the North Koreans in tanks by about a 3:1 margin, in field artillery by a 2:1 margin, and in aircraft by about 400 planes.

Standing at the side of the South Koreans are the 31,500 men and women of the US Eighth Army, along with 2200 Marines and 11,000 Air Force personnel, cooperating since 1978 with their allies under the ROK/US Combined Forces Command. For over a decade the American and South Korean forces have been carrying out their annual Team Spirit exercises with combined forces numbering as many as 200,000 soldiers, including more than 6000 members of the US Army.

US Pacific Command also shares responsibility for the security of Japan, with over 46,000 American combatants (mostly from the Marine Corps and Air Force) stationed

Above: Throughout the 1980s all US armed services trained with South Korean forces in annual Team Spirit exercises. Here, US and ROK Marines practice landings.
Opposite: An Army air assault team begins its perilous descent from a hovering UH-60 Black Hawk helicopter.

on the home islands and Okinawa, plus almost 15,000 military personnel stationed in the Philippines.

Multi-service and multi-national cooperation under unified command is also the hallmark of US European Command (USEUCOM) headquartered at Stuttgart-Vaihingen, Germany. European Command is essentially America's commitment to NATO, but its area of responsibility extends far beyond the borders of western Europe, for this unified command has responsibility for 13 million square miles, from the tip of Norway through the Mediterranean Sea and parts of the Middle East all the way to the southern tip of Africa.

In 1990 there were over 344,000 troops from the Army, Navy, Marine Corps, and Air Force in western and southern Europe. Almost 216,000 of these men and women (63 percent) were Army troops at 82 different sites, with some 207,000 stationed in Germany alone. The primary mission of European Command was originally deterence of aggression from the Soviet Union and its satellites on western Europe. Accordingly, the soldiers in this command have been especially well equipped with sophisticated weapons such as M1 Abrams tanks, multiple launch rocket systems (MLRSs) and Patriot air defense missiles. Their US Navy counterparts have also been equipped with powerful armadas, including the carrier task forces of the Sixth Fleet in the Mediterranean which deploy versatile F/A-18 Hornets, A-6 Intruders, A-7 Corsairs, and F-14 Tomcats and

which include ships armed with such impressive weapons as the 700-mile-range Tomahawk cruise missile. The Air Force too, has been stationing such state-of-the-art aircraft as F-15 Eagles and F-16 Fighting Falcons in the theater to play its part in gaining air superiority in case of conflict.

Equally important to the success of NATO defense has been the skill of the troops of the many nations involved in the alliance. USEUCOM has conducted a large number of training exercises each year, usually with NATO allied troops taking part. The Autumn Forge exercises have at times involved more than 200,000 troops and 400 NATO ships, as well as many thousands of air sorties. Because rapid reinforcement from the United States would be crucial if the US became involved in a general war in Europe, Reforger (REturn of FORces to GERmany) exercises have also been held annually, with as many as 20,000 troops sent to Germany from the United States to test the nation's rapid deployment capabilities. And to assure adequate equipment and supplies once the troops arrive, more and more heavy artillery equipment has been pre-positioned in the theater, with the Army striving to have enough supplies in Europe for six full divisions (60,000 to 100,000 soldiers).

How the forces of European Command will be structured in the future depends on two basic factors. One is strong political pressure in the United States to draw down the number of American military stationed in Europe and thereby save monies spent on national defense (especially in view of the relative economic health of many of the nation's NATO allies, now able to do more in their own defense). The other is the depth and duration of the changes occurring in the still-unstable republics that have replaced the Soviet Union. But until events prove conclusively that a high level of American defensive aid to western Europe is no longer necessary, the areas under the jurisdiction of European Command will continue to be of strategic importance to the US.

Becoming ever more important to American interests beyond its borders are events taking place in Latin America, the area of responsibility of US Southern Command (SOUTHCOM), established in 1963. This unified command has three components: US Army South, the US Southern Air Force, and US Naval Forces Southern Command. US Army South includes approximately 7000 troops and is headquartered at Fort Clayton, Panama City. Its primary mission is to protect the Panama Canal until it is turned over to the Republic of Panama on 31 December 1999. It also supports other missions in 12 Latin American nations, operates the Jungle Operations Training Center at Fort Sherman, Panama, and regularly carries

Top: An MP of the 82nd Airborne crouches behind his M60 during the annual Reforger exercises conducted by NATO armed forces in the Federal Republic of Germany.
Left: Men of the 1st Infantry de-train in Germany to take part in a Reforger exercise.

out multi-national training exercises with names such as Blazing Trails, Kindle Liberty, and Blue Horizon.

Southern Command receives only a small fraction of the Department of Defense budget (0.1 percent), but its missions proved to be of considerable importance in the 1980s, particularly in the two Central American hotspots of Panama and Nicaragua. While difficulties with the Panamanian government of Manuel Noreiga eventually led to successful American military intervention with Operation JUST CAUSE in 1989, the Nicaraguan situation fostered a good deal of insecurity in Central America and led to devisive policy debates in Congress. It is still not clear whether the problem has been completely lain to rest.

After the Sandinistas took power in Nicaragua in 1979 by overthrowing the regime of General Anastasio Somoza, their Marxist-Leninist government, with the aid of Soviet, Cuban, North Korean, Libyan, and PLO advisors, built an army of 80,000 men (120,000 if reservists and militia are counted) equipped with modern Soviet weapons and

Right: US and German troops, standing in the shadow of an M60 tank, discuss tractics during a Reforger exercise.
Below: An M1 Abrams main battle tank in the 1982 Reforger exercise. Such field testing helped to provide information that resulted in the much-improved M1A1 Abrams.

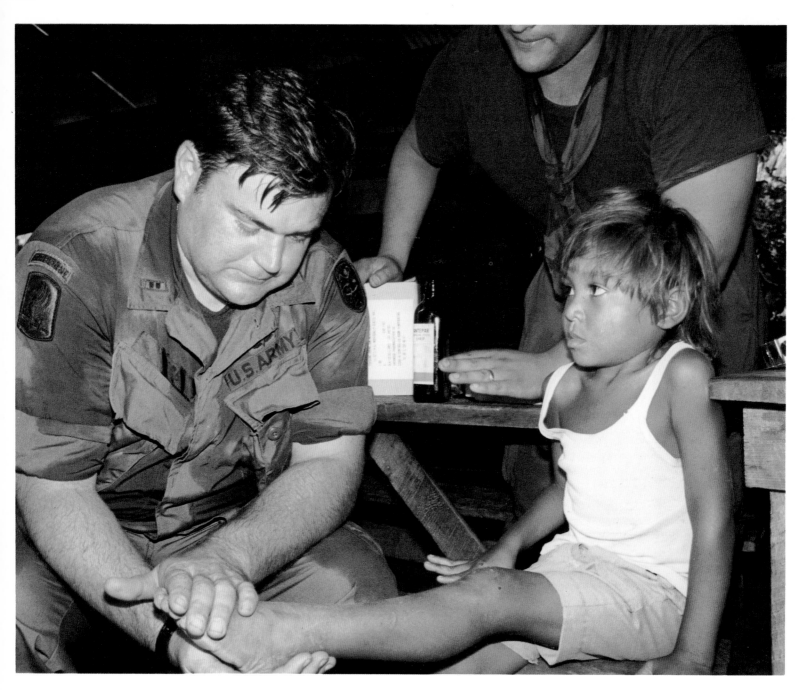

deploying more armored vehicles than in all the rest of Central America combined. Alarmed by the rise of what it considered a new base for potential Soviet subversion – or even direct aggression – in the Americas, the Reagan administration was overtly hostile to the new Nicaraguan government and gave direct military and humanitarian aid to Nicaragua's anti-Sandinista contra rebels. At one point, in March 1988, two battalions of the 82nd Airborne Division out of Fort Bragg, North Carolina, and two battalions of the 7th Infantry Division (Light) from Fort Ord, California, 3200 soldiers in all, were airlifted into Honduras in Operation GOLDEN PHEASANT to stop Sandinista soldiers from making incursions into Honduras in pursuit of contras. By early 1990, however, the Sandinistas had lost power in a Nicaraguan national election, and whatever threat they represented was, if not permanently ended, at least temporarily much reduced.

Fidel Castro's Cuba had also become a secondary problem for the United States and Central America by the early 1990s, despite as many as 14,000 Soviet military personnel

stationed there and Soviet aid of $4 billion each year. Neither Cuba's authoritarian political system nor its collapsing economy provided very attractive models for other Latin Americans, and there was even some doubt about how much longer the USSR would be willing or able to underwrite the inflexible Castro regime.

Whatever the outcome of the Latin American people's struggles for democracy and economic growth as the area emerges to stand on its own in the affairs of the world, Southern Command continues to support American and friendly interests – political, economic, maritime, and military – against those who would turn Latin America's problems into an excuse for violence and further exploitation of its citizens.

US Atlantic Command, established in 1947, is almost entirely a sea command. Its responsibility is to guard US interests in the Atlantic Ocean from the North to the South Pole, an area of 45 million square miles. Headquartered in Norfolk, Virginia, USLANTCOM regularly has but a handful of Army personnel, but it is authorized, as needed, to call up

A member of one of Southern Command's MEDCAP team gives medical treatment to a village lad during the course of an Army exercise conducted in Honduras in 1983.

as many as three combat-ready Army divisions under Army Forces Atlantic.

US Central Command (CENTCOM) was created in 1983 as the successor to the Rapid Deployment Force of the Carter years. It is the unified command for American interests in Southwest Asia, the Persian Gulf, and the area around the Horn of Africa. It is charged with ensuring the uninterrupted flow of oil through the Strait of Hormuz, the Gulf of Oman, and the Persian Gulf: with promoting security for friendly states in the area: and with responding to military challenges such as that posed by Iraq in 1990.

CENTCOM, headquartered at MacDill Air Force Base in Tampa, Florida, has no troops but its own but has the authority to call on and direct more than 400,000 personnel from all the armed services, including ground forces, fighter and bomber wings, Marine amphibious forces, Army Rangers, special forces from the Army, Air Force and Navy, carrier battle groups, and other US Navy forces.

Shipboard pre-positioning and planning for logistical support for Middle East operations has also always been within the purview of Central Command in its preparation of any military eventuality in the 19 countries that constitute its area of authority.

As with other unified commands, CENT-COM has carried out extensive exercises not only in the United States (eg. Gallant Eagle) but also in the Middle East, with its biennial Bright Star exercises utilizing up to 20,000 soldiers, sailors, and airmen, as well as nationals from allied countries in the region. That unified commands in general and Central Command in particular were well prepared for coordinated air, land, and sea warfare was dramatically illustrated by the Gulf War of 1990-91.

The US Space Command, a unified command charged with US military space operations, ballistic missile defense planning, and directing space support operations for the Joint Chiefs and other unified and specified commands, was created in 1985. Head-quartered at Peterson Air Force Base, Colorado, with its nerve center in Colorado Springs, SPACECOM has three components: the Air Force Space Command and the Army Space Agency, both at Colorado Springs, and the Naval Space Command located at Dahlgren, Virginia. The existing North American Aerospace Defense Command (a US-Canadian cooperative radar early warning system designed to thwart trans-polar ICBMs) has been retained to work closely with the Space Command, the commander of each being dual-hatted to assure close coordination of information. The Army plays a slightly smaller role than the Air Force and Navy in Space Command.

The key to the success of this unified command is its ability to gather, assess, and coordinate all space-based intelligence. This information is then disseminated to the Joint Chiefs and the commanders in the field for maximum use in carrying out the technologically sophisticated warfare that marks the present stage of military development. Its role in the Gulf War was vital to the success of that operation.

The US Special Operations Command (SOCOM), mandated in the Goldwater-Nichols Act, came into being in 1987 to provide coordinated covert operations within the American military. Special forces carrying out covert operations had been enthusiastically supported by President Kennedy in the early 1960s, but they were largely subsumed by conventional operations and fell increasingly into disuse and fragmentation in Vietnam and in the years that followed. The

Right: Egyptian troops salute US colors during Bright Star 80, one of a series of exercises that were conducted in the Middle East to hone US desert-fighting skills.
Right: Men of the 101st Airborne unload a UH-60 Black Hawk from a transport aircraft after Bright Star 81. Such desert exercises proved their worth in the 1991 Gulf War.

debacle of the Desert One hostage rescue attempt in Iran in April 1980 revealed their weaknesses and led to the Holloway Commission recommending that special forces coordination, training, and mission specificity were absolutely imperative. With the Reagan administration pushing for these goals, emphasis was again placed on special operations forces working in a unified manner, and Special Operations Command thus came into being.

The SOCOM has four major components: the Army's 1st Special Operations Command at Fort Bragg, North Carolina: the Naval Special Warfare Command at Coronado, California: the 23rd Air Force at Hurlburt Field, Florida: and the Joint Special Operations Command at Pope Air Force Base, North Carolina.

The Army's 1st Special Operations Command is the largest of all and is composed of active duty, reserve, and National Guard forces. Included are eight special forces

groups, a Ranger regiment, a psychological operations group, and aviation and support groups. Cross-training and joint exercises with other special operations forces and with conventional forces are regular parts of the rigorous training given its personnel.

Also created in 1987 was the US Transportation Command (TRANSCOM), designed to provide airlift, sealift, and terminal services, plus commercial air and land transportation, for deploying and sustaining American forces anywhere in the world. The Transportation Command, headquartered at Scott Air Force Base, Illinois, has three major components. These are the Air Force's Military Airlift Command, the Navy's Military Sealift Command, and the Army's Military Traffic Management Command, headquartered at Falls Church, Virginia. With a heavy emphasis on coordination, pre-planning, and full use of data processing, and relying heavily on reserve forces to supplement the regulars in keeping the logistical

pipeline flowing, the relatively new Transportation Command proved in the Gulf War that it would do the job even when faced with exceptional difficulties.

In addition to the unified commands, there are also two specified commands in America's military system. These are the Strategic Air Command (SAC) and the Forces Command (FORSCOM). The Strategic Air Command, headquartered at Offutt Air Force Base, Nebraska, is 'all Air Force,' with 54 units at 39 bases in the continental United States and 16 overseas. With military personnel numbering 124,000, it is America's long-range bomber and intercontinental ballistic missile strike force. As such, it flies more than 2000 aircraft (including B-1, B-2, and B-52 bombers, as well as numerous tankers and reconnaissance aircraft), and it controls over 1000 ICBMs (including Peacekeeper, Minuteman II, and Minuteman III missiles).

The second specified command is Forces

Command. Created in 1987 and headquartered at Fort McPherson, Georgia, FORSCOM's primary mission is to train, equip, and prepare the Army's forces for deployment overseas in support of forward-based contingents. In this capacity, it is in charge of 19 major installations and 1 million soldiers, that is, all the active, reserve, and Guard forces in the continental United States, Alaska, Puerto Rico, and the Virgin Islands.

Its active component is made up of over 250,000 men and women in six armies, three corps, 12 divisions, and four separate brigades. Its reserve component is made up of over 300,000 soldiers in 25 commands, 12 training divisions, and 3 separate infantry brigades. Its Guard component consists of 450,000 guardsmen in 10 divisions, 17 brigades, and four armored cavalry regiments. All must be trained, equipped, and mobilized to augment forward-deployed troops at any time.

A second mission of FORSCOM is defense

Above: President George Bush observes a mock tank battle in the Mojave desert.
Left: The complex gunner's station in the turret of an Abrams tank. Operating modern hi-tech weaponry requires very high levels of skill which must be maintained by both constant training and practice.

of the continental United States and Alaska. To this end it coordinates its efforts with the five continental armies and state units and with the Canadian Forces Mobile Command.

Training for combat-readiness and deployment being its primary goal. Forces Command supervizes training for all its constituent units. Its National Training Center at Fort Irwin, California, is the Army's premier training facility and also operates as a joint training center for all the military services under direction of the Department of Defense. FORSCOM also carries out joint training exercises through the Joint Readiness Training Center at Fort Chaffee, Arkansas, and through amphibious training exercises with the Navy's US Pacific and US Atlantic Commands at Coronado, California, and Little Creek, Virginia. In addition, it con-

ducts joint exercises with the Air Force, as well as deploying its US-based forces overseas to participate in joint training exercises such as Team Spirit in Korea, Reforger in Europe, and Bright Star in the Middle East.

Forces Command is perhaps the best illustration of how the traditional separation in the Army between regulars, reservists, and guardsmen is becoming a thing of the past and how service mission exclusivity, interservice rivalries, and lack of cooperation are coming to an end under the impact of the unified and specified command structures. The positive results of these structural changes became manifest in Panama in 1989 and in the Middle East the following year.

Panama: Operation JUST CAUSE

In February 1988 the Republic of Panama came under the right-wing dictatorial rule of General Manuel Antonio Noriega, whose main sources of power were his 'Dignity Battalions' of about 8000 pro-Noriega irregulars and his army, the Panama Defense Forces. Once he was in authority, there seemed no easy way to get rid of Noriega. When Pana-

manian voters went to the polls and overwhelmingly voted him out of office, Noreiga simply voided the election and refused to allow the winning candidates to be sworn into office. Meantime, Noreiga had been indicted by two US federal grand juries on charges of dealing in illicit drugs and laundering drug profits through Panamanian banks. The United States government wanted him brought to justice.

US-Panamanian relations deteriorated steadily and reached a crisis when Noreiga's men killed an American serviceman and when, in response to US protests, Noreiga made the foolish gesture of declaring war on the United States, American military units stationed within the country, supplemented by additional forces from the outside, were ordered by President George Bush on 17 December 1989 to invade Panama in what

Left: Panamanian strongman General Manuel Antonio Noriega in March 1988, a month after he had assumed dictatorial power in the strategically important republic.
Below: A UH-60 Black Hawk clatters over the streets of Panama City in the aftermath of operation JUST CAUSE, the US invasion of Panama on 20 December 1989.

came to be called Operation JUST CAUSE. Bush's purposes were fourfold: to protect American citizens, to support the thwarted democratic institutions in Panama, to ensure the continued operation of the Panama Canal, and to apprehend General Noreiga.

Long before the H-hour of 1:00 am on 20 December 1989 the 13,000 American troops in Panama were preparing to move against Noreiga, and steps were being taken to airlift in another 9000 troops from bases around the United States. Indeed, some 4500 troops, plus tanks and attack helicopters, had been shipped into Panama in the months before the operation got underway. So well planned and executed was Operation JUST CAUSE that within seven hours after the combined-service operation was launched the 9000 additional American troops had parachuted or been flown into Panama, the initial assault had been completed, Panama City was under the effective control of American troops, the PDF had been neutralized, and Noreiga was on the run and hiding from the American soldiers. JUST CAUSE clearly showed that the changes in force development, unified command, and training regimens instituted in the 1980s were capable of paying rich dividends.

Directing the invasion of Panama was the commander in chief of the Southern Command, General Maxwell Thurman. Days before H-hour special operations forces were shadowing Noreiga's moves, carrying out reconnaissance missions in and around Panama City and the canal, and watching the movements of PDF units. On Tuesday, 19 December, huge Air Force transports were landing at Howard Air Force Base at 10-minute intervals bringing soldiers and supplies into the area.

The on-site and augmenting troops were divided into five task forces, each with its own mission. Task Force Red was ordered to seize the airfield at Rio Hato 90 kilometers southwest of the capital and Torrijos International Airport in the city. To capture the Rio Hato airfield, Army Rangers parachuted in and attacked the two companies of PDF forces there, in the process being aided by Air Force F-117A Stealth fighters which dropped concussion bombs on the defenders, the first combat mission for the new radar-invisible fighters. Some 250 PDF prisoners were taken at Rio Hato as the airfield was secured, and within two hours giant C-130s were landing with additional equipment and supplies. The secondary task of TF Red, the seizure of Torrijos International Airport, was carried out by the men of the 82nd Airborne Division from Fort Bragg, North Carolina, who jumped in two waves and secured the facility.

The men of Task Force Bayonet had three assignments when they started out a little after midnight. First, they attacked the Comandancia, Noreiga's military command building in the heart of Panama City, with tanks and howitzers supported by gunships and attack helicopters. Second, elements of the Navy's special operations Seals (SEA, Air and Land capability) units attached to TF Bayonet rushed Patilla Airport, a private facility in the capital, securing the airstrip and destroying Noreiga's Learjet to preclude his escape by air. Four Seals were killed in this operation because an intelligence failure left them without warning that they would be up against armored troops. In the meantime, other Seals disabled boats that might have been used by Noreiga for an escape by sea. Third, TF Bayonet troops carried out an airborne assault via Black Hawk helicopters to cut off PDF troops at Fort Amador south of the Comandancia, while also securing the United States Embassy, Southern Command headquarters, and the headquarters of US Army South at Fort Clayton.

Task Force Pacific was given the task of reinforcing the on-site troops at Torrijos Airport. They carried this out by jumping in two waves of paratroopers of the 82nd Airborne Division from Air Force C-141 transports. Critics later pointed out that the 82nd could just as well have been landed at the airport

Right: On the third day of the invasion of Panama a US soldier in Panama City pauses in front of a poster of General Noriega. Two days later, Noriega would seek asylum in the Vatican nunciature in Panama City.

Above: An American NCO positions his men outside the Marriott Hotel in Panama City. Some 100 civilians, many Americans, had been held in the hotel by Noriega forces.
Left: Chairman of the Joint Chiefs of Staff General Colin Powell (l) holds a briefing on the Panama invasion in Washington, DC.

rather than carrying out a dangerous night-time jump. Whatever the validity of that criticism, the soldiers of the 82nd joined up with Rangers and other special forces to block the PDF forces from Fort Cimarron from reaching the city. In this blocking operation the soldiers received valuable assistance from AC-130 gunships, which helped drive the PDF forces back to the fort.

While all this was going on Task Force Semper Fidelis, consisting of Marine Corps rifle and light infantry companies stationed in the area, assisted by a TF Bayonet contingent and the Marine's First Fleet Antiterrorism Security Team, blocked the Bridge of the Americas in the southern part of the city to prevent a PDF counterattack on Howard Air Force Base.

Across Panama, at the northern end of the canal, Task Force Atlantic was carrying out its part of the combined operation. Composed of elements of the 82nd Airborne Division and of the 7th Infantry Division, plus other special units, TF Atlantic seized the canal facilities near Colon from PDF infantry and naval infantry units. They also seized the valuable Madden Dam, which feeds the canal locks, and Gamboa Prison, where they released 45-50 political prisoners arrested in the earlier attempt to overthrow Noriega.

In the days that followed these successful assaults PDF forces and Dignity Battalion soldiers continued to hide from the Americans and carry out sniping attacks in Panama City. Much media attention was focused on the successful American operation to secure the Marriott Hotel where some 100 people, many of them Americans, were rescued from Panamanian forces.

Yet the assault on Panama was really over on the first day, as General Colin L Powell, the chairman of the Joint Chiefs of Staff, announced to the American people on television that evening. The one great task remaining was the capture of the elusive Manuel Noreiga. But with his forces killed, captured, or in hiding, he had already been effectively deposed and neutralized, much to the delight of the Panamanian people. A democratically elected government was, in fact, already in power in Panama City, the president-elect, Guillermo Endara, having taken the oath of office at the headquarters of US Army South at Fort Clayton on the evening of the first day of the battle.

With his forces smashed and nowhere to go, Noreiga finally sought refuge in the nunciature of the Vatican on 25 December. Although being thus protected from arrest by the laws of sanctuary, he could not escape, especially as the nunciature was immediately surrounded by American troops. He finally surrendered to US Drug Enforcement Administration authorities on the evening of 3 January 1990 and was flown by an Air Force plane to federal custody in Florida to face the drug charges placed against him.

Operation JUST CAUSE was over. In the successful combined operation only 23 Americans had been killed in action, and 330 had been wounded. Since this was largely an Army operation, it is not surprising that 18 of the soldiers killed and 288 of those wounded were Army personnel. JUST CAUSE had not been without its failures, especially in intelligence, but it had justified the combined forces concept adopted and trained for in the 1980s. As General Edward Meyer, former chief of staff of the Army, said, 'The Panama operation outlined the rationale for the type of forces we will require in the future.'

The Gulf War: the Background

Iraq, a nation of 18 million persons, of whom about one-half are Shiite Muslims, one-fourth Sunni Muslims, and about one-fourth Kurds with their own language, culture, and separatist tendencies, had been governed since 1979 by the Sunni Saddam Hussein in a thoroughly dictatorial fashion. He professed

strongly anti-Western and anti-Israeli sentiments and allowed such renowned terrorists as Abu Nidal refuge in Iraq. But when his 1980 invasion of neighboring Iran bogged down, he was forced to turn to the West and other countries for help. The United States was inclined to be sympathetic to his pleas for aid because the Iran of Ayatollah Khomeini seemed the greater threat to American interests in the Middle East. Besides, there was hope expressed that Hussein might now be more inclined to moderation in his dealings with the West.

In 1982 the United States removed Iraq from its list of countries that supported terrorism, and two years later it restored full diplomatic relations with Hussein's government. By the late 1980s the United States had even agreed to share intelligence information with the Iraqis. When the Iran-Iraq war finally petered out in August 1988, with Iran more-or-less the winner, it appeared that Hussein had indeed moderated his views toward the West and Israel.

But such was not the case. Hussein quickly made it clear that he saw himself as the leader destined to bring the Arab nations back to their deserved glory, by force if necessary, to assume control over the region's oil reserves, and to drive the Israelis out of the Middle East. He did not demobilize his million-man army at the close of the war but, rather, began to spend billions on new weapons (including Soviet Scud missiles, T-72 tanks, and MiG-29 fighters) and pushed ahead Iraqi research and development of chemical and nuclear weapons.

On 17 July 1990 Hussein issued a violent verbal attack on the United Arab Emirates and Kuwait, bitterly accusing the latter of building military installations on Iraqi territory, of stealing billions of dollars worth of oil from the Iraqi portion of the Rumaila oil field

Top: Captured members of Noriega's army, the Panama Defense Forces, mill about in a temporary prison compound.
Above: Iraqi President Saddam Hussein (l) confers with his foreign minister, Tariq Aziz, at a 1987 Arab summit meeting held to discuss the Iran-Iraq War.

that spans their joint border, and of overproducing oil, this driving the world price of crude down. More ominously, he began to amass 30,000 troops along the Kuwaiti border.

Although it had earlier declined to impose sanctions on Hussein, despite his bellicosity, the Bush administration was clearly disturbed by Hussein's threats to Kuwait and to peace in the Middle East. On 25 July the administration sent US Ambassador to Iraq, April Glaspie, to talk with the Iraqi president. Hussein refused to back down but did promise that he would not invade Kuwait

while his current discussions with President Hosni Mubarak of Egypt were continuing. This promise was cynically broken when hundreds of Iraqi tanks and other vehicles rolled across the border into Kuwait on 2 August 1990. The Gulf crisis had come to a head.

The Gulf War: DESERT SHIELD, 2 August 1990-14 January 1991

As Saddam Hussein's force of tanks, armored vehicles, and infantry rolled into Kuwait City, the capital, they quickly seized government buildings, the central bank (where the Iraqis confiscated millions in foreign currency and gold bars), the international airport, and the Dasman palace of Sheik Jaber al-Ahmed al-Sabah. Al-Sabah, the Emir of Kuwait, fled to Saudi Arabia by helicopter: his younger brother, Sheik Fahd, was killed defending the palace. Hussein then announced the annexation of Kuwait as the 19th providence of Iraq.

The United Nations Security Council demanded the immediate withdrawal of all Iraqi forces from Kuwait, but Hussein had no intention of doing so. By annexing Kuwait he had doubled his oil reserves, which now constituted 20 percent of the world's oil supply. If he were next to invade Saudi Arabia, which seemed alarmingly likely, he would control 40 percent.

Hussein had counted on the supposition that the United States would be unwilling to take a strong military stand against him. As he said, 'Yours is a society that cannot lose 10,000 dead in one battle.' He may or may not have been right, but the Bush administration

and the American military, having learned some lessons from the Vietnam experience of two decades before, had no intention of fighting a high-casualty, protracted war of attrition this time around. War with Iraq, if it came, would be fought on an entirely different basis.

Nor were Hussein's suppositions about the weak response that other countries would make to his aggression borne out. The United Nations, with almost universal support from its member states, including the Soviet Union (more in need of Western economic aid than of the continued friendship of Iraq), not only placed a complete trade and financial embargo on Iraq but continued to strengthen its stand thereafter.

Indeed, Hussein failed to get any significant support even from fellow Arabs. Saudi Arabia, under King Fahd, heretofore conciliatory and unwilling to take any action that would endanger its regional friendships and oil revenues, quickly decided to join the US and UN in opposing the Iraqi invasion of Kuwait. Soon thereafter 12 Arab League nations, led by Egypt's President Hosni Mubarak, demanded that Iraq withdraw from Kuwait and pledged their military forces to defend Saudi Arabia and any other Arab state threatened by Iraq. Five nations abstained from these resolutions, but only Saddam Hussein's Iraq, Muammar Qaddaffi's Libya, and Yasir Arafat's Palestine Liberation Organization voted against them. Jordan's King Hussein tried desperately, if none too skilfully, to stay neutral on that occasion and in the months to come, but non-Arab Turkey, a well-armed member of NATO with little to fear from Saddam Hussein, also joined the

Above: On 9 August 1990 the UN Security Council declares Iraq's annexation of Kuwait to be null and void.
Opposite top: Among the first US troops to arrive in Saudi Arabia after the invasion of Kuwait were members of the 82nd Airborne.
Opposite: A massive tent city in Saudi Arabia housing elements of the 1st Cavalry.

coalition being fashioned by President Bush, agreeing to stop Iraq's pipeline across Turkish territory to the Mediterranean.

Thus within weeks a diplomatic and military ring had been formed around Saddam Hussein and Iraq. Yet he still would not back down. If, he reasoned, he could hold what he had and withstand the embargo by causing defections within ranks of the states that had agreed to impose it, he could still emerge victorious and in control of Kuwait. And in the end, it was his army that would be his final trump card.

On the eve of Iraq's invasion of Kuwait, Saddam Hussein had 5000 tanks, including over 1000 modern T-72s with 125mm guns; 6000 armored personnel carriers; 5000 artillery pieces, including Soviet-made multiple rocket launchers and G5 howitzers with a range of 24 miles purchased from South Africa; and some 600 aircraft (these included a limited number of Mig-25 and Mig-29 high-performance fighters and Su-24 and Su-25 attack planes).

Hussein also had Soviet- and French-made surface-to-air missiles in his inventory, plus Soviet Scud surface-to-surface missiles, capable of carrying warheads of 1000 pounds of conventional explosives and modified to fly beyond their designed range of 300 miles.

He also had supplies of poison gas (mustard, tabun, and sarin) and binary chemical weapons, and he was prepared to use them, as evidenced by his earlier use of poison gas against the Iranians and then even against his own people (as in the case of the 5000 Kurds gassed to death in the town of Halabja). There was also some evidence collected by Western intelligence sources which indicated that he might soon have nuclear weaponry.

President Bush had forged and then held together the coalition formed against Iraq, hoping military action would not be necessary, but he nevertheless began working through his military leaders, and especially through Colin L Powell, the chairman of the Joint Chiefs of Staff, to build up American forces in the Middle East should it become necessary to confront Hussein. Responsibility for this operation fell to CENTCOM and its commander in chief, General H Norman Schwarzkopf, 'the Bear', soon to become one of the best known officers in the US military.

Although CENTCOM's war plans had been originally designed to counter an attack by the Soviet Union through Iran toward the Persian Gulf, they proved to be applicable, with modifications, to the new

CENTCOM chief General H. Norman Schwarzkopf led the allied coalition against Iraq in both the buildup phase (DESERT SHIELD) and the combat phase (DESERT STORM).

problem. They called for combat aircraft to be flown to Oman, Saudi Arabia, or Kuwait and for two airborne units to be sent to the Southwest Asia on short notice (the 82nd Division of paratroopers and the 101st Airborne Division, the latter being heavily equipped with troop-transport and anti-tank helicopters, plus specially designed dune buggies and light Sheridan tanks). Three 15,000-man Marine brigades would also be flown into the area, there to be supplied with equipment from three flotillas of ships prepositioned at Diego Garcia in the Indian Ocean. Follow-on equipment in the form of tanks, trucks, and other heavy vehicles would be transported via eight roll-on/roll-off ships docked in the United States and immediately available.

As the UN embargo went into effect in the fall of 1990, and while the United States and its allies persisted in their efforts to solve the problem without war, the overall strategy of the Bush administration in Operation DESERT SHIELD took shape. First, the US would act through the United Nations to build a multi-national military force in Saudi Arabia to protect that country and to free Kuwait by military force if necessary. Second, other nations in whose co-interest the actions were being taken would be asked to help pay for the operation: Germany and Japan, plus Saudi Arabia and Kuwait, promised to pay $51 billion to help defray America's cost. Third, to maintain the coalition aligned

against Iraq, Saddam Hussein's demands at 'linkage' between the Kuwait question and the Israel-Palestine question would be rejected. The United States would promise to work toward a settlement of the Palestinian issue diplomatically after, and only after, Kuwait had been liberated.

By December 1990 American troops in the Gulf totalled 540,000 men and women. Added to these US combatants were the 1st Armored Division, as well as planes and ships, from Britain; the light armored 6th Division, as well as planes, tanks, APCs, and warships, from France; ships from Argentina, Australia, Belgium, Denmark, Greece, Italy, the Netherlands, Norway, Poland, Portugal, and Spain; and warships and planes from Canada. From the Middle East were added two armored divisions and a commando regiment from Egypt; an armored division from Syria; and men, planes, tanks, and ships from various other countries in the region. This represented the greatest multi-national force assembled for warfare since the end of World War II.

Still Hussein would not back down. The United Nations on 29 November gave him until 15 January to get out of Kuwait, and on 12 January, Congress gave President Bush the authority to use the American military to carry out UN Resolution 678 for the freedom of Kuwait. A last-minute flying mission by UN Secretary General Javier Perez de Cuellar on 13 January to plead directly to Hussein to

A Patriot missile roars from its launcher. Though
mainly an anti-aircraft weapon, the Patriot did well
against Iraq's Scud surface-to-surface missiles.

withdraw from Kuwait also failed. All possibilities for a peaceful solution had been exhausted. Now DESERT SHIELD was about to
become DESERT STORM.

The Gulf War: DESERT STORM, 15 January-27 February 1991

DESERT STORM began with an air assault
that lasted from 15 January through 23
February. The American-coalition offensive
started in the early morning darkness of 16
January when dozens of Tomahawk cruise
missiles from the battleships *Wisconsin* and
Missouri were launched against Baghdad.
Simultaneously, hundreds of landbased and
seabased planes and AH-64 Apache helicopters, all equipped with special radar units
and infrared sensors for night vision, swept in
on the Iraqi capital. This was the beginning of
an aerial attack that for the next five weeks
would average 3000 sorties per day.

After one week the coalition air forces had
inflicted such heavy losses on the Iraqi air
force that it faced complete annihilation.
Over 130 Iraqi pilots flew their planes to sanctuary in Iran – where the Iranian government
promptly confiscated them. The coalition air

offensive was technologically aided by
American and Saudi AWACs planes able
both to see all friendly and enemy movement
in the air and on the ground and to direct coalition attack planes against Iraqi targets.

The air offensive made good use of such
amazingly sophisticated ordnance as Pave-
way laser-guided bombs capable of following anti-aircraft laser beams to their sources
and destroying them; HARM antiradiation
missiles that followed enemy air defense
radar beams to destroy them; GBU-15 'smart'
bombs using a TV guidance system to strike
their targets with precision; BLU-82 'daisy-
cutter' bombs that released their explosives
above ground, destroying everything and
everyone below; Maverick missiles with
infrared sensors; and laser-guided Hellfire
missiles capable of taking out a tank from five
miles away.

By the fifth week of the air war about 200
tanks were being eradicated each night; un-
told numbers of artillery pieces had been
destroyed along the Iraqi lines; reinforcement trucks with food, water, and medicine
could not move up to supply the Iraqis night
or day; enemy communications had largely
been wiped out; and the Iraqi troops in their

trenches were being pounded unmercifully,
knowing full well that a ground attack was
sure to follow.

Hussein's reaction to the air assault was to
fire his Scud missiles at Israel and Saudi
Arabia. His hope in launching the missiles
into Israel was to draw that country into the
war and thus split the Arabs away from coalition arrayed against him. But, not without
heated debate between Israeli political and
military hardliners and moderates, the Israeli
government decided not to retaliate (unless
chemical warheads were used) and to let the
coalition forces knock out the Scud launchers
and defeat Iraq without Israel's help. To help
convince Israel of the wisdom of its stand, the
coalition forces made a concerted effort to
find and destroy the Scud launch sites (the
Americans thought there were only a few
dozen Scuds; actually there were over 200 in
Iraq's arsenal) and also rushed in Patriot surface-to-air missile units and their crews from
Germany to help protect the Israeli population. Except for a solitary hit on a US Army

barracks in Dhahran, wherein 28 American servicemen were killed, the Scuds did very little damage to Israel, Saudi Arabia, or the coalition forces.

Hussein's only other response was a 29 January four-unit armor attack on Khafji, a city of 35,000 people six miles below the Kuwait-Saudi Arabia border, in the hope both of forcing the Americans and their allies into a land war before they were ready and of stopping the increasingly effective air campaign against his nation. One armored unit made it into now-deserted Khafji and held it for two days before being driven out by coalition air and ground forces; the other three armored units were stopped in their tracks and destroyed before they could even arrive at their objective.

On 22 February, President Bush announced that the Iraqi leader would have until noon (EST) the next day to begin withdrawing from Kuwait. If not, the offensive against him would continue, a clear signal that the land war was about to begin. Still Hussein would not give in and ordered his forces to begin dynamiting the oil wells of Kuwait in an act of wanton destruction. Thus the die was cast.

While the coalition air units had been pummeling Iraqi airfields, command and control centers, missile sites, storage facilities, and chemical plants, General Schwarzkopf and his CENTCOM staff had been busy refining the details of their projected land offensive. Basically Schwarzkopf's forces, consisting of some 500,000 Americans, 20,000 Syrians, 35,000 Egyptians, 40,000 Saudis, 35,000 British, 10,000 Frenchmen, 7000 Kuwaitis, and 17,000 soldiers from other nations, would carry out three operations.

The first element of the plan was that a 17,000-man Marine amphibious force carried in 33 Navy ships off Kuwait in the Persian Gulf would *not* make an amphibious landing as the Iraqis supposed (the Leathernecks had carried out highly-publicized practice landings on key islands off the Kuwaiti coasts). They would, instead, remain in place to draw Iraqi forces out of the center of the line along the southern border of Kuwait to guard against landings on the eastern shore of the country. In effect, thanks to this feint, many of the Iraqi troops and their defensive ordnance would be facing the wrong direction.

Second, an offensive would be launched into southern Kuwait by Kuwaiti, Syrian, Saudi and other Arab units with the US Marines.

Third, and perhaps the most audacious move of the campaign, General Schwarzkopf lined up the remainder of his assault forces in a 200-mile line well to the east, between the Tapline Road and the Kuwaiti-Saudi Arabian

Left top: Wreckage in Riyadh, Saudi Arabia, caused by an Iraqi Scud missile that got past the defending Patriot batteries.
Left center: An Iraqi personnel carrier wrecked in the battle for Khafji.
Left: An armada of fuel and supply trucks follows the US 1st Armored Division as it moves into position to strike into Iraq in the final days of DESERT STORM.

border, so that they could be used to sweep forward north and then east in a grand envelopment of the enemy forces in southern Iraq and Kuwait. This move was possible because the air campaign had severely interfered with the Iraqi command's ability to know where the coalition forces were at any given moment, and, therefore, to make informed guesses about their intentions. Schwarzkopf later, somewhat loosely, referred to this as a 'Hail Mary' maneuver.

A 'Hail Mary' play in football is a desperation play wherein the quarterback can only pray that a receiver far away in the end zone will be able to catch his pass, but there was no hint of desperation in this brilliantly planned flanking tactic.

By 0400 on 24 February, jump-off time, the coalition ground forces were lined up along the Kuwaiti-Saudi Arabian border from east to west as follows: a Joint Forces unit (Saudis, Kuwaitis, Omanis, and soldiers of the United Arab Emirates); the 2nd marine Division; the Tiger Brigade of 2nd Armored Division; the 1st Marine Division; and a second Joint Forces unit (Saudis, Syrians, Eqyptians, Kuwaitis, Pakistanis). Farther west along the Iraq-Saudi Arabian border, the forces lined up from east to west were: the British 1st Armored Division; VII Corps, consisting of the 1st Infantry Division (Mech), known throughout the Army as 'The Big Red One,' and the 1st Cavalry Regiment; the 1st Armored Division; and XVIII Corps, consisting of the 24th Infantry Division (Mech), the 3rd Armored Cavalry Regiment, the 101st Airborne Division (Air Assault), the 82nd Airborne Division, and the French 6th Light Armored Division.

At 4:00 in the morning of 24 February the attack began, with the 1st and 2nd Marine Divisions breaching the Iraqi deep barrier system along the south central border of Kuwait. They were supported by the Tiger Brigade of the 2nd Armored division, which advanced between them. At the same time, at the far end of the line out to the west, the French 6th Armored and the 2nd Brigade of the 82nd Airborne Division, closely followed by the rest of the 82nd, launched an overland attack toward the As Salman airfield 50 miles inside Iraq. Simultaneously, the Joint Arab Forces along the southern Kuwaiti border near the Gulf broke through Iraqi fortified lines and headed straight up the coast toward Kuwait City.

Four hours later, at 8:00 on the morning of 24 February, the 101st Airborne 'Screaming Eagles' launched the largest helicopter assault in military history as 4000 men were airlifted 60 miles into Iraqi territory to establish a forward supply base. They would then move toward a point on the Euphrates River only 150 miles from Baghdad.

In the afternoon of 24 February the Joint Forces in the center of the line (Saudis, Syrians, Eqyptians, Kuwaitis, and Pakistanis) crossed the border into southwestern Kuwait. To their left, VII Corps also began to penetrate and then rush through the Iraqi defenses, cutting through the Iraqi minefields with no difficulty as it raced north. Meanwhile, the 24th Infantry Division (Mech) tore through on the left and pushed deep into the interior of Iraq.

Much of the success of these attacks could be credited to special forces teams which for weeks had been reconnoitering far behind the enemy lines in helicopters and muffled dune buggies (FAVs, or fast attack vehicles) and now carried out direct-action sabotage and range-spotting missions as the coalition forces pushed into Kuwait and Iraq. Another important factor was that the total allied air cover made it almost impossible for Iraqi forces to move without endangering themselves, even at night.

By the end of the first day the entire network of Iraqi fortified lines had been

Officers of the 1st Armored Division work out some of the battle tactics that helped make the Gulf War so amazingly brief.

penetrated and coalition forces were racing north deep into Kuwait and Iraq. Military leaders in the field and from CENTCOM all the way up to the Joint Chiefs and the Department of Defense were frankly astonished at the success of the first day's fighting, as, indeed, was the whole world.

Days two and three, 25 and 26 February, brought more successes to the coalition forces. The Arab Joint Forces on the east drove north toward Kuwait City while the 2nd Marines, the Tiger Brigade, and the second Arab Joint Forces group on their left, paralleled their moves deep into Kuwait. To their left VII Corps, in the center of the line, continued to drive rapidly northward, then swept to the east to confront Hussein's elite Republican Guards in northern Kuwait. Still farther left on 25 and 26 February, the American armored and cavalry divisions continued to drive deep into Iraq before also wheeling right to take on other Republican Guard units in the southeastern corner of that country and in northern Kuwait. Meantime, the 82nd Division was blocking any counterattacks or reinforcements from the north, and the 24th Infantry (Mech) was sealing off the Tigris-Euphrates valley and preventing the escape of Iraqi forces fleeing north.

Everywhere that the coalition forces moved during these first three days they found their Iraqi adversaries usually willing to surrender with little or no resistance. Deprived of food, water, and medical care and dazed and frightened by five weeks of constant terror from the skies, they seldom put up stiff resistance when faced with the overwhelming firepower and maneuverability of the coalition forces. It is estimated that as many as 100,000 Iraq soldiers

Above: Some of the 100,000 Iraqi troops who surrendered to the allied coalition forces during the 100-hour land war.

Below: Use of such sophisticated weapons in the Gulf War as the Tomahawk cruise missile was a foretaste of what combat might be like in the next century.

surrendered during the ground war, this number matching the 100,000 Iraqi dead and the 100,000 who deserted during the four-day land war.

By the fourth day of the land war, 27 February, it was clear that the fighting was coming to an end. As XVIII Corps was moving into southern Iraq and the city of Basra, VII Corps, in the center, met and soundly defeated the Republican Guards in an all-out tank battle. The 1st Marine Division seized Kuwait International Airport while the 2nd Marine Division blocked all exits from the city in order to allow the Arab Joint Forces from the south and west the honor of moving up to recapture the capital city. President Bush that evening declared that at midnight the fighting would end. The 100-hour land war was over.

Reflections on the Gulf War

An outpouring of analyses and commentaries followed the end of the Gulf War, and from these certain salient conclusions have emerged that both clarify what occurred and have important implications for the decisions the United States must make when considering the nation's armed forces in the years to come:

1. The Gulf War was an overwhelming military victory for the US and coalition forces and surely resurrected both the military services' pride in themselves, much damaged in the aftermath of Vietnam, and the nation's

pride in its armed forces. But the United States must still face the fact that the nation has a plentitude of military obligations to itself and to millions of people around the world. These obligations must be upheld whether or not future wars are ultimately termed 'good' or 'bad'. The United States' military services are not an expensive luxury; they are an expensive necessity.

2. Despite all the criticism of spending for the military in the 1980s, and particularly for

its emphasis on high technology and expensive weaponry, the Gulf War proved that such spending is absolutely critical if a modern military establishment is to be maintained. The high-technology weaponry used by the nation's armed forces in the Gulf War may not in itself have spelled the difference between victory and defeat, but it certainly spelled the difference between less than a hundred US military deaths in the war and the thousands that would inevitably have

been suffered had not such weapons and the trained personnel able to man and maintain them been available.

3. Success in the Gulf War was largely a result of applying the doctrines of coordinated combined-service warfare that had been patiently fashioned for a decade and a half. AirLand Battle worked. Centralized command worked. The ability to deploy highly trained and highly motivated soldiers, sailors, airmen, and Marines worked.

4. The victory in the Gulf War must be credited to all members of the armed services, from the lowest rifleman or technician to the members of CENTCOM and the Joint Chiefs. But it must also be credited to George Bush, not only for forging and holding together a coalition of disparate nations for months on end until a victory had been achieved, but also because, unlike Lyndon Johnson in Vietnam, he established the parameters of the war and then let the military fight it. Sound military theory and practice demand such a controlled stance on the part of the supreme commander in all military conflicts, great or small.

5. Saddam Hussein's military incompetence undoubtedly contributed much to the ease with which he was defeated, but we must be wary of drawing the wrong conclusions from that fact. General Schwarzkopf was certainly right when he said at a news conference regarding Hussein as a military leader: 'He is neither a strategist, nor is he schooled in the operational art, nor is he a tactician, nor is he a general, nor is he a soldier. Other than that he's a great military man. . . .' But in its next war the United States might not be so lucky.

6. The war fought in the deserts of the Middle East was almost tailor-made for the application of overwhelming ground and air power, plus rapid, almost unimpeded, maneuverability. Any future wars, large or small, will probably not be fought under the same conditions. The US must therefore be prepared for all military contingencies through the now-proven doctrine of flexible response. If not, it could face a defeat somewhere else every bit as great as its victory in the Gulf War.

Continued Challenges of the 1990s

The Gulf War had, indeed, been won in decisive and dramatic fashion. The Army, along with the other US armed forces, won accolades from the public, who had viewed the successes of the war on television. For the first time since the Vietnam War the nation's fighting forces had faced a major challenge, and no one could doubt that they had won a resounding victory over a dangerous foe. Perhaps of greater importance, the Gulf War illustrated that the military had learned from its mistakes of the recent past, had made substantial changes in its warmaking capabilities, and had shown that it was capable of preparing for future conflicts realistically, rather than 'fighting the last war.' This change of outlook has been crucial to the Army and its sister services, their bywords for the 1990s and beyond being change and adaptability when faced with new challenges-some in historically familiar areas, some not - in a rapidly changing world.

A member of the 10th Mountain Division guards a street in Mogadishu, Somalia, in 1993.

One of the most unsettled areas of the world in the 1990s is sub-Saharan Africa. Nation after nation has seen political instability, turmoil, civil war, and famine in the decades since the rapid decolonization movement took hold in the aftermath of World War II with its resulting weakening of the former colonialist European powers. Chaos and heartbreak have been the watchwords of these countries, caught between their former subservient stage of development from their colonial days and the political and economic demands of the late 20th century. One of the most unfortunate of these nations is Somalia.

Gaining its independence from Great Britain in 1960, Somalia, on the eastern horn of Africa, witnessed nothing but chaos thereafter. Born out of the former British Somaliland and a former Italian possession, the new Somali Republic in 1969 fell under a one-man rule that lasted until January 1991 when Gen Muhammed Siyad Barrah fled from the capital of Mogadishu. Thereafter it fell into civil war between rival factions, the most dangerous being the Somali National Alliance led by Mohammed Farah Aidid. An estimated 40,000 casualties bore grisly witness to military bloodshed, banditry, and drought.

Faced with the likelihood of mass starvation of 1.5 million people in Somalia, the United Nations secretary general declared the country to be 'without a government' in July 1992 and accepted the United States' offer

Above: Army troops land in Port-au-Prince, Haiti, in September 1994.
Below: Members of the 10th Mountain Division patrol the streets of Port-au-Prince, Haiti.

to send in troops to ensure delivery of food to the starving populace. Thus, at the direction of President Bush, Operation RESTORE HOPE was launched by the US in December 1992. The Army eventually sent in 25,000 troops, the first consisting of 10,000 soldiers from the 10th Mountain Division (Light Infantry) from Fort Drum, New York. Troops from Canada, France, Italy, and Belgium joined them. The next year the UN took control of the humanitarian mission and attempted to convince all sides in the civil war to engage in negotiations to end the bitter fighting.

In March 1993 the United States began to withdraw its peacekeeping forces, leaving that duty to the Untied Nations, although 3,000 American logistical and 5,000 other troops remained behind. But violence between the tribal factions seeking to control the country continued, encouraged by weak UN decision-making and a failure to capture Gen Aidid in May. Firefights between US soldiers and Somali guerrillas in the streets of Mogadishu intensified, culminating in a series of tragic incidents in which 18 US soldiers were killed and 78 wounded in an ambush in Mogadishu on 3-4 October, causing Congress to call for a withdrawal of all US forces.

President Bill Clinton thereupon made the decision to withdraw all US forces from Somalia by mid-March 1994. By that time all United Nations-sponsored troops had pulled out of the country, leaving its people still mired in the horror of civil war and famine. The American forces had done their best to carry out their humanitarian mission and had enjoyed some success, but it was a mission launched without the military being given the authority to bring the country out of chaos and ruin by disarming the various political factions that kept the nation in chaos. The lives of US soldiers, it seemed, had been lost in vain, and Somalia's survivors were left with a future without hope of peace and stability.

The problem faced by the United States in the Caribbean nation of Haiti dated back to 1986 when the 26-year dictatorship over that country ended when President Jean-Claude Duvalier fled into exile and a military junta seized control. After further rapid turnovers of government, in 1990 a priest, Jean-Bertrand Aristide, was elected president but within a few months had been expelled as another military junta seized control. Thereafter conditions in Haiti deteriorated rapidly, economically and politically, forcing 35,000 Haitians to flee their native land for the United States. At first welcomed, their increasing numbers persuaded first President Bush and then President Clinton to have them returned to their homeland or to temporary shelter at the Navy's Guantanamo Naval Base in Cuba.

As conditions in Haiti continued to deteriorate, the United Nations imposed a near-total embargo of the country, and in 1994 the UN Security Council authorized a multinational force under US control and command to restore democracy in Haiti and secure the return of Aristide to office. President Clinton alerted the Army and the other services to prepare for an invasion, a move not approved of by most Latin American governments, the US Congress, and American public, according to the polls. Nevertheless, plans for carrying out Operation SUPPORT DEMOCRACY went forward, and on 14 September 1994 Clinton announced that an invasion of Haiti was most certainly forthcoming. Two days later, however, a special US delegation headed by ex-President Jimmy Carter, ex-chairman of the JCS General Colin Powell, and the influential Senator Sam Nunn of Georgia arrived in the Haitian capital of Port-au-Prince. Faced with a clear warning from the delegation that US land, sea, and air forces would be loosed on Haiti if the military junta did not come to terms with the UN resolution, four days later the military leaders agreed to leave office, paving the way for the restoration of Aristide.

The first US troops to land in Haiti to ensure that the agreement would be carried out and that order would be maintained were 3,000 soldiers of the Army's 10th Mountain Division from Ft. Drum, New York. They landed on 19 September 1994 and they were followed by 15,000 more troops from 25 countries. Only minimum bloodshed followed, and on 15 October Aristide was returned from exile in the United States to be restored to power. Thereafter the UN sanctions were lifted, and by 31 March 1995, all foreign troops had left Haiti (except for some assigned to police duties).

The most troubling and controversial use of the Army in the 1990s came when 18,500 of its men and women were sent as peacekeepers into Bosnia-Herzegovina in late December 1995 and early 1996 as part of a United Nations protection force 21,000 strong. With the breakup of Yugoslavia and the declaration of independence by Croatia and Slovenia in 1991, fighting between ethnic Croats and ethnic Serbs began with Serbia sending arms and supplies to Serbian rebels in Croatia.

troops already being stationed there. Fearing more instability in the volatile Middle East, on 7 October President Clinton announced that US air, land, and sea forces would be sent to Kuwait to protect its territory against any move by Saddam Hussein. Accordingly, in Operation VIGILANT WARRIOR of October-December 1994 some 40,000 ground troops, including the 24th Infantry Division (Mechanized); 28 Navy ships; and 650 aircraft were sent into the area to join the 12,000 US men and women already on duty there. Many of these latter were members of Operation SOUTHERN WATCH, inaugurated in August 1992, in which Air Force and Navy air crews patrol a 'no-fly' zone over southern Iraq to ensure Saddam Hussein's compliance with the United Nations Security Resolution 688. Faced with this show of strength, the Iraqi dictator backed down and began to withdraw the Republican Guards from the border area, and, in turn, the Defense Department

Left: The 1st Armored Division crosses the Sava River into Bosnia, 30 December 1995. *Below:* A US soldier on Operation JOINT ENDEAVOR speaks with a Bosnian child in early 1996.

The next year Serbia and Montenegro proclaimed themselves to be the Federal Republic of Yugoslavia and sent supplies to Serbian rebels in Bosnia and Herzegovina. Within three years some 200,000 people had been killed or wounded in the ensuing fighting. The continued bloodletting between Serbs, Muslims, and Croats, and campaigns 'of ethnic cleansing' in which Serbian forces killed all Muslims and non-Serbs in areas under their control, led to the United Nations imposing sanctions and finally calling for the creation of a multinational military force to impose peace on the troubled countries.

As a result, the 18,500 Army troops were dispatched to Bosnia in Operation JOINT ENDEAVOR, part of a larger United Nations force already in the country and the first time Army troops served in Eastern Europe in appreciable numbers. Aiding in the peacekeeping were Navy jets off carriers in the Adriatic and Air Force planes stationed in Italy that overflew the UN-occupied areas to ensure the safety of the troops on the ground. The massive air strikes in Operation DELIBERATE FORCE by these planes and those of other NATO nations in August 1995 on Serb positions had resulted in the lifting of the siege of Sarajevo and drove the Serbs to the negotiating table, resulting in the Dayton Accord in November of that year. According to this accord, a ceasefire was to be put in place and 60,000 NATO troops, about 20,000 of them from the US, were on duty in the troubled remains of Yugoslavia.

As 1996 came to a close, US troops remained on station in Bosnia, the promise made by President Clinton when the troops were dispatched that the deployment of US forces would be for no more than a year now long forgotten. It appeared that US and UN military intervention in the former Yugoslav state had led to few longterm positive results, and the combatants only waited to resume their ethnic warfare at the first opportunity.

But if the Army's mission to Bosnia led to no positive results, its role in Kuwait in 1994 showed it and the other US military forces to

be extremely effective when given a role commensurate with their designated missions, training, and capabilities. In October 1994 Saddam Hussein began to deploy 20,000 of his Republican Guards to just north of the Kuwaiti border, 50,000 regular Iraqi

limited the deployment of US troops to 13,000 ground forces, 275 combat aircraft, and one aircraft carrier battle group. These UN sanctions imposed on Iraq remained in effect, to be lifted only when that nation disposed of its weapons of mass destruction, recognized as inviolable the border between itself and Kuwait, and acknowledged Kuwait's rights of sovereignty over its territory.

Hussein continued to challenge the terms laid down by the United Nations. He occasionally sent Iraq's planes into the no-fly zones, he occasionally had his radar "lock onto" Coalition planes flying over their inspection zone, and in a few instances even fired on these planes. In the case of all serious incidents, the US military responded with either airplane or missile attacks on Iraqi military installations. Although none of these incidents involved the US Army, thousands of US Army personnel remained stationed in Saudi Arabia and Kuwait in the event they would be needed to deter a more serious challenge by Hussein.

As in the case of Haiti, US Army troops are sometimes assigned to intervene in what are effectively civil wars in other nations. This can be a controversial move, both domestically and internationally, but the United States has long maintained its right and responsibility to do so, especially with countries with which its has a "special relationship." One such country is Liberia in Africa, which was founded by former slaves from the United States. In the spring of 1996, civil war broke out in Liberia. In April US Army paratroopers were flown in to bolster the small US Marines guard unit assigned to the US embassy in Monrovia. Shortly thereafter a large force of Marines arrived to relieve the Army troops of this duty.

A more persistent trouble spot involved the new nations that had once formed Yugoslavia. Serbia continued to be plagued by so much internecine violence that the original plan to withdraw all US troops had to be set aside. In December 1997,

President Clinton announced that the US Army troops would remain in Bosnia-Herzegovina for an indefinite term. Meanwhile, in the Former Yugoslav Republic of Macedonia (FYROM), which split off from Serbia in 1991, the United States continued to maintain a force of some 500 US Army troops because of ethnic divisions and violence there.

Things remained relatively calm in these two states until in February 1998 a virtual civil war broke out in the Serbian province of Kosovo between the Serbians and the ethnic Albanians there. Although the ethnic Albanians were the majority in terms of population, the Serbians had the overwhelming advantage of the military units and police assigned there by Slobodan Milosevic, president of Serbia. As the violence spiraled out of control and Serbia refused to accede to the demands of a treaty negotiated in Rambouillet, France, in February-March 1999,

NATO on 24 March 1999 launched air strikes against Serbia and the Serbian forces in Kosovo. In fact, the vast majority of the air strikes were made by US forces—Air Force, Navy, and Marines—but as Milosevic continued to resist, on 27 April President Clinton called up 25,000 Army reservists. Meanwhile, the Army had assigned 24 Apache helicopters and their supporting units (including tanks, armored vehicles, and howitzers) to the Albania-Kosovo border region. In the end, these Apache helicopters were never sent into action over Kosovo because NATO was never able to gain total control of the airspace there; in other words, the US forces could not be certain that they might not take casualties. (In fact, one of the Apache helicopters crashed on a training mission in Albania.) By the time the bombing and the fighting stopped on 10 June, the only US Army "casualties" of the Kosovo action turned out to be three soldiers captured by Serbians while on patrol along the Kosovo-Macedonia border; after being held by the Serbians for a month, they were released unharmed. Some 7,000 US Army troops were then quickly assigned to southern Kosovo as part of the NATO-sponsored

Above: US Army soldiers in Skopje, Macedonia in April 1999 continued peacekeeping efforts in this troubled region.
Below: Shown through a night vision lens, Special Forces troops embarked on a night raid near Kandahar, Afghanistan, 20 October 2001.
Opposite, top: US Special Forces troops took to horseback to cross the Afghan terrain as they assisted members of the Northern Alliance in November, 2001, as part of Operation Enduring Freedom.
Opposite, bottom: Troops of the 1st Battalion 87 10th Mountain Division arrived at Bagram Airfield in Afghanistan on 16 December 2001, where they were to take over from the departing Marines.

Soon thereafter, members of the Army's Special Operations Force began to be inserted into Afghanistan—their exact numbers and missions kept secret for security reasons.

Meanwhile, US Army troops throughout the world were not only on high alert but in some cases were receiving special training for possible assignments in Afghanistan. Among these were members of the 82nd and 101st Airborne Divisions, which were likely to be among the first to be sent in if large units were called for. And as it happened, during October 2001, units of the US Army were among the 65,000 military personnel from 10 different countries in Exercise Bright Star, a multi-national exercise held biennially in northern Egypt. Scheduled long before the events of September 11, this was the largest and most significant such exercise conducted by the US forces in the Middle East, and the US personnel clearly participated with a special focus, given the situation in Afghanistan. Although the first major US ground forces put into Afghanistan were Marines, on 28 November the first units of the Army's 10th Mountain Division began to enter northern Afghanistan, and more units of the US Army were certain to follow.

Throughout the world, whenever they are called upon, Army personnel are conscious that end of the Cold War has not meant the end of conflict or personal danger to themselves. New and better conventional vehicles and weapons and theater ballistic missiles possessed by increasing numbers of nations have now been joined by the threats of chemical and biological weapons, not to mention the methods of terrorists. All these continue to endanger not only US lives and security but also those of the nation's friends and allies throughout the world. Given the realities of the 21st century, the US Army, as a basic component of the international defense system, is committed to remaining the best-trained and best-equipped army in the world. It is clear that the Army intends to maintain its proud tradition as the bulwark of America's land fighting forces while preparing itself for the future.

Kosovo Force (KFOR), under which Kosovo was divided into five regions to be controlled temporarily by troops from five NATO members (USA, Britain, France, Italy, Germany).

After the activities in the Balkans calmed down, the Army, along with the rest of the US military branches, seemed to go into a state of hiatus. Matters such as cutbacks in the defense budget, closing of bases, and declining active duty personnel seemed to dominate the news, along with public policy issues such as gays ("Don't ask, don't tell") and sexual harassment in the military. When the new administration of President George W. Bush took over in January 2001, still other issues came to the fore. The new secretary of defense, Donald Rumsfeld, for example, was a proponent of developing multiservice military units that would be prepared for rapid deployment in the early stages of an overseas crisis. At the same time he indicated that among his priorities were "quality-of-life" issues—improving pay and other conditions to maintain re-enlistment and morale in what appeared to be a largely peaceful world.

On 11 September 2001, three of four terrorist-hijacked airplanes crashed into the World Trade Center and the Pentagon and brought the United States, and indeed, the world, to a state of highest alert. The crash into the western part of the Pentagon, killed some 80 Army personnel and civilians associated with the Army. In addition to responding to the disaster at the Pentagon, personnel of the Army Corps of Engineers were at "Ground Zero" in New York within two hours after the hijacked airliners struck the World Trade Center. They continued for weeks afterward to provide support for many aspects of the recovery operations.

Meanwhile, the Army was prepared to move into action from the moment President George W. Bush declared a war on terrorism and launched Operation ENDURING FREEDOM against Osama bin Laden and his Taliban protectors in Afghanistan. The operation began on 7 October with air and missile strikes from US Air Force and Navy personnel, while the Army participated in the preparation and dropping of emergency food supplies into Afghanistan. On 19 October, a small unit of US Army Rangers parachuted into southern Afghanistan on a daring night raid on two Taliban sites. The US soldiers met with some resistance but suffered only mild casualties, including two paratroopers who were injured in the jump. Two Rangers were killed in a helicopter crash in Pakistan that same night in an unrelated accident.

ACKNOWLEDGMENTS

Many pictures throughout the text, and a majority of those relating to the 20th century, were supplied by the US Department of Defense, the US Army, the US Navy and the US Air Force. the publishers thank these agencies and the following whose pictures appear on the pages noted:

Anne S. K. Brown Military Collection, Brown University: 7 bottom, 20 bottom, 23 bottom right, 34 bottom, 39, 50 top right, 55 bottom, 59 bottom, 68 bottom, 71 top, 77 top, 78–79, 88 top, 97 top, 115
Black Star: 203 bottom

Christopher Morris/Black Star/Timepix: 252 top
Dwight D. Eisenhower Library: 208
Library of Congress: 11 top, 19 top, 22, 30, 41, 51 top left, 60-61 bottom, 63 bottom, 64 bottom, 73 top, 81 top, 86 bottom, 92, 96-97, 108, 111, 114 top, 116 bottom, 118
Lincoln Library and Museum, Fort Wayne Indiana: 65
Martin Marietta, Inc.: 221 top
National Archives: 13, 44 top, 64 top, 99 bottom, 106 bottom, 107 top, 112, 113, 120-1, 128 bottom, 139 top, 150-1, 179 bottom
National Gallery of Art, Washington, DC: 20 top

National Portrait Gallery, Smithsonian Institution: 54
New York Historical Society: 45 bottom
Peter Newark's Western Americana: 6 bottom, 12, 16, 17 bottom, 23 top, 24, 25 top, 28 bottom, 29, 33 bottom, 38 bottom, 40, 42, 46, 50, 52, 53, 56 bottom right, 57, 58 top, 63 top, 66 top, 70, 72, 75, 77 bottom, 79 top, 83, 86 top, 87, 89, 94, 95 bottom, 98 top, 99 top, 100, 101, 105
Remington Arms Company: 95 top, 112 top
Reuters/Bettmann: 224-5, 228 top, 230, 238 both, 239, 240 both, 241 both, 242, 243 both, 244, 245, 246 all, 247 both, 248 both

Reuters/DOD/TimePix: 252 bottom, 253 top
Reuters/TimePix: 253 bottom
Roosevelt Library and Museum: 134 top
State Historical Society of Wisconsin: 15 top
UPI/Bettmann: 237
US Military Academy Library: 90-1, 222 bottom
WWP: 199 bottom, 200, 201 top and bottom left, 208 top
Yale University Art Gallery: 34 top